THEODORA

THEODORA

· PORTRAIT IN A BYZANTINE LANDSCAPE ·

ANTONY BRIDGE

Academy
Chicago
Publishers

Published in 1993 by
Academy Chicago Publishers
363 West Erie Street
Chicago, Illinois 60610

First hardcover edition published by Academy Chicago: 1984

Printed and bound in the United States of America.

Library of Congress Cataloging in Publication Data

Bridge, Antony.
        Theodora: portrait in a Byzantine landscape.
        Reprint. Originally published: London: Cassell, 1978.

        Bibliography: p.
        Includes index.
        1.   Theodora: Empress, consort of Justinian I, Emperor
of the East, d. 548.   2. Byzantine Empire—History—
Justinian I, 527–565.   3. Byzantine empresses—Biography.
I.   Title.
DF572.5.B7   1984   949.5'01'0924 [B]   84–434
ISBN 0-89733-394-2 (paperback)

CONTENTS

Photo section between pages 104 and 105

PREFACE

One of the most glaring gaps in most people's knowledge is their almost total ignorance of the thousand years of Byzantine civilisation, without which neither western civilisation as we know it nor that of Russia and eastern Europe could have existed. They have heard of Constantine; they know that at some time or another he transferred the capital of the Roman world from Rome on the banks of the Tiber to Constantinople on the shores of the Bosphorus, though few of them have much idea of when or why he did so. Most people have also heard of Justinian, though they are very vague as to when he lived and what he did. Lastly, the name Theodora is faintly familiar and has slightly naughty associations; but that is all. The rest, as Hamlet said in a very different context, is silence.

This remarkable ignorance is at least in part the fault of Edward Gibbon, paradoxical as that may seem, for he wrote the first and in many ways the greatest history in the English language of Byzantine civilisation; but he was so blinded by the enlightenment of his age that, in the process, he misrepresented Byzantium and misjudged it more completely than anyone else, and was thus responsible for the universal contempt in which all things Byzantine were held for over a century, and the almost equally universal neglect with which they were treated. Happily, however, within the last hundred years there has been a change of heart amongst historians, many of whom have reassessed the Byzantine achievement, rejecting Gibbon's judgement of it. At the same time, the ease of travel which everyone now enjoys and the excellence of modern means of reproducing paintings and mosaics in colour have led to the rediscovery of Byzantine art, which is probably more widely and deeply appreciated today than it has been since the days of men like Cimabue and Giotto, and this in its turn has led to a rebirth of curiosity about Byzantine civilisation and history. Unfortunately, this curiosity is not very easily satisfied; few people can return to the original Greek sources of information, even when they are easily accessible, which with a few exceptions they are not; meanwhile, most of the standard works on the subject in English, French, and German, let alone those in Russian, are either difficult to obtain or rather daunting in appearance by reason of their size, their obvious erudition, and sometimes their cost. So many ordinary, interested, and intelligent readers decide that Byzantine history is not for the likes of them; they would probably enjoy it greatly if they read it, but they seldom do so, and this is a pity.

Indeed, it is because I think it such a pity that I have written this book, which is intended for the person who would like to know more about the civilisation of which Byzantine art was the mirror and the people of whose hopes and dreams and beliefs it was the expression and the glory. To get to know a civilisation you can do one of two things; you can take a sweeping bird's-eye view of it, or you can focus your historical telescope on one period of it in all its variety, colour, and living detail. It is probably a good idea to do both, but you can only do one or the other in a single book, and I have chosen to look at the life and times of Theodora in as much detail as is available, partly at least because there is so much of it; for the events of her life and time are extremely well documented. Her contemporary, Procopius, a brilliant if at times violently prejudiced historian, who copied the style of Thucydides, left a mass of detailed information about her personally and about the events of her day in a large number of works, and he was by no means the only man to do so. Several other Greek historians, notably John Malalas, covered the same period, as did the Syriac historian John of Ephesus. Their works, as well as a mass of other contemporary documents of one kind or another, have been the sources to which all modern historians have returned, and the results of their labours have been legion. I have listed many of these modern histories, both of the particular period covered by this book and of Byzantine civilisation in general, in the bibliography at the end of this book, but I must acknowledge here my debt to two men: the French historian, Charles Diehl, whose biography, *Théodora, Impératrice de Byzance*, together with his history of her time, *Justinien et la civilisation byzantine au VIe siècle*, and his many other works are still invaluable, even though most of them were published sixty or more years ago, and Diehl's equally great English contemporary, J. B. Bury, whose *Later Roman Empire* is not only a classic but also a mine of information about the life, times and contemporaries of both Justinian and Theodora. Of course, I am in the debt of many others too, but they must forgive me if I do not mention them all by name here.

As for my own book, it is in no way a work of original scholarship, as any historian will be able to see at a glance; I have picked the brains of other scholars and raided their works unmercifully, and I am grateful to them for the wealth of detailed information and local colour which they have provided. If my book manages to rouse the enthusiasm of some people for the Byzantines and their achievements, and thus encourages them to take a greater interest in one of the world's greatest, yet most misunderstood and undervalued civilisations, I am sure that its real historians will forgive me for raiding their territory and invoking their assistance in the process.

A.B.

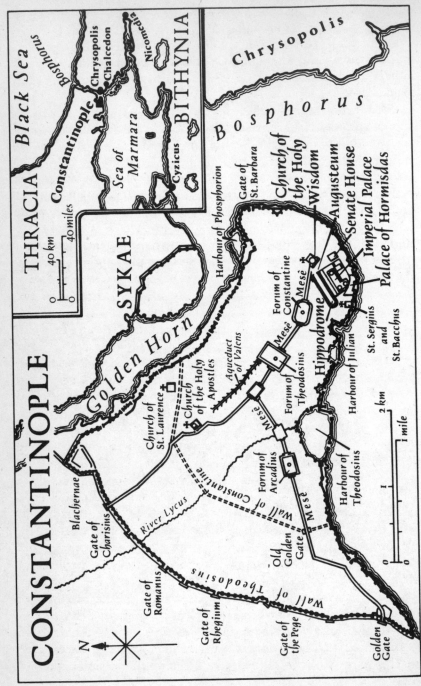

CONSTANTINOPLE

Inset map (top left)

THRACIA

Black Sea

Bosphorus

Chrysopolis
Chalcedon

Nicomedia

BITHYNIA

Constantinople

Sea of Marmara

Cyzicus

40 km / 40 miles

Main map

SYKAE

Golden Horn

Chrysopolis

Bosphorus

Gate of St. Barbara

Church of the Holy Wisdom

Augusteum

Senate House

Imperial Palace

Palace of Hormisdas

Harbour of Phosphorion

Forum of Constantine

Mesē

Mesē

Hippodrome

St. Sergius and St. Bacchus

Mesē Constantine

Forum of Theodosius

Gate of Julian

Harbour of Julian

Church of St. Lawrence

Church of the Holy Apostles

Aqueduct of Valens

Mesē

Harbour of Theodosius

2 km

1 mile

Blachernae

Forum of Arcadius

Forum of Theodosius

Gate of Charisius

River Lycus

Wall of Constantine

Old Golden Gate

Mesē

Gate of Romanus

Gate of Rhegium

Gate of the Pege

Wall of Theodosius

Golden Gate

N

© Cassell Ltd. 1978

I

ΘΈ ΟΔΨ ΡΑ Each year on a day in late August or early September, the storks of northern Europe, western Russia, and the Ukraine rise into the air on great black and white wings, almost as if they had been given a signal to do so, and begin their journey to Africa where they spend the winter. In their tens of thousands they converge on the Bosphorus, until the sky above the narrow waters which separate Europe from Asia is filled with birds wheeling and soaring on the thermals of late summer as thick as motes of dust in a sunbeam. In A.D. 500, far below them on the triangle of land between the Golden Horn and the Sea of Marmara, lay Constantinople. Its houses, with their red-tiled roofs warm in the sun, were interspersed with parks and gardens, orchards and green fields; its streets and squares and forums stretched three miles westwards to the most formidable city wall the world had ever seen, running from sea to sea right across the peninsula. No doubt then as now, at a lower level than that at which the storks flew, the ubiquitous Byzantine pigeons circled in a noisy flurry of wings, and scavenging kites hung on the hot air in search of food, while the sounds made by a city of three-quarters of a million inhabitants rose up above the house-tops like the sound of a distant sea. A few noises stood out sharply from the groundswell: dogs barking in the distance, children calling and laughing as they played together, a donkey braying somewhere as if in pain, and down by the sea and the harbour the noise of men hammering or shouting the price of fish.

It was a cosmopolitan place. For centuries the Roman Empire had been a melting pot in which the races of mankind living around the Mediterranean had been mixed together, while others from farther afield had been drawn into it as immigrants in the hope of sharing its way of life and its riches. The result was a new kind of citizen; in origin the people of Constantinople might be Roman, Greek, Armenian, Syrian, Arab, or even Gothic, for a large number of blue-eyed, fair-haired Germans could be seen in the city, where they worked as labourers in menial jobs or slaves in rich households, but by the beginning of the sixth century they all felt themselves to be Byzantines, and they nearly all spoke Greek. Latin was still spoken by some people, chiefly on formal and official occasions, but it had been in decline for years throughout the eastern half of the Empire, where Greek had increasingly become the common language of the people since the days of Alexander of Macedon. It was Greek which you heard spoken in the streets, and it was in the streets too that the people of the city could be seen in all their variety.

The *beau monde* and the rich, whether on foot or in carriages drawn by white mules, were always attended by a retinue of servants without which no one who was anyone dreamed of moving about in public; bejewelled and dressed in the height of fashion, they were unmistakable. Fashions in dress had changed since Constantine had founded the city in the year 330; the old flowing Roman toga had disappeared, especially from the wardrobes of the upper classes, in favour of a straight ankle-length tunic with narrow sleeves, which was often elaborately embroidered and richly decorated, and which had probably been copied in the first place from the robes of a Chinese mandarin. Members of the new order of Patricians were easily recognised too, for they wore pure white edged with purple and had scarlet girdles round their waists. Priests were to be seen everywhere, recognised not only by their traditional clothing which had not changed with changing fashions, but also by their beards; the clergy had worn beards since apostolic times, and because the Church was a profoundly conservative institution, they still wore them. Monks were even more numerous than the clergy, for Constantinople was above all a city of monasteries, and the monastic profession was held in such popular esteem that a particularly holy or ascetic monk could, and often did, become the idol of the people and even a rival of the Emperor of the day in his influence over them.

Eunuchs, though rarer than either the clergy or the monks, were omnipresent too, for most of the civil servants who worked in the vast Byzantine bureaucracy and staffed the central government of the Empire were eunuchs; but they were not particularly easy to distinguish from other men, for contrary to common belief they were neither fatter nor smoother than anyone else. They were trusted in positions of power precisely because they were eunuchs and could therefore have no dynastic ambitions of their own, and parents often had their sons castrated in infancy in order that in later life they might qualify for the highest and most powerful government posts.

There were always soldiers in the streets, strolling about the city in their short green tunics with red facings and white stockings, enjoying an hour or two off duty; but there were seldom many of them, for the Byzantines maintained only a small professional army, most of which was stationed in the eastern provinces or on the northern frontiers during peace time; they preferred to rely upon diplomacy rather than upon military force for the protection of the Empire whenever it was possible to do so. In an emergency, when all else failed, there were large military reserves which could be called up to reinforce the regular soldiers. During the day, children were at school, but in the evening and during the holidays they could always be seen playing in the streets or dancing at street corners in the hope of earning a few pence. Meanwhile, of course, workmen of all sorts went about their business, and peasants from the country driving carts full of vegetables, shepherding flocks of sheep or goats to market, or walking behind donkeys with panniers full of fruit or dairy produce were commonplace.

But perhaps the most common of all were the merchants and shopkeepers, for Constantinople was the greatest mercantile centre in the world, lying as it did across the trade routes between east and west, north and south. All roads might have led to Rome in the old days, but to the new capital of the Roman world on the shores of the Bosphorus ran the caravan routes from China, India, and Ceylon, the roads from the steppes of Scythia and the forests of Germania Magna, and the sea-ways from Africa, the Mediterranean, and the Aegean. So the streets of the city usually contained a few people from almost every corner of the known world who were there as traders, ambassadors, or simply as sightseers. In times of peace on the eastern frontier little parties of Persians in exotic clothes mingled with the crowds, gazing up at the statue of Apollo with the head of the Emperor Constantine on its tall porphyry column in the Forum which bore his name; barbarians from the tribes which lived somewhere north of the Danube stared at the aqueduct of Valens which brought water to the city's vast underground reservoirs; Egyptian sailors on shore leave from the corn-ships which brought grain from Alexandria wandered down the Mesê or Central Street, which ran its splendid marble way from the oldest square in the city, the Augusteum, past shops selling silk, jewellery, perfume, and other luxuries in the arcades at its sides to the Golden Gate almost three miles away in the great wall built in 413 by the Emperor Theodosius II; and others whose nationality could not be guessed from their appearance were usually to be seen somewhere amongst the crowds in the city, for people lived in the open air much more than we do, and the main thoroughfares were perpetually busy.

Behind them lay a maze of narrow and confusing streets, which followed the contours of the hilly ground upon which Constantinople was built, and opened up frequently into little squares. Churches were everywhere, and so were monasteries, though some of them held no more than one or two people, while others were the homes of a hundred or more monks or nuns. By the sixth century a law had been passed to regulate the width of the back streets; none of them was supposed to be narrower than twelve feet, though some of the older streets were mere alleys, and the authorities could do little about them, for they had existed for a hundred years or more; similarly the balconies on the houses were not supposed to extend nearer to the opposite side of the street than ten feet or be lower than fifteen feet above the ground, although once again in some of the older parts of the city this regulation was not observed. Balconies were common on the poorer houses, where the inhabitants—especially the women of the place—when they were not working liked to sit and watch the life of the street go by beneath them. Since most of these houses were built of wood, which stood up to the earthquakes which rocked the city from time to time better than brick or stone, there was an ever-present risk of fire; and although there was an efficient fire-fighting force, when fire did break out it often did extensive and appalling damage, especially in the older and more overcrowded districts. But there were no slums in the modern sense and no fashionable residential areas either; rich and poor lived in the same streets, though the houses of the rich were far grander than those of their less affluent neighbours. Like some of the older houses in the cities of the Arabic world today—Cairo, for instance—the houses of wealthy Byzan-

4

tines presented blank faces to the streets, being built round courtyards on to which their rooms opened; sometimes these inner courts were covered with roofs, but more often they contained gardens, fountains, and little arbours where the occupants of the house could sit under the shade of vines or flowering shrubs.

Perhaps it was because the rich and the poor lived side by side, or perhaps it was because the poor knew that Byzantine society was a society in which people could rise from the humblest beginnings to positions of great power and dignity—whatever the reason may have been neither racial prejudice nor class distinction divided them; at least, it did not usually do so. There had been a time in the fourth century when there had been a good deal of prejudice against the Gothic minority which lived in the midst of Byzantine society; rather like the black minority in the United States and in England, the Goths were racially recognisable, economically under-privileged, and mostly employed in the most menial jobs. Everywhere you went there were these German barbarians. They worked on the land; they did the dirty jobs in the cities; most households had one or two as slaves or as badly paid servants; and worst of all the army was full of them. The idea that they might revolt one day was terrifying, and to many Byzantine citizens the sight of these immigrants with their fair hair, blue eyes, and pink skins was both disturbing and disgusting. But by the sixth century the Goths had been assimilated by Byzantine society, and there was no longer any prejudice against them on account of the colour of their skin.

Class distinction was not a feature of Byzantine society either. In the nature of things only a few people rose from rags to great riches, but the mere fact that some did so in every generation seems to have been responsible for the acceptance by most people of the basic order of society. Moreover, although the poor were often very poor indeed, they were seldom destitute; there was no poverty in Constantinople or elsewhere in the Empire comparable to the poverty of modern Calcutta, for although the social pyramid of Byzantine society was crowned by an Emperor with autocratic and almost unlimited power, the state over which he presided was in many ways a welfare state. There were free hospitals where the sick were nursed by monks and nuns, almshouses for the needy and the old, free accommodation for the homeless, and orphanages subsidised by the state. Both prices and wages were strictly controlled by law, and rationing was often introduced in times of need, so that the poor did not suffer while the rich thrived. But the absence of social divisions in Byzantine society was not merely a negative quality; it was the result of three positive forces which united nearly everyone: Roman citizenship, Christian faith, and a passion for chariot racing.

As many people in the United States of America during the first half of the twentieth century, who were born of Polish, Italian, Russian, Jewish, German, Irish, or native American parents, were nevertheless united by their American citizenship and welded into one people, so the Byzantines were united by their Roman citizenship. They were not all Roman by blood or birth, but from the highest to the lowest every Byzantine was intensely conscious of being an heir of the eternal world of Rome. It was a world which seemed to everyone, both its citizens and its enemies, to be coterminous with civilisation itself: a steady and a splendid light in a dark and barbarous world. For a thousand years the Empire had grown, absorbing into itself all that was best in classical Greece and the Hellenistic world which had followed it, and taking peace and the rule of law to people of different races and beliefs from the Atlantic Ocean to the deserts of the Middle East, and from the Danube to the Sahara. The collapse of the West under barbarian invasions during the fifth century had only made the citizens of the East more conscious of their role as guardians of civilisation in a world where barbarism seemed to be inexorably spreading; and curiously enough this was a verdict with which the Gothic conquerors of Italy would almost certainly have agreed. The last thing the invaders of the Roman world wanted was to destroy it; they wanted to share its riches and its way of life, which they admired above all things. Moreover, there was nothing they desired more passionately, once they had established themselves within the borders of the Empire and had built their petty kingdoms, than to be recognised by the Byzantine Emperor, who claimed to rule by divine authority as God's representative on earth, arrogating to himself and to his office not only the secular powers of Caesar but also the God-given powers of the western Popes; as a result the Goths regarded him with a respect bordering on idolatry as almost a god in his own right. All this the Byzantines knew, and their pride in themselves as Romans became even greater than it had been before the barbarians had begun to encroach upon the Empire; but it was a pride tinged with a certain self-mockery and an urbane

6

cynicism about their own chances of escaping the fate of the West in the long run. Their role as defenders of civilisation often seemed a very lonely one and their chance of ultimate success rather forlorn.

A cynic might say that it was as a result of this pessimism that the Byzantines turned to religion for comfort, and there would be a measure of truth in such an accusation. In a world which seemed to be crumbling around their ears, the Byzantines found very persuasive the voices of men like Augustine of Hippo in the West and, nearer home, Basil the Great of Caesarea in Cappadocia, both of whom advocated rejection of this mundane world as a vale of tears, a deceitful and untrustworthy place in which only a fool vested his hopes. Certainly they were obsessionally religious almost to a man. It is difficult, if not impossible, for us living in the secular society of the twentieth century to imagine what it must have been like to be a Byzantine. He lived his life between two worlds; like us he was born into the physical world of human desire, power politics, war and peace, life and death, and the everyday business of getting and spending, but he did not feel himself to be primarily its citizen. He was first and foremost a citizen of the world represented in the glittering mosaics which surrounded him when he entered one of his churches: a world ruled by Christ and the supernatural hierarchy of heaven and hell and erupting with miracles. The darkly luminous world of his icons, where martyrs and saints and confessors, silhouetted against golden skies, moved about in a strange and timeless landscape not subject to the mundane dictates of perspective, was his true home. It was far more real to him than the humdrum world of material reality; it was the primary reality in which he lived, and hoped, and planned his future in the prospect of eternity and judgement. Not surprisingly, therefore, his great passion was for theological debate, and this was taken to astonishing lengths. A contemporary historian remarked how, towards the end of the fourth century, 'the imperial transport system was quite disorganised by bands of bishops travelling hither and thither in government conveyances' to synods where they disputed minute points of Christian doctrine for weeks on end. But this Byzantine passion was by no means limited to the ranks of the clergy; laymen were possessed by it too. At about the same time—that is to say towards the end of the fourth century, when the controversy over the doctrine of the Trinity was at its height—one of the great doctors of the eastern Church, Gregory of Nazianzus, complained

7

that, if you went into a shop in Constantinople to do something as apparently simple as to buy a loaf of bread, it was almost impossible to do so without being drawn into a religious discussion; for 'the baker instead of telling you the price will argue that the Father is greater than the Son. The money-changer will talk about the Begotten and the Unbegotten instead of giving you your money, and if you want a bath, the bath-keeper assures you that the Son surely proceeds from nothing.' In fact, the average Byzantine citizen got as excited over religious arguments of this kind, and as divided by the religious issues arising from them, as party politicians are today excited and divided by politics. Indeed, in a very real sense religious issues were political issues in the world of the sixth century, for it was the Christian faith which united the Empire against her enemies, many of whom were her enemies principally because they were adherents of another religion. The over-riding aim of all Byzantine Emperors in foreign politics was to convert the enemies of the Empire to Christianity and thereby to turn them into allies, rather as Russian Communists today try to convert non-Communist countries to Communism in the belief that they will thus gain political and military allies. It is impossible to understand the Byzantines unless the fact that they were obsessed by religion is constantly remembered; almost to a man they were religious, and some of them were grossly superstitious too.

But the pessimism with which they viewed the secular world, from which they withdrew into the world of Christian hope, fell away from all Byzantines like an old cloak when they indulged their other great passion: chariot racing. The world might be a deceitful place in which only a fool would put his trust, and the rising tide of barbarism might one day wash up to the very walls of Con-stantinople until the last citadel of civilisation succumbed to its dark waters, but in the meantime while there was life there was chariot racing. It had been the absorbing passion of the Roman people since the days of the Republic, and when the capital of the Empire was moved from the banks of the Tiber to the shores of the Bosphorus, the cult of the circus was transplanted to Constanti-nople. The advent of Christianity made little or no difference to the popular mania for the sport, even though it was denounced again and again by churchmen; in fact, it reached the peak of its popularity in Byzantine days when it was organised by the celebrated circus factions known as the Greens and the Blues,

Prasinoi and *Venetoi*. These organisations fulfilled a function rather like that of the big professional football clubs of our own day, organising and financing the competing teams of charioteers and other athletes in the Hippodrome, and attracting to themselves the fanatical loyalty of their supporters; and nearly everyone was a supporter of one side or the other. Indeed, partisan feeling often ran so high that the races ended in violence. One historian of the sixth century declared that 'chariot racing gives rise to madness rather than pleasure, and has already brought a number of great cities to ruin . . . For the faction a man will squander his property, endure martyrdom and death, and commit crime. Party interest takes precedence of family, house, country and law. Men and women suffer from a sort of mental disorder, and general insanity prevails.'

This power of the Greens and the Blues to engage men's allegiance was due only in part to the fact that they were sporting clubs; they were more than that, for they played two other roles in the lives of the people of Constantinople as well as dividing their sporting loyalties between them. The Blues tended to be politically conservative, supporting the cause of the wealthier classes, and most of them were strictly orthodox in religious matters. The Greens on the other hand were the party of the workers and the champions of those who opposed a rigid religious orthodoxy; though, of course, the divisions were not as neat as that. But the fact that each faction combined the role of a sporting club with that of a political party as well as that of a religious denomination inspired its supporters with the ferocious tribal loyalties and sectarian hatreds usually aroused by all three, and as a result they could be extremely dangerous. But they also had their value, for the Hippodrome was the one place where the voice of the people could make itself heard: the one place where the absolutism of the Byzantine state could be challenged by its ordinary citizens. On more than one occasion an Emperor was toppled from his throne by the factions in the Hippodrome, and the fall of an unpopular minister was, if not regularly engineered there, at least quite often accomplished by either the Blues or the Greens or both working together; they provided a kind of popular parliament which, if it had no legal or constitutional standing, exercised a very real power and performed a very necessary function in Byzantine society.

It is no exaggeration to say that on a day when there was to be racing in the Hippodrome, the eyes of the entire population of the city were turned upon it almost to the exclusion of everything else, and the defeat of one of the factions was treated by its supporters as being more disastrous than the defeat of the imperial army by the Persians. Early in the morning people began to converge on the circus from all over Constantinople through streets which had been watered during the night to lay the dust of dry animal manure reduced to powder by the traffic. Everyone came. Young and old, rich and poor, priests and laymen shared a common passion for the sport; only respectable women who valued their reputations kept away, for it was considered improper for them to be seen there. As people approached the place, they had to make their way through a confusion of small shops, traders' stalls, and booths clustered thickly round it, running the gauntlet of astrologers, tipsters, and fortune-tellers, all of whom claimed to be able to predict the winners of the coming races and competed with each other to sell their information to the gullible public. The Hippodrome was an enormous U-shaped building copied from the Circus Maximus in Rome, and it was capable of holding about a hundred thousand spectators; the race track was laid out around the curve of the U, while thirty or forty tiers of stone seats rose up round it; the Emperor had his special place—a royal box named the *kathisma*—in a miniature palace built by Constantine at the northern end of the track near the winning post, and this he could enter by a private way which led up a spiral staircase from the Imperial Palace itself. The public entered by a gate on the west side through corridors crowded with side-shows; barkers, hucksters, and hawkers vied with each other and with conjurors, dancers, and strolling players for people's attention and for their money; the place was alive with stable-boys, grooms, and keepers of wild beasts, while petty criminals, pimps, prostitutes, and con-men mingled as unobtrusively as possible with the crowd and preyed upon their respective victims. A German historian has described the Hippodrome on such a day, probably without exaggeration, as 'a mad menagerie in which grotesque beasts mingled with their even more grotesque keepers and multifarious freaks . . . clowns leading gilded crocodiles, mountebanks riding on ostriches with their feathers dyed lilac, acrobats, monstrosities, the disproportionately large and the disproportionately small. From the jaded audiences of the Byzantine circus, nothing but the preposterously unusual could raise a cheer.'

But the races themselves raised the loudest cheers. The chariots were two-wheeled, and usually they were driven by four horses, though beginners sometimes raced with two-in-hand or three-in-hand teams. The charioteers, some of the most successful of whom were the idols of the people, stood upright in open cars dressed in short tunics, their arms bare, crash helmets on their heads and covering their foreheads and cheeks; each was armed with a whip and a knife to cut himself free from entangling traces in the event of a crash. Waiting for the beginning of a race, the crowd became more and more tense, and when a white handkerchief was dropped as the signal to start, there was a roar of excitement as whips cracked, charioteers yelled, and the horses plunged into a violent gallop in a cloud of dust. Usually a race consisted of seven or eight laps of the course, which was about a kilometre in circumference, and the chances of all the chariots surviving without mishap were small; that was part of the excitement. Sometimes a driver fell off as he cornered too fast, and was dragged along by the traces; at other times he cut himself free only to be run over by the wheels of the next chariot or injured by the horses' hoofs; occasionally two or more chariots became locked together in a collision, and animals and men spilled on to the track in a struggling confusion of kicking limbs and splintered wood; but even the death of a charioteer did not dampen the hysterical enthusiasm of the crowd. As the excitement mounted, people stood in their places screaming abuse or encouragement at the charioteers, waving their arms about, jumping up and down in the passion of the moment, and as the end came either hugging each other in a rapturous embrace if their faction had won, or howling with despair if it had lost. At the end of the day they went home purged of emotion and flushed with enjoyment, leaving the Hippodrome to those who lived there: the freaks, the owners of side-shows, the stable-boys, the keepers of wild beasts, and a large and varied riff-raff who managed to make a living in a number of unlikely and usually disreputable ways.

One such was a man named Acacius (Akakios in Greek), who was bear-keeper to the Greens; he made a slightly better living than most, for bear-baiting, bear hunts, and fights between bears were popular, but his job was a menial one, and both he and his wife belonged to the lowest order of society. In about A.D. 500, however, Acacius' wife gave birth to a daughter who was destined to become the most notorious woman in Byzantine history, though no one who was a witness of her very humble beginning could possibly have predicted such a fate for her. She owed it, not only to the fact that she led an extraordinary and dramatic life, but also to a brilliant historian, Procopius by name, who knew her when she was at the height of her fame, and hated her with such an obsessional loathing that he wrote a scurrilous *Secret History*, in which he did everything in his power to blacken her memory. It was secret because it was so libellous that he did not dare publish it in his lifetime, and in fact it remained unknown for centuries; but since it was discovered about three hundred years ago, the subject of its author's implacable dislike has enjoyed such a *succès de scandale* that her name has become the one name in the voluminous annals of the Byzantine Empire known to almost everyone, even to those entirely ignorant of everyone and everything else connected with its thousand years of history. It was Theodora.

II

Θ Έ
Ο Δ ώ
Ρ Α

     It is difficult to imagine a tougher environment in which to be born and to grow to maturity than that of the Hippodrome in Constantinople in Theodora's time. It was not perhaps as hostile or as squalid as the slums of London and other great industrial cities in Victorian days, but there is a sense in which it epitomised everything from which most parents try to protect their children in infancy. When Constantine had taken over the old Greek colonial city of Byzantium, he had renamed its main market place the Augusteum after his mother, the Augusta Helena, whose statue he had set up there; and then as if symbolically to enshrine at the very heart of the new capital of the Roman world the gods of the Roman soul, he had built round it a remarkable group of buildings. On the one side lay the great basilican Church dedicated to Santa Sophia, the Holy Wisdom, witnessing to the newly adopted Christian faith of the Roman people; opposite to it on the other side of the square was the Imperial Palace, embodying their older belief in the divine right of the Emperors of Rome to rule the world; over to the east could be seen the Senate House, paying formal tribute to the even more ancient, but by this time largely empty, belief in their own political right to a say in the government of their own world; while next to the Palace rose the Hippodrome as a kind of temple to the most ancient of all the Roman gods: the gods of the primordial and unchanging human libido which could not be bottled up for ever, whatever the official religion of the people might be.

    The Hippodrome was theirs. It was a place dedicated to passion, violence, group aggression, mob excitement, and the shedding of blood; for fights staged between men and animals and between animals themselves were almost as popular as chariot racing, and roused much the same sort of blood lust in the spectators as the old gladiatorial contests had excited before they were abolished by Theodosius the Great in the fourth century. Apart from the officials of the two factions, the Blues and the Greens, who managed the day-to-day business of the place, the permanent staff were mostly illiterate and uncouth, while those who hung around the fringes of the circus were often from the dregs of society. Here Theodora was born, and here she spent her childhood. It is difficult to imagine how she could have picked up a ready-made set of conventional middle-class morals in such a setting during the course of her early life, and this is something which her many pious detractors have usually chosen to forget or ignore. It was a time better suited to teaching her how to hold her own and survive in a human jungle, where toughness, courage, a quick wit, and shrewd judgement of people were more valuable than a nice ethical sensitivity; and these were qualities which she did indeed exhibit in later life.

She was not an only child. She had an older sister, Comito, and in due course another girl was born and named Anastasia. It used to be said that the family came from Cyprus, though more recently Syria has been suggested as their place of origin; the fact is that no one knows for sure where they came from. As if their circumstances were not already bad enough, shortly after the birth of the youngest child, when Theodora was about four or five years old, the father of the family died. Nothing is known about his wife, but the death of her husband, Acacius the bear-keeper, must have been a bitter blow to her; for, if it is seldom easy for a widow to bring up three children alone and unaided, it was an even more formidable task in the cut-throat world of the Hippodrome in Byzantium. With commendable speed and good sense, if with little regard for conventional ideas of mourning or morality, she quickly found another man to take her dead husband's place as bread-winner for the family. Whether she married him is not known, but she started to live with him in the hope that she would be able to secure her late husband's job for him. In order to do so, the manager of the Greens, a man named Asterius, had to be persuaded to appoint him, and unfortunately for the widow, he had already accepted a bribe from someone else who wanted the job. So when the unlucky woman sought an interview with Asterius and begged him to make her new consort bear-keeper, she discovered that she was too late.

This could only have been a tragic disappointment to the mother of the three small children. She could not hope to out-bid the other candidate for the post by offering a larger bribe than his, even if Asterius would have accepted it, for she had no resources; but she could make a bid for the support of the ordinary members of the Green faction in the hope that they would help her in her extremity, and this she decided to do. So one day when the Hippodrome was packed with people waiting for the races to begin, she appeared in the arena with her three small daughters; driving them before her, their heads crowned with little chaplets of flowers and their hands held out in supplication, she explained her plight and that of her children to the crowd, begging the Greens to employ her daughters' new father so that the family might not starve. Appeals of every kind, including appeals to the Emperor himself, were not uncommon on such occasions, and they were made through a spokesman trained for the purpose. There could seldom have been a more touching appeal than this, but it left those to whom it was addressed completely unmoved; indeed, the Greens roared with laughter, and both mother and children were driven back whence they had come with their ill-judged merriment ringing in their ears.

The Blues, however, who were always on the look-out for ways of winning supporters away from their rivals, saw a chance of scoring a few points off them by offering the family employment similar to that which they had lost, and they promptly offered Theodora's stepfather a job, thus solving the immediate problem. In all probability they then forgot the whole thing, dismissing it as one more trivial brush with the Greens and of no great consequence; but the long-term consequences of the whole affair were enormous, for Theodora never forgot the humiliation inflicted on her and her family on this occasion. For the rest of her life she was bitterly hostile to the Greens. This is not surprising when the probable impact of such an event on a child of four or five is estimated; it must have been shattering. The mother must have rehearsed the children in their part, and like all children they must have been excited, nervous, and desperately anxious to please and to succeed. When eventually they ran out into the arena and found themselves the sole objects of attention by perhaps as many as a hundred thousand pairs of eyes, they would hardly have been human if they had not been overcome with a mixture of terror and determination to do their part as well as they possibly could. Their feelings, when they found themselves assaulted by waves of mocking laughter and knew that they had failed, do not bear thinking about, and when they were chased from the arena in ignominy with their mother, their bewilderment at the injustice done to them must have been as unbearable as their sense of rejection and injury was memorable.

Nothing else is known of Theodora's early childhood. According to Procopius, however, who is our only source of information about this time of her life, a little later, when she was of an age to do so, her sister Comito went on to the stage as an actress; probably this was when she was about fourteen or fifteen, and Theodora was eleven or twelve. At the time, the stage was regarded as a proper place only for the lowest of the low, and the profession of an actress was treated as much the same as that of a prostitute. For instance, in common with anyone who had ever been a servant girl, a barmaid, or a whore, girls who had been on the stage were forbidden by Roman law to marry senators or anyone else of high rank. For obvious reasons, however, such legal disincentives were unlikely to deter anyone born in the Hippodrome and brought up amongst the dregs of society, as were Theodora and her sisters, from embarking on any of these careers; few other occupations were open to them, for one thing, and for another their chances of marrying anyone of exalted social position were so small as to be negligible. So probably Comito had no misgivings about adopting the stage as a way of life, with all that such a decision implied. It is possible, even probable, that her mother had been on the stage in her younger days, or had been employed in one of the many side-shows which clustered round the circus, and that Comito was simply following in her mother's footsteps; but this is conjecture. What is certain is that, although at first she was given only the smallest parts in bawdy plays or slapstick farces, it was not long before she became a minor success.

The Byzantine theatre in the sixth century had long ceased to resemble the Greek theatre in the days of such men as Euripides and Aristophanes, from which it was separated by nearly a thousand years of history, and indeed so had the Roman theatre before it. The plays in which Comito appeared were as unlike one of the great Greek tragedies or comedies of the fifth century B.C. as a performance in a London or a New York strip-tease club is unlike a play by Shakespeare. All Comito needed in order to be a success on the stage of the day was to be pretty, uninhibited, and unembarrassable; and while she had been lucky enough to be born pretty, there was perhaps some poetic justice in the fact that the misfortune of being born in the Hippodrome could at least be set against the fact that there was nowhere else on earth better adapted to teaching anyone to be both wholly without inhibitions and almost proof against embarrassment of any kind. Meanwhile, Theodora went along with her as a dresser, and even appeared on the stage with her, dressed as a young slave in a short tunic and carrying a stool on her head for her sister to sit on. She must have been an engaging child at this time, as pretty as Comito and with an impish sense of humour, for it was not long before she was making the audiences roar with laughter by pulling faces and making childish and vulgar gestures to please them. As sharp as a needle, she picked up the ways of the theatre with precocious rapidity, and soon she was given minor parts of her own. As a result, by the time she was fifteen or sixteen she had left Comito behind her and was fast becoming the star of the Byzantine theatre in her own right, with a growing reputation for daring immodesty.

Her success seems to have been due at least in part to her appearance. She was no longer the *gamine* little creature she had been a few years previously; she had developed into a ravishingly beautiful girl with a lovely if diminutive figure, a small oval face with huge dark eyes, a skin as smooth and almost as pale as ivory, and a miraculous grace and vivacious charm which even her worst enemies acknowledged to be irresistibly attractive. 'To express her charm in words or to embody it in a statue would be, for a mere human being, altogether impossible,' Procopius said of her in one of his public works, though he hated her, and even in his vicious *Secret History* he admitted that she was 'fair of face and in general attractive in appearance'. She could not sing; she played no musical instrument; she had no talent as a dancer; and she could not act in the usual sense of that term; but she had a ready wit, a flair for making people laugh, a perfect sense of timing, and a genius for stripping with such suggestive and consummate indecency that the whole of Constantinople flocked to see her with mixed delight and shocked disapproval. According to Procopius, she did her various acts without the smallest scruple or inhibition and with great inventive bawdiness. For example, part of her repertoire was a comic burlesque of the story of Leda and the Swan, during which she would lie on her back on the stage with virtually nothing on, while a domestic goose pecked at some grains of corn secreted between her thighs, and she rolled about in an amorous frenzy, wriggling and twisting and grimacing in an apparent paroxysm of abandonment, to the uproarious delight of her audience. Some people were outraged, but they came in their tens of thousands to see her nevertheless, and she soon became the talk of the town.

But the stage was not the scene of her most notorious exploits. Procopius discharged his heaviest moral broadsides at her for supplementing her earnings in the theatre by becoming a highly successful and highly paid courtesan in her spare time. Her supper parties, he said, were a scandal, and the things which she was prepared to do for the men upon whom she bestowed her favours were infamous. Indeed, her unsavoury reputation and notoriety are based largely on Procopius' highly coloured and lurid account of her sex life at this time; some historians have hinted at it coyly without going into detail, while others have quoted Procopius in his original Greek on the rather specious grounds that such details 'must be veiled in the obscurity of a learned language', as Gibbon put it, as if pornography was suitable reading for those with an academic training and for no one else. In fact, what Procopius said about her was that she was both sexually insatiable and also perverse.

She was extremely clever [he wrote], and had a biting wit, and she soon became popular as a result. There was not a scrap of modesty about her, and no one ever saw her embarrassed; she would do the most shameless things without the smallest hesitation, being the sort of girl who, if you slapped her bottom or boxed her ears, would make a joke of it and roar with laughter: and she would strip herself naked and exhibit bare those parts of her body, both before and behind, which are properly hidden from men's eyes, and should be so. She used to titillate her lovers by keeping them in suspense, and by constantly toying with new ways of making love she never failed to capture the interest of the lecherous; nor did she wait for men to accost her, but she took the initiative herself by wiggling her hips to attract their attention and by cracking suggestive jokes to all who came her way, especially if they were still in their teens. No one has ever been such a total slave to sexual pleasure and indeed to all forms of pleasure as she was. Often she would go to a party with ten young men or even more, all of whom were at the height of their physical powers and devoted to a life of sexual indulgence, and she would sleep with every one of them, one after the other, throughout the night; then, when she had exhausted all of them, she would proceed to seduce their servants, even if there were as many as thirty, lying with each of them in turn; yet even so she would end the night unsatisfied . . . Moreover, although she pressed into service three entrances into her body, she often complained that nature had not made the openings in her nipples larger so that she could have invented a new way of making love there too. Naturally, she often became pregnant, but nearly always she managed to have an abortion.

This deliberately sensational picture of Theodora as a raging nymphomaniac is difficult to reconcile with what is known of her later life, but it would be foolish to react against it by trying to whitewash her altogether; it is no good pretending that she was a paragon of virtue at this time, for it seems sure that she was no such thing. There are some grounds for believing that at the age of about sixteen she had an illegitimate son, though there is no unimpeachable evidence to prove this; but there can be no doubt at all that at about eighteen she had an illegitimate daughter, for much of the girl's subsequent career is well known. So there is probably some truth in Procopius' account of her life at this time. But even so for two reasons his *Secret History* must be taken with a large pinch of salt where it speaks of Theodora: first, he does not claim to have been one of her lovers, and so his detailed account of her sexual practices can be based on nothing more substantial than lascivious gossip and malicious tittle-tattle, neither of which is a source which inspires much confidence; and secondly, every line of his narrative reveals the hatred with which he wrote it as well as the fact that he himself was very obviously not without his psychological problems. He loathed Theodora with a neurotic and obsessional loathing which drove him to accuse her and the man whom she later married, whom he also detested, of being possessed by devils. 'These two people,' he wrote in another part of his *Secret History*, 'never seemed to be human beings but rather avenging devils . . . Assuming human form and becoming demons in human shape, in this disguise they harassed the whole world.' This kind of thing makes him highly suspect as a witness. Even if Theodora did behave as most girls on the Byzantine stage behaved, practising the oldest profession in the world as a side-line, this hardly makes her the she-devil of Procopius' sick and unbalanced imagination, or even such a bird of ill omen, as he also alleged, that respectable people crossed the street to avoid being contaminated by meeting her. Once again his tendency to exaggerate makes him suspect, for the people of Constantinople were far too accustomed to the presence of a few young prostitutes in their midst and far too sophisticated to behave in such a naïve and unlikely fashion. So on the whole Theodora must be given the benefit of the doubt as far as Procopius' most unpleasant and lurid accusations are concerned, though she probably did lead the life of a courtesan at this time. It was one of the few ways of earning a living open to anyone born into the poverty and ignominy of life on the fringe of the Hippodrome, and to a beautiful girl like Theodora it must have seemed a natural and obvious way of bettering herself; moral objections would hardly have been likely to deter her, even if she had been aware of them. Like Eliza Doolittle's father in Bernard Shaw's *Pygmalion*, Theodora's mother and her children could not afford morals; they were too poor. But despite Procopius' accusations to the contrary, she does not seem to have enjoyed her life as a courtesan, for she abandoned it when the first opportunity to do so presented itself.

In about the year 520, when Theodora was approximately twenty years old and at the height of her notoriety, she suddenly disappeared from Constantinople. She had taken a lover in the person of a man named Hecebolus, of whom nothing is known except that he came originally from the city of Tyre in Syria. He was appointed governor of the Pentapolis, the province around Cyrene in North Africa, and when he left to take up his new job, Theodora gave up the stage and her life in Constantinople to go with him. But for once her charms failed her; after only a very short time in Africa, she quarrelled with Hecebolus, who turned her out of his house, piling insults on her as he did so, though why they fell out is not known. It was a disaster for Theodora; she was a thousand miles from home, penniless, and totally alone in a country where she knew no one. Procopius, in an even more nauseatingly self-righteous and prurient mood than usual, wrote of her at this time that 'she was at a loss for the necessities of life, which she proceeded to provide in her usual way, putting her body to work at its unlawful traffic. She first went to Alexandria; later, making her way round the whole East, she returned to Byzantium, plying her trade in each city (a trade which a man may not call by name without forfeiting forever God's compassion), as if heaven itself could not bear that any place should be ignorant of the viciousness of Theodora.' No doubt it was a time of great unhappiness for her, and probably she had no alternative to making a living, in the way gloatingly suggested by Procopius, as a common prostitute, though it is not easy to imagine where he discovered the evidence upon which to base his accusation. By his own admission she was alone in Africa, where no one knew her, and it is highly unlikely that many people even noticed her, let alone took an interest in her or her way of life during this time of unhappiness and insecurity. So it is worth at least wondering where Procopius found anyone who knew how she made a living during these difficult days.

But however she may have managed her affairs, somehow she succeeded in making her way to Alexandria, five hundred miles away. Probably she travelled there by sea rather than by land, for although Roman roads were good in most parts of the world, the journey from Cyrene to Alexandria by road would have been a daunting one. The country between the two cities was hot, desolate, and inhospitable; inns where travellers could spend the night were few and far between, and even in more civilised parts of the world they were often rough places which many people feared; and the North African climate made travelling uncomfortable except during the winter months. By sea, on the other hand, the journey would have been both easier and more peaceful, for during the centuries of Roman rule, the Mediterranean had become ever more and more crowded with shipping going about its lawful business in peace. The pirates, who had infested the seas and had been the scourge of all sailors in earlier times, had been wiped out long before, and merchantmen of all shapes and sizes carried the trade of the Byzantine world from province to province, country to country, without having to worry about being attacked or robbed on the high seas; wheat from Egypt, olive oil from Spain, wine from France, marble from Greece, and a hundred other things were shipped to and fro along the shipping lanes of the Empire, keeping the ports perpetually busy and their inhabitants perennially prosperous. Merchant ships varied very much in tonnage, just as their modern counterparts do today; some were little coasters, which could be handled by a crew of five or six men, about the size of the modern fishing boats which put out to sea from the small harbours of Cornwall and Brittany; while the Egyptian corn ships

The Byzantine Empire

Milan

Rimini

ITALIA

Adriatic Sea

ILLYRICUM

DALMATIA

DA

Corsica

Rome

Thessaloni

Apollonia

MACEDONIA

Sardinia

Naples

Tyrrhenian Sea

Ionian Sea

N

Sicilia

Patras

Carthage

Melita

Mediterrane

NUMIDIA

AFRICA

Cyrene

THE PENTAPO

Byzantine Empire before Justinian I

Territory conquered by Justinian I

0   600

0   300 miles

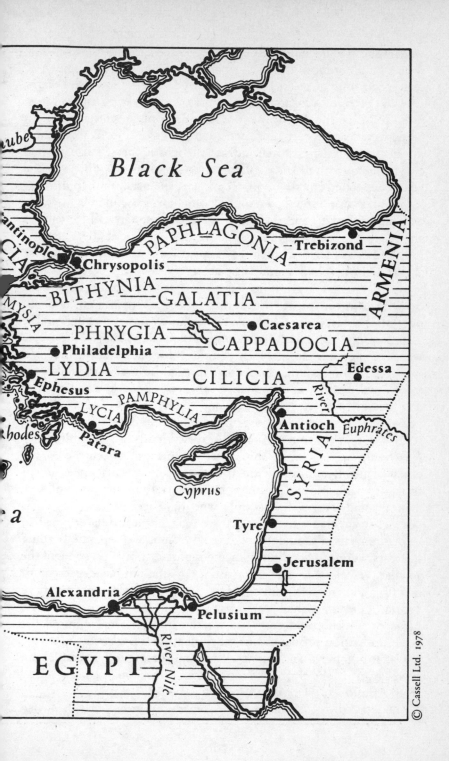

Black Sea

PAPHLAGONIA

Trebizond

ARMENIA

Chrysopolis

BITHYNIA

GALATIA

PHRYGIA

Caesarea

Philadelphia

CAPPADOCIA

LYDIA

CILICIA

Edessa

Ephesus

PAMPHYLIA

River

LYCIA

Antioch

Euphrates

Patara

Rhodes

SYRIA

Cyprus

Tyre

Jerusalem

Alexandria

Pelusium

EGYPT

River Nile

© Cassell Ltd. 1978

were huge by the standards of the day, some being 180 feet long with a beam of more than 45 feet and a hold 40 feet deep, in which over 1000 tons of grain could be stowed. Their prows and sterns rose up gracefully in gradual curves to end in carved figureheads, often representing the Mother of God or a popular saint, who might be expected to protect those who sailed in the ship. Roman ships did not carry much canvas; indeed, the smaller vessels usually had only one square sail on a solitary mast amidships, while even the giants depended chiefly upon a big square mainsail, though this was sometimes surmounted by a topsail, which was useful in light winds and calm weather, and they also had a small square sail forward as an aid to manoeuvring the ship. At the mast-head there usually fluttered a banner on which was depicted yet another saint whose aid could be invoked in times of danger.

Storms were a Byzantine sailor's worst enemy, and they were dreaded. No one put to sea during the winter months if he could possibly help it, though in emergencies it was sometimes impossible to avoid doing so; and even in summer most ships hugged the coasts wherever possible, so that they could run for shelter at the first sign of danger. But as long as prudent precautions of this kind were taken, sea travel was reasonably safe, and since it was far more comfortable than travelling overland, many people preferred it to riding at a snail's pace in horse-drawn or mule-drawn coaches with solid wheels over roughly paved or dusty roads. So, in addition to merchantmen, passenger ships plied regularly between the coastal cities of the Byzantine world carrying civil servants, government officials, bankers, and business men, as well as tourists, holiday-makers, and even a few people who had been ordered by their doctors to spend a week or two at sea for their health. Everyone had to bring his own food and bedding with him, and separate sleeping quarters were provided for men and women, though in some of the smaller vessels this was often done by the simple expedient of dividing a single deck-house down the middle with nothing more substantial than a thick canvas sheet. In larger vessels, however, some of which could carry six hundred passengers or more, the accommodation provided was more elaborate; but such ships were fewer in number than their small competitors, and if Theodora did travel by sea, she probably took passage in a small coastal vessel from Apollonia, the port of Cyrene.

She stayed in Alexandria for several months, and her visit

changed the course of her life. As a city it was magnificent. It had the best natural harbour in the eastern Mediterranean; the approach to the place by sea was marked by one of the seven wonders of the world, for in 279 B.C. Ptolemy Philadelphus had built a great marble lighthouse over four hundred feet high on the little island of Pharos at the entrance to the harbour there; its streets, which were laid out on the gridiron principle, ran from the sea in the north to the shores of Lake Mareotis in the south, whose fresh waters were constantly replenished by the Nile; and its history was as splendid as the architecture of its principal buildings. For years it had been the proud possessor of the greatest library in the world, until eventually it had been wantonly burnt by some over-enthusiastic Christians. In the third century B.C. Euclid had founded a mathematical school there which was destined to endure for 700 years; in the same century the geographer Eratosthenes had measured the diameter of the earth correctly to within fifty miles; and four centuries later, another Alexandrian, Ptolemy, had mapped the known world so accurately that one of the greatest British archeologists of the twentieth century, Sir Mortimer Wheeler, used to claim that he had used Ptolemy's maps at opposite ends of the compass in India and in Britain with profit. In view of all this, it is not surprising that after the sack of Rome by the barbarians at the beginning of the fifth century Alexandria claimed to be second only to Constantinople itself amongst the cities of the Byzantine world, although Antioch disputed her right to do so. Above all, it was a great commercial centre, an enormous international market place; through its wharves and storage depots passed the corn which was exported from Egypt to Constantinople to make the bread which was issued free to the people there by the government; its warehouses were stacked with fruit and olive oil from the Levant, gold from Ethiopia, and ivory from central Africa destined for the markets and luxury shops of cities throughout the Empire. Naturally, most of its merchandise came from Africa or the near East, but some goods from the far East found their way into the Roman world through Alexandria too; aloes, cloves, and sandalwood from Indo-China could be bought there; pepper came from Malabar, silk from China, musk from India, and rubies from Ceylon.

It was renowned for its wealth, its elegance, its corruption, and the beauty of its courtesans; but it was also one of the great capitals of the Christian world, and the fame of its saints, theologians, Patriarchs, and monks had spread far and wide. The great and uncompromising Athanasius had been made archbishop of Alexandria when he was only about thirty years of age; Antony of the desert, whose sanctity was as evident to all as the fact that he had not washed for forty years, had drawn admiring crowds of people after him through the streets of the city, when he had visited it at the height of the bitter religious dispute between Athanasius and the heresiarch Arius; Clement had lived there and written his elegant and lucid denunciations of ignorance and error, condemning them as greater evils than sin, thus earning for himself a reputation for doubtful orthodoxy; and the monastic movement, which had been born in the Egyptian desert nearby, had thrived there so mightily that the suburbs were full of monasteries and the city crowded with monks.

Theodora arrived at a time of great political and religious unrest. Since the beginning of the fourth century when Constantine had adopted Christianity as the official religion of the Empire, successive Emperors and their governments had tried to force religious unity upon their millions of infinitely varied subjects as a means of binding the Graeco-Roman world together, for the disunity of their enormous and unwieldy realm was their perpetual nightmare. Disunity had nearly destroyed the Empire in the second and third centuries. Constantine had grown up at a time when he and three other men were contending for the throne of the Roman world and tearing it apart in the process. He had eventually eliminated his three rivals, and having done so one of his major motives for making Christianity the official religion of the Empire was that he saw in it a powerful means of welding it together and strengthening its precarious unity. Thus from the earliest days of Byzantine civilisation, which was heir to the older civilisation of pagan Rome, any deviation from the accepted doctrines and creeds of the Church, the sudden emergence of any new interpretation of Christian belief, anything in fact likely to set Christians arguing and disagreeing with each other rather than agreeing was regarded with apprehension by the rulers of the Byzantine world as a threat to its political unity. Since anything was preferable to the disastrous disunity of the days before Constantine, Emperor after Emperor tried to force agreement on his Christian subjects, though some sided with the Orthodox party and others sided with the opponents of the strictly Orthodox party line. Persecution after persecution was launched upon those Christians who dared to threaten the unity of the Empire by disagreeing with the doctrines supported by the Emperor of the day, and anyone who had the temerity to deviate from the narrow path of contemporary orthodoxy did so at his peril. The Communist heresy hunts of our own century and the bitter disputes between orthodox Marxists, Trotskyites, Maoists, supporters of Tito, and disciples of the unfortunate Dubček have been very similar to the violent and polemical conflicts between the Orthodox ecclesiastical party and those whom they considered to be heretics in Byzantine days; and this similarity is not entirely coincidental. Both the Russian state and the Russian Orthodox Church, which were the parents of Soviet Russia, were themselves children of Byzantine civilisation, and the Communist world is therefore its grandchild, inheriting many of Byzantium's faults as well as some of its virtues.

But the struggle of the rulers of Byzantium to enforce religious uniformity upon their subjects from Spain to the borders to Persia and from the Crimea to Upper Egypt was made formidably difficult by one simple but awkward fact: those same subjects behaved as though they were divided into two irreconcilable camps by a fundamental psychological difference of approach to religion, which made it impossible for them to see each other's point of view or even to agree on the very nature of the Christian faith. This is not the place to describe in detail the complex and abstruse theological problems which so excited the Byzantines and their world: problems which are infinitely remote from our own world and its way of thinking; but since Theodora herself was deeply involved in the passions aroused by them and the fights which they caused, a brief look at the nature of the differences which so bedevilled the world in which she lived is unavoidable, if she herself and the ideals which inspired her are to be understood. It would be an over-simplification to say that the people of her day were divided into Protestant and Catholic prototypes, and yet it would not be wholly misleading as a rough analogy. It would be nearer the truth to say that they were divided into those who were primarily conscious of the mystery and transcendence of God and those to whom the fact that he had given himself an image in Christ was the supreme, unique, and pre-eminent truth of the Christian faith; but of course people in both groups acknowledged both truths, and it

27

was only a difference of emphasis which divided them. It was a difference which was compounded, however, by the fact that both sides used the same or similar words to describe different ideas or beliefs in much the same way as Communists and social democrats today both use the word 'democracy' to describe radically different political concepts. Difficult as it is neatly to define the fundamental difference between the two great opposing groups of Theodora's day, the fact is that on the one hand nearly all the people of the eastern provinces of Syria and Palestine together with the people of Egypt were deeply attracted to the simplicity and purity of a belief in one transcendent God, of whom there could be no image and no likeness, while on the other hand the people of the western provinces including Italy and Greece liked to surround themselves with icons and mosaics and other images as reminders of the central and glorious fact that Jesus had been the image of God.

It may not seem much of a difference to us, but it bitterly divided Theodora's world, as disputes about the interpretation of the word 'democracy' and its implementation in practice divide our world; and as if this argument was not enough to divide the people of the day, there was a further and even more profound difference in the way in which their minds worked, which made it more difficult to unite them or even to persuade them to live in peace together. While the Greek mind was profoundly analytical, and the Roman mind had a fondness for legal definition, both had a natural dislike of unsolved mysteries. When these two minds came together, as they did in the Orthodox councils of the Byzantine Church, they drove men to attack the intellectual problems posed by Christian belief in very much the same way that the physicists and cosmologists of our own century have attacked the problems posed by the nature of the physical universe; and such men were not content until they had found a verbal formula or set of formulae in which to define the findings of their brilliant, subtle, and profound intellectual analysis of the problems they tackled. Although they were prepared to admit that the final mystery of God was indeed a mystery, they had little or no use for mystery or darkness as such; the enigmas of the Christian faith had to be forced to reveal their secrets if at all possible, until their darkest corners were uniformly illuminated by the light of human understanding in an orderly, well-articulated way and with as much clarity as was attainable, very much as the atoms, which physicists have examined in our own day, have been forced to reveal the secrets of their nuclear composition.

But to the middle eastern and mostly Semitic people of Syria, Palestine, and Egypt this way of thinking about God was close to blasphemy; their minds worked in a different way from that of the Greeks, for they were descendants of Abraham, Moses, and the great Jewish prophets, who had moved in a world of mystery and encounter: a world heavy with silence and shadow, where the appropriate response to the ultimate mystery of God, whom no man could see, let alone analyse and define, was reverence, not intellectual arrogance. Job, who had tried to reason and argue with God until, confronted with the overwhelming reality of his presence, he was forced to repent in dust and ashes, was a very typical Semitic man. Greek ways were not his ways, and he was convinced that they were not God's ways either; so a great gulf divided the two sides. Matters were made worse by the fact that to many of these near-eastern men the doctrine of the Trinity, which was the crowning glory of both western intellectual achievement and strict ecclesiastical orthodoxy, seemed to come very close to blasphemy by encouraging people to believe in three gods instead of the one transcendent God of pure monotheism.

The dust had settled on the Trinitarian battlefields of the fourth century before Theodora was born, but the Byzantine world was still divided into two opposing camps, as it had been a hundred years earlier and for much the same reasons, except that at this time the subject over which the two sides were arguing was not the nature of God but the nature of Christ. The Graeco-Roman lust for analysis and definition had been at work again, and the result was that strict orthodoxy demanded that all Christians should believe that in Christ two natures, one human and one divine, had co-existed side by side without interfering with each other. It was a highly technical point, yet it split the Christian world down the middle; for the people of Syria, Palestine, and Egypt could not bring themselves to accept this official party line, preferring to believe that, although Christ had been both God and man, his human nature had been absorbed into his divine nature during his life on earth. Since this could be presented as a belief that Christ had had only one nature, those who took this view were called Monophysites from the two Greek words, *monos* (single) and *phusis* (nature). Unintelligible as it is to most people today that anyone should become violently excited by such an issue, the fact is that it seemed to everyone then to be so crucial that passions ran immensely high for many years; and since Theodora's life was destined to be spent in the midst of the storm roused by those passions, no account of her life can afford to ignore them.

When she arrived in Alexandria, the Byzantine world was in a ferment as a result of a change of official government policy in religious matters, which had recently taken place in Constantinople. For some years the Emperors had tolerated and even favoured the Monophysites in an attempt to keep their eastern provinces happy, but with the accession of the Emperor Justin there had been a sudden reversal in favour of their Orthodox opponents, and instructions had been given to the authorities in the provinces to order anyone whom they suspected of being a Monophysite to give up his deviationist beliefs and his nonconformist ways and embrace a full Orthodoxy or take the consequences. The result had been a full-scale persecution of thousands of people who refused to bow to force or to deny their most deeply held convictions; no one was exempt from inquisition; archbishops and bishops were evicted from their sees if they would not conform; monasteries were burnt to the ground and their inhabitants chased into the hills like criminals; churches were deprived of their priests and deserted by their terrified congregations; and in some places blood was shed and lives were lost when people stood up to the imperial commissioners and their agents. The brunt of all this fell on the people of Syria and Palestine, many of whom fled to Egypt, which had been exempted from persecution by the express order of the Emperor despite the fact that it was full of Monophysites.

The Emperor did not dare offend the Egyptians for two very good and practical reasons. First, the Patriarch of Alexandria was known to be sympathetic to the Monophysites, and he was also known to be surrounded by so many monks, who were devoted to the Monophysite cause, and who were prepared to fight for it with passion and ferocity if needs be, that any force short of an army of persecutors despatched against him would have been torn to pieces in no time. Secondly, Constantinople depended so heavily upon Egypt for corn, all of which was shipped from Alexandria, that no Emperor in his senses dared to stir up a hornets' nest by offending the Alexandrians for fear of creating a famine and provoking a revolt in the rest of his Empire, when the supplies of corn were cut off at the source. So Alexandria became the principal sanctuary for those who fled for their lives from Syria and Palestine, and when Theodora entered the city it was full of refugees. Finding themselves hospitably welcomed by the Patriarch, a man named Timothy, many settled in the city, and attempted to gather up the threads of their lives all over again and make a new beginning; but hundreds of others, who had lost everything they ever possessed, including wives and families, passed through Alexandria into the solitude of the Egyptian desert, which stretched away to the south and to the west, its horizons lost in the heat-haze, its barren wastes alternately dancing and shimmering in the glare of the African sun and smothered in suffocating dust storms. Here the founders of the solitary life had lived, prayed, and died in a desolation of poverty and an exaltation of spirit which had so impressed the Roman world that their example had been followed by thousands of men and women in search of God; and here in 'the desert of the saints', as it had come to be called, because it was full of hermits, monks and anchorites, many Syrian and Palestinian Monophysites sought the freedom of the wilderness to believe what they believed, to worship as they wished to worship, to live in poverty, and to die in peace.

With all this going on in the city and in his archdiocese, it is astonishing that Timothy, the Patriarch of Alexandria, should have got to know Theodora in view of the eminence of his position and the many calls on his time which must have been made by other people; indeed, it is difficult to imagine just how he could have met her in the first place, for with the city full of fugitives from the persecution in Syria and Palestine, the arrival of a 21-year-old girl of doubtful reputation, with no letter of introduction or other claim upon him, was not an event which he was likely to notice. But there is no room for doubt that he did indeed meet her, for he made such an impression on her at this time that for the rest of her life she referred to him as her spiritual father, a title which she gave to no one else. Although we shall never know how they met, it is easy enough to guess why Theodora was so impressed by him; when she was washed up in Alexandria by a tide of misfortune, the last thing she could have expected was to be welcomed there by the archbishop, let alone to be kindly welcomed. It is unlikely that she had known much kindness either during her life in the Hippodrome or during her career on the stage; people do not as a rule treat the Theodoras of this life kindly. They may treat them generously, passionately, and amorously or, of course, callously, brutally, and impersonally, but they seldom treat them with ordinary human kindness. Theodora was overwhelmed.

Nothing much is known about Timothy, who had only just become Patriarch, except that he was a Monophysite by conviction, though he tried to play a moderating role in the theological disputes of the day, and that he deeply impressed Theodora. Most accounts of him are uncomplimentary, but this is not surprising, for the history of the people whom the early church condemned as heretics has been written almost exclusively by their enemies, who were far from impartial. More often than not they have been blackened and misrepresented in much the same way as opponents of the official Communist party line are blackened and misrepresented by spokesmen of the Kremlin in our own day. Though some of the leaders of the heretical parties in the church were men of less subtle minds than the best of their orthodox adversaries, tending to over-simplify deep and complex issues, it was by no means always so, and some of them were men of great intellectual ability and equally great integrity. Even more important, they were often as loving and as saintly as the best of their enemies, and sometimes more so. This was something which Theodora soon discovered in Alexandria, for Timothy seems to have been such a man, and his impact on her was decisive; from this time her way of life was completely changed. Whether she was converted from a state of total religious ignorance at this time, or whether some sort of rudimentary Christian faith picked up in her childhood was greatly deepened while she was in Alexandria, the evidence all points to the conclusion that she underwent a deep and lasting religious experience there, and that Timothy was largely responsible for it. But she also met another eminent Christian, while she was in the city, who may have had a hand in her conversion, if conversion it was; and for him too she formed a lasting respect and affection.

His name was Severus, and he was the Patriarch of Antioch. Together with many other exiles, as a Monophysite he had been forced to leave his own archdiocese while the persecution was at its height and seek safety in Egypt. He had had a stormy career, beginning life as a pagan and a student of law, at which time he had been a great admirer of Aristotle; but later he had been converted to Christianity and had become a monk in Alexandria. He had not been there long, however, before he was expelled from the city by the Orthodox archbishop of the day as a turbulent heretic;

whereupon he had promptly gone to Constantinople with a band of like-minded monks, and he had remained there until his activities on behalf of the Monophysite cause had provoked a riot. But in spite of this history of trouble-making he had so many virtues and intellectual qualities that in A.D. 513 the Emperor Anastasius, whose ecclesiastical policy was to favour the Monophysites, made him archbishop of Antioch. As Patriarch of that great and ancient city he became a leading propagandist and teacher of his own brand of Christian doctrine, and almost certainly it was from him that Theodora learned how to hold her own in theological argument and debate. While she could not have had a more brilliant tutor, he could scarcely have had an apter pupil, for Theodora was both highly intelligent and extremely articulate, though she had probably never had an opportunity before meeting Severus to exercise her mind or to develop a taste for intelligent conversation.

Her stay in Alexandria lasted for several months, though exactly how long is not known. Before returning to Constantinople she went to Antioch for a time, where she made friends with a celebrated dancer named Macedonia. It has been said that Macedonia was accustomed to moving in exalted circles, and that it may well have been through her instrumentality that Theodora, when eventually she returned to the capital, met the man who was destined so radically to change her fortunes; but there is no real evidence as to how this happened. All that is known for certain is that in A.D. 522 she returned to the scene of her former notoriety in Constantinople, perhaps visiting Paphlagonia on the southern shores of the Black Sea *en route*, but not to her old haunts or ways. Instead, she found some sort of modest accommodation, where she lived, and earned an even more modest living by spinning wool, as the women of Rome had done in earlier and less corrupt days. But she had not been in the city for long before she did indeed meet the man with whom her destiny was to be indissolubly linked for the rest of her life. His name was Justinian, and he was the heir to the throne of the Roman world.

III

ΘΕ
ΟΑΫ
ΡΑ

Justinian was a man of medium height, slightly on the plump side, with a round face and curly dark hair; he was pleasant enough to look at but by no means exceptionally handsome. He had been born in a village named Tauresium in the Roman province of Dardania not far from the modern city of Nish in Yugoslavia, and Justinian was not the name given to him by his parents, who had called him Petrus Sabbatius. They were peasants, and he owed the extraordinary change in fortune, which altered the course of his life when he was about eight years old, to an uncle who adopted him, took him to Constantinople, and re-named him Justinian. His uncle too had begun life as a peasant in the neighbouring village of Bederiana. It was a part of the world which had been thoroughly Romanised over the centuries, and although most of the peasants were of Thracian stock and spoke the original Thracian language—an Indo-European tongue related to Armenian—they also spoke Latin, and some bore Latin names. Such was the case with Justinian's uncle, whose name was Justin, and who seems to have been one of the younger sons of a small peasant farmer. He grew up in a part of the world in which the normal lot of the peasants was poverty, and since Justin was not the heir to the family farm, at the age of about fourteen or fifteen he decided to leave home and seek his fortune elsewhere. With two other young peasants of whom nothing is known except their names, Zimarchus and Dityvistus, and with some food for the journey in a bag on his back, he set out to walk to Constantinople, where he joined the army. Being a strong, well-built lad he was drafted into the Palace Guards, with whom he might easily have served without distinction for the rest of his life, in which case he would eventually have been sent home with a small pension to die in his native village; but such was not to be his fate. He must have been

34

a man of considerable ability and intelligence, for as the years went by he rose from the ranks, serving in a number of increasingly senior and responsible military posts.

At some time during his military career in the army he bought a slave-girl and made her his concubine. Her name was Lupicina, and she followed Justin wherever he went, even when he was on active service, living in camp with him and looking after him as well as she could under the circumstances. He must have had other virtues as well as ability and intelligence, for he treated the girl with great kindness, and eventually became so fond of her that he married her. It may have been on the occasion of his marriage to her that she changed her name to Euphemia, which had a less proletarian sound to it than Lupicina, and was thus more suited to the wife of someone who was beginning to move in increasingly lofty social circles as he was given higher and higher command in the army. A soldier's profession was one in which a man of ambition could expect to better himself, but even by Byzantine standards Justin's progress was remarkable, and when, in his fifties, he was made Count of the Excubitors (or Commander of the Imperial Guard in Constantinople), he seemed to have reached the highest position open to any soldier. But it was not so.

At that time, the Emperor was an old man named Anastasius, who had been on the throne for twenty-seven years when, on 9 July 518, he died at the age of eighty-seven. His death created an immediate crisis in Constantinople for reasons which need not be described here in detail, but which included a very real possibility of a bid for the throne by a rebel general in command of some Gothic troops stationed about ten days' march away to the north on the coast of the Black Sea not far from the mouth of the Danube. Since this man might have decided at any time to march on the capital at the head of his men, it was imperative that the throne should not be left unoccupied for longer than was absolutely unavoidable; a new Emperor was needed at once, and he had to be a man who could cope with this threat of a military *coup d'état*. Anastasius had been childless, and although he had had three nephews, for one reason or another none of them was thought to be suitable as his successor. So someone else had to be found as quickly as possible.

One obvious candidate was a man named Celer, who was Master of Offices (or head of the huge Byzantine civil service), and he was backed by some of the household troops who were stationed in the capital, but not by those under Justin's command. Celer hastily summoned the Senate, the Patriarch, and the highest government officials to the Palace to press his own candidacy upon them, while the people of Constantinople, who revelled in this kind of thing, crowded into the Hippodrome and began to call for a new Emperor. While negotiations were going on in the Palace, officers of the Palace Guard, who favoured Celer, appeared from time to time in order to keep the crowd happy by putting forward names of possible candidates, none of whom were serious suggestions, but were meant to be rejected by the crowd, which in every case they were; it was a delaying tactic pure and simple. Meanwhile, however, some of Justin's men arrived on the scene, and began to call his name, whereupon fights broke out between them and those who supported Celer. Justin himself then appeared in the Hippodrome, ostensibly to restore order there, and his men began to call even more vociferously for him as Emperor; but he refused. Fighting then again broke out, and the crowd joined in with the rival bands of soldiers, as names were bandied about and passions began to run high, until pandemonium became general. It was not long before an angry mob was beating on the ivory doors behind which the Senate was in session; by this time Celer was deeply alarmed, and he and the terrified Senators turned to Justin, who seemed to be the one man with the power to control the situation, and begged him to accept the throne. Once again, he refused; but as the rioting spread and threatened to get totally out of hand, Justin at last yielded to the increasingly urgent entreaties of the Senate. Immediately, he was escorted into the Hippodrome by his own troops, who raised him shoulder high on a shield as custom dictated, and an officer put a golden chain on his head in symbolic coronation. The standards of the soldiers, which had been lowered in sorrow at the moment when Anastasius had died, were raised again in triumph, and as the Patriarch stepped forward to place the diadem of the Roman Emperors on Justin's head, the crowd rose to the occasion and cheered their new imperial master to the echo. The crisis was past, and the peasant boy from Bederiana had indeed bettered himself.

As Emperor, Justin often found himself out of his depth. He was over sixty when he ascended the throne, an old soldier of great practical ability but little sophistication and less education. Procopius, who disliked him, declared in his *Secret History* that he was illiterate and could not even sign his own name, but this is extremely unlikely. He could hardly have been promoted to high command in the army if he had been wholly unable to read or write; Byzantine standards were higher than that. But even so, the job of a military commander, however senior, was very different from that of an Emperor who was the undisputed ruler of a realm stretching from the Adriatic to the deserts of the Middle East and from the waters of the Danube to the sands of Nubia, and Justin turned more and more for advice and help to his nephew Justinian.

Very little is known about Justinian's early life except the bare fact that he had been adopted by his uncle and given a first-class education, of which no one could have taken greater advantage than he did, for intellectually he was far above most people, with the temperament and the tastes of a scholar. He had the kind of mind which was capable both of greatness of vision and of minute attention to detail, and as if this rare combination of virtues was not enough for any man, he also had a passion for work; in order to indulge it, he disciplined himself with monastic severity, sleeping as little as possible and rising in the early hours of the morning in order to return to whatever task was currently absorbing him. The investment which his uncle had made in his education could therefore hardly have paid higher dividends, and it is not surprising that, as the years went by, Justin came more and more to rely on his brilliant nephew for help and advice. Indeed, Justinian became the power behind the throne, and those who sought favours of any kind from the Emperor tended increasingly to approach Justinian rather than his uncle. This was not difficult, for although he led the frugal life of a dedicated scholar and cultivated austere habits, he was not in the least austere as a man; on the contrary, he was easy in manner, affable, readily approachable, always in control of his temper, and naturally kind.

Nothing is known about his social life before he met Theodora. Self-indulgence was foreign to his nature, but he must have enjoyed some moments of relaxation from time to time, and presumably it was at such a time that he met her. The mere fact that he moved occasionally in the kind of circles where he could meet a girl with her reputation and background, even if by this time she had become a reformed character, may perhaps be an indication that he was not averse to sowing a few wild oats when the opportunity arose; it would have been odd if a man in his social position had never done so. But however this may have been, he did indeed meet her, and he seems to have fallen deeply, passionately, and hopelessly in love with her from the first moment he saw her; and despite the difference between them, both of age and of temperament, he was destined to love her without reserve until the day of his death. Not surprisingly, when the news of their romance burst upon an astonished world, the citizens of Constantinople were so staggered by it that they attributed Justinian's infatuation to the use of love philtres and magic potions administered to him by Theodora. But the truth was simpler: she had always been devastatingly attractive to men, and Justinian was no exception to the rule. Moreover, he found in her exactly the right complement to himself, for she supplied the qualities which he lacked; they were equally intelligent, but where Justinian had the brilliant mind of an academic visionary, dreaming dreams of restoring the Empire to its former glory, Theodora had a firmer grasp of reality than he had. She had not been brought up in the Hippodrome for nothing, and her mind was in some ways more practical and more penetrating than his, so that her political judgement was nearly always the sounder of the two; and although she was eighteen years younger than him, she had a strength of will and character upon which he was destined to rely again and again in times of crisis.

Meanwhile for her part Theodora would hardly have been human if she had not been elated by the extraordinary reversal of fortune, which had been brought about by her meeting with Justinian. In any age a girl in Theodora's position would have been excited when a man of Justinian's standing fell in love with her, whether she happened to return his love or not. In a state not far removed from penury, she was suddenly offered great riches; after her time of dereliction in north Africa, a position of complete security was hers for the taking; and however disreputable her past may or may not have been, an august future now stretched away invitingly before her eyes. It would be impossible to blame her if she had accepted Justinian's advances without loving him in return, but there is in fact no reason to doubt that she did indeed love him. Even Procopius never suggested that Theodora was anything but completely faithful to Justinian; in every crisis of his career she stood by him, and although it will remain for ever impossible to know what went on in their most private life together, by far the simplest explanation of their known behaviour over many years is

38

that she loved Justinian as much, if not as demonstratively, as he loved her. If anyone was foolish enough to threaten their relationship, she reacted with cold and immediate ferocity, and nothing could save that person from her undying enmity. Justinian was hers, and she would brook no rival.

Shortly after meeting him, she became his mistress. He was living at the time in the Palace of Hormisdas, which had been built by Constantine and given to a Persian prince of that name, who had sought political asylum in Constantinople; the house lay close to the shore of the Sea of Marmara near the mouth of the Bosphorus, and here Theodora moved in with him. He was so in love with her that he piled presents on her with an immense and delighted prodigality. She had been born in poverty, so he loaded her with riches; she was used to being treated as of no account, so he persuaded his easy-going uncle to raise her to the rank of Patrician; no one had ever asked her opinion on important matters of state, so Justinian made a point of consulting her in everything, and usually took her advice; he was staunchly orthodox in religious matters, but when he discovered Theodora's affection for the Monophysites, he persuaded the Emperor to call a halt to their persecution and to issue orders that they should be treated with greater consideration than they had known for some time. But even these marks of his love for her were not enough for him; until he could marry her, Justinian refused to be satisfied. However, there were formidable difficulties in the way of such a plan. The law against a man of his station marrying anyone who had ever been on the stage could not be conveniently ignored or forgotten, as though it had never been put on the statute book in the first place; and to Justinian's surprise and dismay Justin's consort proved to be implacably opposed to the mere idea of such a marriage. She herself might have started life as a slave-girl with the undignified name of Lupicina, but now that she was the Empress Euphemia, she had no intention of being succeeded on the throne by a wanton little tart from the Hippodrome, who was no better than she should be despite her pretty face. Complete deadlock would have followed, and Justinian would have had to postpone his marriage indefinitely, if the old lady had not suddenly and most conveniently died in about the year 523; the exact date of her death is not known. If she had to die, she could not have chosen a more opportune moment to do so from her nephew's point of view, for now nothing stood in the way of his marriage to the girl whom he adored except the law which forbade anyone who had been an actress from marrying a man such as himself. It was not difficult to persuade his uncle to have that particular statute changed in such a way that, in future, those who had abandoned their careers on the stage, and had shown some evidence of repentance for their past way of life, could marry whom they pleased.

As soon as they could decently do so after the death of the old Empress, Justinian and Theodora were married by Epiphanius, the Patriarch of Constantinople at the time, in the Church of the Holy Wisdom, which had been built originally by Constantine only to be partly burnt down and rebuilt in A.D. 404. Nothing remains of it now, but it is known to have been a great rectangular basilica lit by mullioned windows which were glazed with plates of translucent marble, while its walls were decorated with inlaid marble and mosaic, and the whole interior was crowded with hundreds of statues of saints and Emperors. Here under the carved eyes of Constantine's mother, Helena, who was represented by three statues, one in porphyry, one in silver, and another in ivory, and in front of a crowd of courtiers, Patricians and Senators, officers of the Excubitors, the Scholars, and other *élite* regiments, ministers of the Crown and top-ranking civil servants, all resplendent in their uniforms or their long embroidered silk robes sparkling with jewels, Justinian pledged himself to Theodora and she to him. The galleries were packed with an even more dazzling gathering of ladies-in-waiting, maids of honour, and the wives and daughters of the assembled dignitaries in the nave below. Her sisters, Comito and Anastasia, must have been present, for Theodora's loyalty to the people whom she had loved in the old days never wavered, but no one knows whether her mother was still alive to witness her daughter's improbable triumph. After the marriage vows had been administered and duly taken, the liturgy wound its endless and sonorous way like some solemn and sacred ballet through clouds of incense and drifts of prayers chanted by bearded priests and deacons; Justinian and Theodora were given the sacrament of Christ's body, followed by that of his blood in a silver spoon, and then Epiphanius blessed them in God's name while a veil was held over them. Then and only then, with nuptial crowns placed on their heads where the veils had been, did they turn hand in hand and walk slowly out of the church through the assembled dignitaries in the nave and the little crowd of beggars and cripples who were always to be found in the narthex, a kind of vestibule or ante-chamber to the church, to remind everyone of the existence of poverty and misfortune. Outside the church they showed themselves to the crowds of people who thronged the Augusteum in the hope of catching a glimpse of Justinian's new bride. It seems that they liked what they saw, for no one protested against the marriage. Social rigidity was never one of the vices of Byzantine society, and on the whole people accepted Theodora. A few, who already disliked Justinian and considered that both he and his uncle were upstarts, were not surprised that he had chosen such a wife; what else could be expected from someone with Justinian's peasant background, they asked each other with sour satisfaction. But many more, who must have remembered going to watch Theodora strip on the stage a couple of years earlier, did not hesitate to offer her their congratulations or to pay their humble respects to someone who in all probability would one day be their sovereign. Despite her diminutive stature, she received them all with ineffable grace and consummate dignity as to the manner born. Her new way of life suited her perfectly.

IV

For nearly three years after his marriage to Theodora, Justinian remained no more than heir presumptive to the throne and the power behind it, though at least one attempt was made to persuade the ageing Emperor to proclaim his nephew to be co-Emperor with him; but Justin refused. Nevertheless by this time there was little doubt in anyone's mind that Justinian would succeed his uncle when eventually the old man died. His only serious rival had been eliminated in unpleasant circumstances a few years earlier by being murdered during a banquet in the Palace and some people suspected that Justinian had been responsible for his death, though his guilt was by no means certain. He already held the post of Count of the Domestics, which was equivalent to Commander-in-Chief of the army, as well as the rank of Master of Soldiers or Field Marshal; and even more significantly from the point of view of the realities of power politics, he was the acknowledged champion and hero of the Blues, who were powerful enough in the capital itself to act almost as king-makers in a political crisis, if they chose to do so.

Since the relationship between Justinian and the Blues was destined to have a dramatic effect on events in the future, it is worth looking at it in some detail here, and at the way in which it had developed during the first years of Justin's reign. For during this period some of the Blues had become increasingly arrogant in their disregard for the law, and Justinian's enemies alleged that they were able to ignore it with impunity because they were protected by him from legal retribution; and there is reason to believe that this may have been true. Certainly, if Justinian was not protecting them from the legal consequences of their actions at this time, someone was. Not all the Blues were criminals by any means, but at the centre of both factions, Blues and Greens, there was a small nucleus of young men who cared nothing for law and order. Dedicated hooligans, they were known as 'the Partisans', and were greatly feared, for they roamed the city in gangs, and terrorised law-abiding citizens. Like most of the very similar gangs of youths who roam our own city streets from time to time, they were easily recognisable by their appearance; they let their hair grow long at the back, shaved their foreheads, and wore beards. Their clothes were equally distinctive, separating them at a glance from all ordinary citizens and acting as a kind of para-military uniform; for where everyone else wore normal full-length Byzantine tunics falling to the ankles, the Partisans went around in short coats with wide sleeves, which they drew tight at the wrists, over trousers which they had copied from the Huns. The result was that they looked more like some new species of barbarian than civilised citizens of the world's greatest city, and they behaved like barbarians too. Indeed, they stopped at nothing, fighting bloody battles between themselves whenever a bunch of Blues met a gang of Greens, beating people up and robbing them of their jewellery, their money, and even their clothes, and raping any attractive woman who was foolish enough to cross their path. If the civil authorities tried to interfere with them, the over-taxed police were lucky if they got away with their lives, and on the rare occasions when they succeeded in bringing some of these criminals to justice, nearly always they were quietly released without being punished or even brought to trial.

It had been suspected for a long time that these gangs accepted commissions to murder anyone against whom someone else had a grudge, and the culminating scandal came when a well-known and respected citizen was openly murdered by some Partisans in the Church of the Holy Wisdom. Justinian happened to be seriously ill at the time, and the crime was brought to the attention of his uncle Justin by some senior ministers, who did not want to miss the opportunity of dealing with the gangs while their protector, if he was indeed shielding them from retribution, was unable to prevent the law from taking its course. They urged the old Emperor to take drastic action against the Partisans immediately on the grounds that they were an intolerable social cancer which needed cutting out of the body politic once and for all. Justin agreed. He was appalled at what he was told, and he ordered the Prefect of the city, a certain Theodotus Colocynthus, to take whatever measures were necessary to wipe out these enemies of society.

With the authority of the Emperor behind him, the Prefect, who had smarted for years from the insolence of the Partisans, bitterly resenting their virtual immunity from reprisals, declared something very like war on them. They were hunted down without mercy and arrested in their hundreds, to the delight of the ordinary men and women in the street, who thanked God that at last these thugs and assassins, who had made life impossible for everyone else for far too long, were being given a taste of their own medicine. The Partisans fought back with their accustomed violent ferocity, but they were no match for the forces of law and order once they were fully mobilised against them, and they could not avoid arrest. At first, this did not unduly worry them. Indeed, when they were arrested many of them laughed at their captors, for they fully expected to be released without coming to any harm, as had always happened in the past; but they were soon to be disillusioned. All of them were tried, and most of them were found guilty of a number of serious crimes; many were hanged, some were burnt, and others were beheaded, while a few lucky ones were allowed to live on condition that they took religious vows and spent the rest of their days in monasteries.

Shortly after this campaign against the Partisans, Justinian recovered from his illness, but it was too late to save those who had been condemned; they had already been executed for their crimes. However, Theodotus Colocynthus was dismissed from office as Prefect of the city and exiled to Jerusalem, and it is not surprising that people attributed his disgrace to Justinian's recovery of health and his desire for vengeance. Whether it was true or not that he was responsible for getting rid of Theodotus, the two circus factions believed it to be so, and the Blues in particular were duly grateful to him as a result; so, although their wings had been clipped, they remained his staunch supporters. It was not long after his marriage to Theodora that it became known that she detested the Greens; since this meant that she too was a supporter of the Blues, the news served to strengthen their traditional loyalty to Justinian's cause, and with the old Emperor visibly failing, their backing was a factor which reinforced Justinian's chances of succeeding him when the time should come.

Meanwhile from Theodora's point of view the years between her marriage and the death of the old Emperor were invaluable, for they gave her time in which to get to know the formal and resplendent

44

world of the Imperial Palace and to become accustomed to living in its rarefied and Olympian atmosphere, before she became its acknowledged mistress. The Palace itself was not a single large building like Buckingham Palace but a great complex of buildings more like the Kremlin in Moscow, covering a considerable area and housing the whole apparatus of the central government of the Empire.

It had been built piecemeal by various Emperors over the years around a series of courtyards and gardens, where fountains played in summer, and icy winds from the Black Sea whistled in winter. It has almost entirely disappeared now, but in its heyday there must have been as many as two dozen buildings or more within the Palace precincts, all built on a hill overlooking the Bosphorus and the Sea of Marmara; pavilions, banqueting halls, and state rooms for the Emperor and his guests stood side by side with baths, churches, and offices for Ministers of State, while the Palace Guard had its own quarters. It was very magnificent, for the world had been ransacked to embellish it; red granite columns had been brought by barge from Egypt, porphyry from Ptolemais on the coast of Palestine, and marble from the hills of Attica to adorn its buildings, while in the more sumptuous of them the floors were covered with mosaic, and everywhere there were tapestries, damask hangings, furniture of ivory, rare wood, silver, and even of gold, silken brocades, and ceramics from Persia and China; even the chamber-pots were of silver. The impact of all this magnificence on visiting Goths, Slavs, and other suppliant barbarians was overwhelming, and of course it was meant to be so.

After their marriage, Justinian and Theodora continued to live in the Palace of Hormisdas, which was only a little less splendid than the Imperial Palace, where Justin dwelt in rather sad and lonely state after the death of old Euphemia, nursing a nasty ulcer on his foot, where he had been wounded by an arrow during one of his old campaigns. Entry into the precincts lay through a building known as the Chalkê, or Brazen House, which probably took its name from bronze doors across the actual gateway; it was manned at all times by Palace Guards, and opened every morning at seven o'clock by a senior court official known as the *Curopalates,* to whom the honour of being entrusted with the great key was given, and who was accompanied by a retinue of minor functionaries and guards as he made his ceremonial way to perform his morning duty.

The life of the Palace was as impressive as its buildings and trappings. It revolved around the Emperor in a manner as formal as the liturgy itself, and once again the formality was intended, for the Emperor was regarded as being God's vicegerent on earth, while his court was a symbolic version of the court of heaven. Its ceremonies were endless, and its etiquette almost oriental in its complexity. As if they were taking part in some splendid and stately ballet, courtiers and ministers of state, bishops and chamberlains, eunuchs and ladies-in-waiting, prefects and military governors approached the Emperor and Empress, withdrew, re-formed, and approached again, weaving patterns around them in a slow, courtly, and intricate diplomatic dance. The reality of power was so well hidden beneath the ordered surface of this politely formal world with its unchanging rituals that it seldom showed itself openly or vulgarly; but when from time to time a sudden eruption of violence shattered the elaborate social texture of life in the Palace, then the whole Byzantine Empire was plunged into crisis, as Justinian and Theodora were to discover in the years to come.

Meanwhile, however, Theodora revelled in the luxury of her new life. Wherever she went she was accompanied by a bevy of ladies-in-waiting and maids of honour amongst whom, however pretty they might be, she shone with a natural grace and beauty which everyone acknowledged, for she was breathtakingly lovely. Indeed, she was so radiantly beautiful that she could get whatever she wanted from the old Emperor, who adored his ravishing new daughter-in-law, as he liked to call her, and Justinian could refuse her nothing; so that she had not been married for six months before everyone realised that she was very much a power to be reckoned with. People began to treat her with even greater respect and deference than before, and this she accepted as being no more than her due; in fact, like many another parvenu before and after her time, she soon became as great a stickler for strict etiquette and proper protocol as any autocrat, and anyone who was foolish enough to take liberties with Theodora soon learnt not to do so a second time. But she did not allow her new dignity to go to her head, or to blind her to the fact that, beneath the surface of the glossy and urbane world of the Palace, it was not very different from the world of the Hippodrome, in which she had been brought up and trained in the techniques of survival; it might be more polite at first glance, but in brute fact the world of Byzantine power politics was quite as savage as the world of her childhood. If she was to survive in it, it was just as important for her to take the measure of its other inhabitants as it had been in the old days for her to learn who to trust and who to fear in the underworld of the circus. First and foremost that meant getting to know the people close to her husband, Justinian.

From the moment when the Emperor Justin was placed on the throne by the army, Justinian had been the chief dispenser of power behind the scenes, and in the process he had collected around him some extremely talented people, all of whom were destined to play leading parts in the drama of Theodora's future life, and who are therefore worth looking at for a moment here before that drama unfolds. The first one she got to know well was a man named Sittas, an old friend of Justinian's, who married her sister Comito. Apparently he met her in the house of a man named Antiochus, who lived near the Hippodrome, and fell in love with her. Little is known of Sittas's origins except that he came from Thrace. Like the other members of Justinian's private circle, he was of humble birth, but he did not come from so low a social stratum as did Theodora and her sisters. Although he became the Empress' brother-in-law, he was destined to play a smaller part in her life than some of her husband's other intimate friends, for he was a brilliant soldier, whose duties took him away from the capital much of the time, and he was killed before he was forty in a minor skirmish in Armenia.

Belisarius, an even more talented soldier than Sittas, played a much greater part in Theodora's affairs as the years went by. He was astonishingly young at this time, being not much older than Theodora herself, but despite his youth he had greatly distinguished himself on active service against the Persians; the fact that Justinian had already picked him out for preferment is a proof of the older man's shrewdness and judgement. Belisarius had been born in a village near the city of Adrianople, and thus like his friend Sittas he too was a native of Thrace. His family seems to have been of some substance, for he began his military career as an officer in one of the regiments of Palace Guards; but nothing is known of his youth, and his father was probably no more important socially than many other small landowners. As a young man he had all the attributes of a popular idol; he was tall, handsome, and dashing, 'the very epitome of a cavalry officer', as someone has said, and he was lucky enough to be endowed by nature with an almost unerring instinct for making the right military move at the right moment, without which no man can hope to become a really great and inspired soldier. His troops loved him for two main reasons: first and foremost, he led them from victory to victory as no one had done before; but they loved him too for his bravery, generosity, and unceasing care for their welfare. As a result, as the years went by, they were willing to follow him anywhere, knowing that his name was enough to turn the tide of a battle and terrify the enemy.

In his private life too, he was loving, generous, and trusting; indeed, he was too trusting as far as his wife was concerned, for he was so unwilling to believe ill of her that again and again he became the laughing-stock of Byzantine society, as the world watched her deceive him under his very nose, while he alone remained blind to what was going on. Her name was Antonina, and she was older than her husband; like Theodora she was reputed to have been no better than she ought to have been in her younger days, and as time went by the destiny of the two women became ever more closely linked, Theodora acting as Antonina's protectress, and Antonina in turn acting as Theodora's devoted friend and willing agent. It was an arrangement which worked well, for Theodora felt safe in the knowledge that, if needs be, she could control Belisarius through his wife; and there were times when he became so popular and powerful that he could have made a most dangerous challenger for Justinian's throne, if he had chosen the path of rebellion, and this Theodora was determined to prevent. Meanwhile Antonina felt safe, under Theodora's protective wing, to indulge her passion for adultery, knowing that if she was discovered by her husband, Theodora would shield her from the consequences. In fact, Belisarius was not ambitious for supreme power; he was the soul of loyalty, and he loved Justinian, so Theodora need not have worried about him; while Antonina could have relied on her husband's extraordinary blindness to her philanderings to protect her from discovery and upon his natural generosity and eagerness to forgive her almost anything, on the rare occasions when he did catch her *in flagrante delicto*, to ensure her immunity from his revenge. But neither of the two women knew that.

Then there was Narses. He began life as a slave somewhere in Armenia, and he was made a eunuch by his parents in the hope that it would help him to better himself when he grew up. Nothing is known of his early life, nor of how Justinian found him; but find him he did, and he first appears in history as commander of Justinian's bodyguard of eunuchs. The year of his birth is not known for certain, but probably he was born about A.D. 480, for he was about forty years old when Theodora first met him. A contemporary historian, who knew him personally, described him as 'a slight, frail-looking man', and added that 'he had incredible courage and ability'. In fact, he was the exact opposite of today's popular idea of a eunuch as a sly, fat, lazy, and degenerate creature, fit only for a servile position in the women's quarters of an eastern household: an unmanly monstrosity given to evil intrigues. On the contrary, Narses emerges from all the accounts of the time as a man who always behaved with dignity and humanity even under the most difficult and trying circumstances. No one, not even the venomous Procopius, has a word to say against him, and it is evident that he commanded universal respect and something very near to universal affection. Although he received no formal education in his youth, he was so intelligent that it was impossible to guess that he had never been to school, for what he had not learned as a child, he taught himself with extraordinary speed and ease in later life. At the age of about fifty he even learned to be a soldier, and despite the gentleness of his nature he became a general as well known for his bravery and military skill as Belisarius himself, though he did not have the younger man's genius or his panache. Justinian trusted him above all his other intimate associates and ministers, and so did Theodora; indeed, as the years went by, he became one of her closest and most devoted friends. He outlived them both, and died at the age of about ninety-five.

John of Cappadocia was a man of a very different stamp. Coarse, uneducated, crude in speech and manners, he was a man of limitless appetites, a drunkard, a lecher, and a glutton; but he was a brilliant organiser, a hard worker, and a man of immense personal force, which made him useful to Justinian as head of the huge Byzantine bureaucracy, without which the Empire could not possibly have been governed. John began his career by joining the civil service as a junior clerk in the office of the local military commander in Caesarea, the capital of Cappadocia in what is now central Turkey, where he was born. How he attracted Justinian's attention is not known, but as soon as he did so he was moved to Constantinople, where his promotion was rapid. Since he was extremely able, completely ruthless, and afraid of no one, as the years passed and his power grew, he made himself very unpopular. The rich in particular loathed him, for he treated them with the same brutal contempt with which he habitually bullied the poor, and wealthy people were not used to such roughness and lack of consideration. But though he made a multitude of enemies, their hatred did not worry him, for he knew that he was virtually indispensable to Justinian, and he counted on him for protection, while at the same time going everywhere surrounded by a formidable bodyguard of his own private thugs to make doubly sure that he was not molested by anyone with a grudge against him. All would therefore have probably been well with him despite the number of people who longed to see him dead, if he had not made one bad error of judgement: he made an enemy of Theodora, and that was a fatal mistake.

The last of Justinian's inner circle of picked men to play a major part in the story of her time was Tribonian. He had been born in the ancient city of Side in Pamphylia of a pagan family, and he had never become a Christian. In many circles, this would have been an insuperable obstacle to his advancement, but for some reason this anti-pagan prejudice did not affect a man's career in some of the intellectual professions. Tribonian was a man of great erudition, and he became the leading lawyer and academic jurist of his day. Justinian enlisted his aid in the monumental task, for which he himself is best remembered, of codifying the laws of Rome, and much of the most original and brilliant work involved in that enormous enterprise was Tribonian's. It was by no means limited to collecting together all the existing laws, but embraced their modification and interpretation too, and in this field Tribonian excelled. Personally, he was charming and attractive, a graceful and talented speaker, and a man of unlimited intellectual energy, and it is easy to see why Justinian singled him out for special service; but unfortunately there was another side to his character, for he had an insatiable appetite for money and no compunction whatever about the ways in which he made it. When Justinian made him Quaestor, which was roughly equivalent to Minister of Justice and Lord Chief Justice rolled into one, he did not hesitate to change and manipulate the law, making and unmaking petty regulations at will to suit his own financial book or as a favour to people who paid him to do so for their own benefit, and he also openly sold his verdicts as president of the Court of Appeal to the highest bidders, thus making a vast private fortune while ruining other people and making a mockery of the administration of justice. As a result, he earned the bitter hatred of the Byzantine people and especially of those of Constantinople, who suffered most from his activities.

There was one other man close to Justinian who should be mentioned here, though he was not one of the men he had singled out for preferment to high office; he was his cousin. His name was Germanus, and like Justinian himself he had been brought to Constantinople by his uncle Justin as a boy, and had been educated by him. But unlike Justinian, he chose the army as his career, where he distinguished himself as a brave and competent officer, and where he gained a reputation for great courtesy, honesty, and natural generosity. Being the Emperor's nephew, promotion came quickly; he was made Master of Soldiers in Thrace, while he was still in his late twenties or early thirties, and to crown his success and good fortune he married into one of the richest and most aristocratic families in the Roman world, the Anicii, who had moved to Constantinople from Rome when the Ostrogoths had overrun Italy. Justinian seems to have got on well with this paragon of all the virtues and to have been fond of him, but Theodora detested him, and it is not difficult to guess why. The relationship between Germanus' wife, who traced her ancestry back a thousand years through most of the noble houses of Rome, and the girl who had been born in the Hippodrome was plainly destined to be strained at the best of times; and Theodora's punctilious insistence upon the minutiae of protocol must have been more than enough to ensure that in fact it was at all times frigid in the extreme.

Her relationships with all these people developed slowly, and when she first married Justinian she could have had no idea which of them would prove to be her friends and which her enemies. For their part, they watched her power grow as she mastered the ways of the Palace and established herself ever more firmly in the love of her husband and the affections of the old Emperor, who showed clear signs of his age as time went by. As the old man's powers failed, he delegated more authority to his nephew, and even though he still refused to make him co-Emperor, no one could doubt any more that Justinian was his choice of successor. In the spring of A.D. 527, however, Justin fell dangerously ill. His chief ministers and members of the Senate immediately became alarmed lest he should die before the succession was finally and openly settled, for there was always the chance of trouble in such an eventuality; the nephews of Justin's predecessor, Anastasius, were still alive, and though none of them seemed to be ambitious for the throne, there were people who did not particularly like Justinian, and who might use one of the nephews to oppose his candidature, whether the young man wanted power or not. So a large deputation of Senators and senior officers of state waited upon the Emperor as he lay on his bed of sickness and prayed him to co-opt his nephew as his colleague on the throne. Perhaps the old man was too tired to resist them, or perhaps he did not very much care any more what happened, but at all events he yielded to their entreaties and told them to go ahead. If they wanted to have Justinian as co-Emperor, they should have him. Let them make the necessary arrangements as soon as possible.

On 4 April, in front of members of the Senate, serried ranks of senior officers from the army, the navy and the Palace Guard, and assembled dignitaries of the Empire, the Court, and the government Justinian was crowned in one of the great halls of the Palace known as the Triclinium of the Nineteen Couches. (In fact the word 'triclinium' is the Latin equivalent of a Greek word which simply means 'three couches'.) In origin it was a banqueting hall, though by this time it was probably used as a throne room too, and the couches of its curious name were those upon which the Byzantines, like the old Romans before them, reclined during meals. In the absence of old Justin, who was too ill to be present at the ceremony, the diadem was placed on Justinian's brow by Epiphanius the Patriarch. However, it was not by virtue of his own office that he crowned him, for the Emperor was God's vicegerent on earth, and he alone had the right to confer upon another man God's gift of sovereignty; so on this occasion Epiphanius acted on his behalf. Once he had done so, Justinian became as much a true Emperor of the Romans, both legally and in the eyes of God, as his uncle Justin or any of his imperial predecessors.

But even if the substance of his coronation was thus complete, the full splendour of the traditional Byzantine ceremonial of king-making had only just begun, and three days later, on Easter Day, Justinian, accompanied this time by Theodora, went to the Church of the Holy Wisdom for the Patriarch to play his own distinctive part in their consecration and anointing. Once again the great basilica was crowded with the pomp and pageantry of

Byzantium as Justinian and Theodora arrived, attended by a retinue of court officials and maids of honour, to be welcomed by the Patriarch at the entrance to the nave. Justinian was dressed in full imperial splendour in a tunic of cloth of gold, his feet shod with the purple shoes which only an Emperor might wear; around his waist he wore a sash which sparkled with emeralds, while by his side, her dark hair studded with pearls and wearing a long dress embroidered with precious stones, Theodora stood as stiff and still and straight as a figure in an icon. Each of them lit a little cluster of candles, and then Epiphanius led them up the aisle with slow and measured steps as hundreds of faces turned to watch their solemn progress. Before the sanctuary, once again they lit a small forest of candles, and as the light was reflected by the jewels they were wearing in little points of fire, they mounted the steps from the nave to stand by a table on which lay the imperial regalia. A deacon began to chant a litany, and a small choir of bearded priests sang the response, 'Kyrie eleison', over and over again, while Epiphanius turned to the table to bless the two purple cloaks and the two imperial diadems which were lying there. One by one, Justinian and Theodora were robed in purple by an official known as the *vestitores,* who fastened the cloaks upon their shoulders with golden brooches, but it was the Patriarch who placed the crowns on their bowed heads, saying in a loud voice, 'In the name of the Father and of the Son and of the Holy Ghost', as he did so. 'Holy, holy, holy,' everyone in the Church shouted in reply, 'glory to God in the highest and on earth peace!'

When the religious ceremony was over, they went in slow and splendid procession through cheering crowds held back by soldiers to the Hippodrome to be acclaimed by the people of Constantinople, who had 'crowned the town', as they called it, for the occasion, decking the streets with sprigs of myrtle, rosemary, ivy, and box; bunches of spring flowers adorned the windows along the route; silks and brocades, moving like flags in the breeze, hung from the balconies of the houses, and everyone had brought out their family treasures of gold and silver to sparkle in the sun and in the light of the torches which many people carried in their hands. Carved and gilded, the state coach in which Justinian and Theodora sat was drawn by four white horses; with heralds and trumpeters going before, it was surrounded by a company of Palace Guards, while Narses and the imperial bodyguard of eunuchs brought up the rear. The newly-crowned couple entered the Hippodrome by way of the Palace and through the private corridors and spiral staircase which led directly into the *kathisma* from the rear. On their appearance, the standards in the centre of the racecourse were raised by Guards already stationed there, and Justinian stepped forward holding Theodora by the hand, while with the other he made the sign of the Cross over the enormous crowd of more than a hundred thousand people who were packed into the arena and on to the tiers of stone seats to greet them. 'Justinian Augustus, be victorious! Theodora Augusta!' they cried in a great gale of delighted noise; 'Lord have mercy on us! Long live the Augusta! God bless our Christian Emperor and Empress!' No one will ever know what Theodora's thoughts were, as she stood beside Justinian in this place where she had grown up in abject poverty, and where she had been humiliated when she and her sisters had made their pathetic appeals to the crowd for help in their extremity; but whatever they may have been, this moment of her triumph must have been full of bittersweet memories of a past which was almost unbelievably different from the present.

Although the old Emperor rallied for a time after his nephew's coronation, and it even seemed possible that he might recover from his illness, a few months later he relapsed; the ulcer on his foot turned gangrenous, and on 1 August 527, he died. In his place, Justinian and Theodora became the supreme rulers of the Roman world.

V

From the moment when Theodora was made Empress, the tempo of her life was determined by the political situation in Constantinople and the Empire, and this was moving slowly but steadily towards a crisis. On the surface, things looked peaceful enough, although Justinian inherited a war with Persia from his uncle's time; but the barbarian pressures which had overwhelmed the western half of the Empire had been successfully resisted in the eastern half, and the shadow of the Bulgars and the Slavs, who would become such a desperate menace after Justinian's death, was not yet darkening the political landscape; everywhere the borders of the realm were at peace. Internally too there were no serious problems for the new Emperor to contend with, or so it seemed. Once again, however, appearances were deceptive; Justinian not only inherited some political problems which were more or less chronic, but he adopted a policy which was guaranteed to make them worse in the long run.

Even though the old Roman provinces of Gaul, Britain, Spain, and its original heart-land of Italy had been lost, the Empire was still enormous, and it was not easy to govern. There was a natural and very understandable tendency for those who lived 600 miles away from Constantinople in provinces on the periphery of the Byzantine world to pay no more attention to the central government than was absolutely necessary, and much the same could be said of people living in the fastness of the Taurus mountains, the rugged country of northern Greece, and the oak forests of Serbia, even though these were nearer the capital. Communications were slow, for though the roads were good, they were few, and the distances were huge. So there was an ever-present tendency for the Empire to disintegrate into its constituent parts, many of which were ethnically different one from another, consisting as they did of peoples who had only been united in the first place by Roman rule, and who had been held together subsequently more by growing cultural and religious bonds than by bureaucratic control either from Rome or later from Constantinople. The unifying powers of their Roman citizenship and a common allegiance to the Christian faith succeeded in binding the Byzantines together most of the time, despite the various geographical and political forces which tended to pull them apart; but when, for one reason or another, the central government began to exert unpopular pressure upon the people of the provinces, trouble usually followed. Even before he ascended the throne, Justinian, acting as the power behind the scenes, began to steer the Empire on to a course which was destined inevitably to bring the most unpopular pressure of all to bear on everyone: namely, financial pressure. But during his uncle Justin's reign, the effects of his new and expensive schemes did not show themselves, for the old Emperor Anastasius, who had been a parsimonious man, had left enormous reserves in the imperial treasury, which lasted for several years. But by the time that Justinian became sole ruler of the Roman world, he and his uncle had spent them; the imperial coffers were empty, and if his various policies were to succeed, the money with which to pay for them had to be found somehow, and this inevitably meant increased taxation.

It would be both untrue and unfair to say that Justinian was a man with an obsession, if that is taken to mean that he was unbalanced and neurotic, for he was nothing of the kind; but he was a man driven by an idea which preoccupied him to the virtual exclusion of everything else, and in that sense it would not be unfair to say that he was obsessional. His one over-riding aim in life was to restore the Empire to its former extent and former glory; everything he did was done to further that end. The *imperium romanun* had brought greater blessings to mankind than any other political system since the creation of the world, and since the Empire had embraced Christianity, it had become co-extensive with the kingdom of God on earth; to push back its boundaries once again, until they reached and then exceeded their former limits, was therefore an enterprise which would bring to more and more people the dual blessings of civilisation in this world and salvation in the next, and plainly there could be no more desirable consummation than that. This was the grand idea which obsessed Justinian. It is possible that he thought of himself as a man of destiny, who had been singled out from other men when he was a boy in his native village of Tauresium, and raised to the purple by God for the express purpose of rebuilding the glory that had once been Rome; as David in biblical days had been taken away from tending his father's sheep to become king of Judah, so he, Justinian, had been taken away from his father's farm, and charged with the task of enlarging the kingdom of Christ. A man with his extraordinary personal history and even more extraordinary personal endowments of intellect and character could hardly be accused of suffering from delusions of grandeur if he had thought of himself in some such way, but there is no direct evidence that he did so. There is conclusive evidence, however, that everything he did, whether it was his attempt to impose Orthodoxy on all Christians within his realm, or his attempt to reduce the power of the large landowners, or his military attempt to reconquer the lands which had once been Roman before they fell to various barbarian invasions, was done in order to further his great endeavour to widen the borders of the Christian Roman Empire. Unfortunately for him, directly or indirectly, each of these aims involved him in trouble with his subjects.

The large landowners were a recurring source of trouble to Emperor after Emperor for as long as Byzantine civilisation lasted, and in the end they were to be one of the principal causes of its downfall. For the Empire depended for its health and vigour on the existence of a large class of free, landowning peasant farmers, who worked their small farms themselves with the help of their sons. Not only were they the primary source of state revenue as tax-payers, but they were also the primary source of recruits for the army; and of course, as long as they flourished, the land was cultivated. But their lives were hard, and it was only too easy for the large landowners to expropriate their land one way or another by fair means or if necessary by foul. Throughout the Byzantine period by far the best and safest investment was in land, so the central government was faced again and again with the problem of how to curb the power of the great landed families, rapacious and acquisitive as they often were, and thus prevent them from destroying their smaller and weaker neighbours who were so necessary to the life of the Empire. This was not easy, for the small freeholder led a hard life; unlike richer men, he had few reserves, so that a bad harvest, the death of an animal, or some minor calamity in his family might make it impossible for him to pay his bills or to meet the demands of the tax-collector. In such a case, either he could borrow enough money to pay his way, or he could sell his land to one of the land-hungry aristocracy. Even if he chose the former alternative and retained his land, borrowing enough money to tide him over his immediate financial difficulty, all too often he found that he had delivered himself into the hands of his creditor, who did not rest until he had forced him out of business and had acquired his land.

This kind of thing had been going on for so long by the time that Justinian had reached the throne that the peasant free-holder had almost disappeared, and the great landlord had taken his place everywhere. Some of these magnates were almost incredibly rich and commensurately powerful. One of the Apions, an Egyptian family, had vast estates scattered in various parts of the country, owning whole villages as part of his private inheritance; he lived like a petty king surrounded by a quasi-regal household; he employed hosts of secretaries, an army of stewards, and thousands of workmen; he organised his own private tax-collectors; he ran a private postal service, and he may also have organised a private army, as many large landowners in other parts of the Empire certainly did, though it is not known for sure that he himself did so. But where these private armies existed, the small landowner, if he had not already been squeezed out of existence and dispossessed by legal means, faced the very real possibility of being deprived of his land by brute force, even if he and his family had owned it and worked it for generations. Justinian was appalled by this.

> News has come to us [he wrote to a Proconsul in Cappadocia] about such exceedingly great abuses in the provinces that their correction can hardly be accomplished by one person, however high his authority may be; we are positively ashamed to describe how improperly the managers of landlords' estates march around surrounded by bodyguards, how they are followed by mobs of thugs, and how shamelessly they rob everyone . . . State property has almost entirely gone into private ownership, for it has been stolen and plundered, and so have all the herds of horses; and not a single man has spoken out against all this, for everyone's mouth has been stopped with gold.

It soon became known that the new Emperor was determined to

clip the wings of these over-powerful subjects, and needless to say they bitterly resented his intentions; so that within a very short time after Justinian's accession he had made enemies of this particular class of men.

They were not his only enemies. He antagonised the senatorial class too. The Senate had long ago lost all real power, but membership of it was regarded as an honour, and the polite fiction that its members played a part in the government of the Empire had been sedulously maintained by a long series of tactful sovereigns. It was much the same with the Imperial Council, whose members exercised no more real authority than the Senators; but they enjoyed the dignity conferred on them by their membership and the semblance of power which went with it, when they were formally consulted by the Emperor on matters of state. It was well understood by all concerned that they could do nothing but give their approval to the Emperor's decisions, but as long as the custom of consultation was observed they were happy. In fact, the Emperors were autocrats pure and simple, and had been such for centuries; they did not have to consult anyone, whether Senators, Imperial Councillors, or Ministers of the Crown; they simply gave orders, and they were obeyed. But when Justinian decided to recognise the reality of their position, and made it clear to both the Senate and the Imperial Council that he had no intention even of pretending to consult them any more, they were bitterly offended. How did this upstart dare to abolish a custom as ancient as that of consulting the Senate and the Imperial Council? they asked each other angrily. The Senate, after all, represented the people, and it was monstrous that the people should be deprived of all say in the government of the Empire, even if they had no more than a formal say in it. Many Senators and members of the Council, coming as they did from old and often Patrician families, had not been exactly overjoyed when this peasant had come to the throne in the first place, even though snobbery was not a Byzantine disease; but now their initial dislike turned into hatred, and with the big landowners they joined the ranks of Justinian's sworn enemies. It was a dangerous coalition.

But perhaps the most dangerous thing he did was to antagonise his old favourites, the Blues. Whether it was true or not that in the past he had protected them and treated them with special consideration in return for their political support, the Blues certainly believed this to have been the case; and when he came to the throne, they were understandably delighted. But as soon as he was safely seated on it, he adopted a new policy towards the circus factions, which seemed to him to be more appropriate to his new imperial dignity, treating both Blues and Greens alike with scrupulous justice and impartiality and refusing to take sides with his old supporters. The Blues were furious. They felt that they had been cast aside like an old glove with cynical ingratitude as soon as their political support was no longer needed; so they too joined his enemies.

Justinian's growing unpopularity during the first few years of his reign would probably never have come to a head if it had not been compounded by his financial policy. He desperately needed money: money to pay for the war with Persia; money for his grandiose schemes of reconquest in Italy, north Africa, Spain and elsewhere; money for his almost equally grandiose building schemes, for he had a passion for building fortresses, churches, and palaces which amounted almost to an addiction; money for his diplomatic policy of buying the support and alliance of barbarian nations in strategic positions beyond the frontiers of the Empire, wherever they were well placed to act as buffer states between the Byzantines and the ever-restless, ever-menacing nomadic peoples of Asia and northern Europe; and finally money to behave with the kind of regal generosity which alone befitted a Roman Emperor, and which in any case came naturally to him and to Theodora, who were generous people by temperament and inclination. Only one example of this generosity of theirs need be given here, but it was typical of many other instances. On 29 November 529 when Justinian and Theodora had been on the throne together for just over two years, Antioch was shaken by a violent earthquake, suffering appalling damage, and nearly five thousand people were killed. The city had only recently been rebuilt after an earthquake three years earlier, when the number of dead had been even greater in the worst natural disaster the Empire had suffered for centuries. Justinian and Theodora, who is specifically mentioned with her husband in the contemporary accounts of the event, immediately sent a princely sum of money to the stricken city, virtually emptying the imperial treasury in the process; and the next year, when another earthquake killed 7,000 people in Laodicea, they did not hesitate to do the same again. But this royal munificence had to be paid for somehow, and so did all Justinian's other projects, whether they happened to be architectural, military, or diplomatic; there was only one way in which the money could be raised, and that was by taxation.

No one likes being taxed, and it is even less enjoyable if it is done callously, ruthlessly, and with brutal efficiency by a man like John the Cappadocian. Yet it was to him that Justinian entrusted the task, making him Praetorian Prefect of the East, and sending him to the rich provinces of Syria and Asia Minor with the necessary powers to reform the whole tax system and the tax-gathering apparatus there. Reforms were badly needed. For years the burden of taxation had fallen on the shoulders of those least able to afford it, for the peasants and the poorer urban classes were easy game for the tax-collector; they had neither the power nor the means to dodge him. Other classes were much more adroit. Both the large landowners, upon whom Justinian had virtually declared war in any case, and the merchants and tradesmen, who knew a thing or two when it came to feathering their own nests, were accustomed to fiddling their books, bribing people in the right places, and taking advantage of every loophole in the fiscal regulations; many of them were also past masters in the arts of shady dealing and near-racketeering, and even when they were detected, the rich at any rate were not much worried; for though they might be fined from time to time, it had come to be accepted that men in their station were virtually immune from the more serious forms of punishment which were reserved for the erring poor.

John of Cappadocia changed all that. He was completely fearless; indeed, it was said of him that 'he did not fear God nor regard man', and as soon as he was installed in the office of Prefect he began to make a series of sweeping changes and long-overdue reforms. Despite the fact that he could hardly read or write, having received no formal education in his youth, he was a brilliant administrator; and this combination of fearlessness and efficiency made him a very formidable figure indeed. Much of what he did was good; he dismissed a number of lazy and inefficient civil servants; he put a stop to a host of little private rackets and fiddles; he forebade many wasteful and extravagant practices; he abolished some jobs altogether, either because they were comfortable sinecures, or because they overlapped unnecessarily with others; and he made some stringent economies.

But some of the measures he took were ill-judged, and one or two were disastrous. For instance, one of his major economies was to cut down or to reduce the state post with the exception of that which ran on the main road to the Persian frontier, which he left alone; on some routes, however, he abolished the postal service altogether, while on many others in Syria and through Asia Minor he ordered that asses should be used instead of horses in the future. Money was saved, but the speed of travel was greatly reduced, and news took much longer to reach its destination than before. Far more serious was the effect on farmers in the inland provinces who were suddenly deprived of the means of public transport, upon which they had always relied to carry their goods to the ports, from which they were then shipped to Constantinople and elsewhere. Many of them could not afford to hire private transport, even where it was available; they were reduced to trying to carry their goods to the ports, and the roads were filled with straggling parties of men and women heavily laden with bales and sacks of farm produce on their backs, many of whom did not survive the arduous journey. Others, seeing the roadsides, if not strewn with the corpses of people who had died of exhaustion at least punctuated by them, decided to let their corn rot in the fields or in the granaries rather than lose their lives; everywhere farmers went bankrupt, while both the quality and the quantity of bread and other foodstuffs in the big cities suffered badly. This was especially true of Constantinople, where an acute shortage of food developed, which was made much worse as thousands of countrymen deserted their farms and their small holdings, where they could no longer make a living, and invaded the city in search of employment, turning the shortage of food into something like the beginnings of a famine. Constantinople and the other cities of the Byzantine world were crowded with angry, resentful, and frightened men, who blamed the Cappadocian and his employer, the Emperor, for their plight; and the ranks of Justinian's enemies were once again dangerously reinforced.

But if some of John's reforms misfired and bitterly antagonised many people, the brutal manner in which he did his primary job of collecting taxes offended thousands more. There was a popular saying that 'Cappadocians are always bad, worse in office, worst where money is concerned, and worse than worst when set up in a grand official chariot'. The way in which John set about making everyone pay their taxes more than confirmed that popular judgement on his countrymen. Being afraid of no one, he treated the rich and the powerful with as little respect as the poor and the weak, throwing anyone, whoever they might be, into gaol without the smallest hesitation or compunction, if they would not pay what was demanded of them. No excuses were accepted; protestations of inability to find the money were not believed; and it was said that defiance and refusals to pay were greeted with physical violence.

It is always difficult to be sure how much truth there is in accusations of this kind; there is no one more bitterly hated or more likely to attract libellous stories than a ruthless and successful tax-collector. But it seems probable that John, who was a man of immense physical strength and unbelievably coarse manners, did not scruple to have people physically ill-treated when they crossed him, for he is known to have tolerated such abuses of power in some of his subordinates. He appointed another Cappadocian, also named John, as governor of Lydia, and there is ample evidence that this man freely resorted to extreme violence in order to attain his ends, and moreover that he did so with the full knowledge and consent of the Praetorian Prefect. This other John was a grossly fat man with an enormous jowl, who was nicknamed *Maxilloplumacius* or 'flabby chops', and he made himself both feared and detested throughout the province of Lydia and especially in its capital city, Philadelphia. His treatment of a man named Petronius, a leading and respected citizen of the place, was typical. He discovered that Petronius owned a collection of jewels, which had been in his family for generations, and he decided to confiscate them in payment of a supposed new tax on inherited wealth, of which no one had even heard. When their owner flatly refused to hand them over, he was chained in a stable and beaten; but news of his arrest and ill-treatment spread through the town, and the bishop of Philadelphia decided to intervene. Surrounded by junior clergy and holding a bible in his hand, he sought out the fat-faced extortioner; but he was greeted with such a torrent of foul and abusive language accompanied by threats of violence that he withdrew in alarm and dismay. The wretched Petronius, who was eventually reduced to despair, promised in the end to do what he was told, if only he was released. He was duly set free, whereupon he gathered up his jewels, and carrying them to the Praetorium threw them contemptuously on to the floor of the entrance hall in a heap.

In another case in the same town, an old soldier hanged himself after he had been tortured in order to force him to hand over money which he did not even possess, whereupon his body was kicked into the street like the corpse of a dog, and left lying in the gutter for all to see. After a few more such incidents, very few people refused to pay whatever was demanded of them.

If his subordinates behaved with such brutality, it is altogether possible that John himself resorted to physical violence, when it suited him to do so, and that his enemies were right when they accused him of keeping a well-equipped torture chamber in the basement of his Praetorium. But whether this was true or not, it is certain that people soon began to believe such stories of his cruelties, and it was not long before everyone, rich and poor, was terrified of him. As a result, money poured into the imperial treasury as it had never poured before, and Justinian, who probably had no idea how this money was being extorted from his subjects, was delighted. He would have been less pleased if he had discovered how much of it was being diverted into John's own pocket in the process; it was probably only a small percentage of the whole, nevertheless the Cappadocian became immensely rich during his tenure of office in the East, a happy state of affairs which gave him the chance to indulge his grosser appetites. He was not the man to miss such an opportunity, and his daily orgies of gluttony and drunkenness soon became common knowledge, while it was also said of him that 'he did not leave a wife, a virgin, or a youth unviolated', if they came within his reach. Meanwhile, his agents left no house unpillaged; thousands of people were ruined, and hundreds of thousands learned to hate John the Cappadocian with as bitter a hatred as that of the farmers whom he had already bankrupted by his ill-considered economies. Like the farmers too, they blamed Justinian for the depredations of his Prefect, and the Emperor's unpopularity reached a new peak in the provinces.

Consequently he and Theodora had not been on the throne for five years before the unrest throughout the Empire was so serious that civil disturbances became more and more common. The situation was at its worst in Constantinople itself, for the city was packed with disaffected people who could find no work, and the shortage of food got worse almost daily; so when there was a riot in the Hippodrome early in January 532, Eudaemon, the Prefect of the city, deciding to take no chances, put it down promptly and firmly.

64

It was not a particularly serious affair, but during its course some people lost their lives, and a number of those arrested by the Prefect were charged with murder. Both Blues and Greens were amongst those who were put on trial, and after an exhaustive inquiry, which seems to have been fairly conducted, seven of the accused men were found guilty; four were condemned to be beheaded, and three to be hanged. This was unusually severe punishment by Byzantine standards, for the death penalty was seldom enforced except for the most callous murders and for treason; the worst that most murderers could expect was to be blinded in order to render them innocuous in the future, and often they suffered nothing worse than perpetual banishment to a monastery, where they had to take religious vows and live a life of repentance until they died. But doubtless Eudaemon, well aware of the tense political situation in the capital, wanted to make an example of the condemned men as a deterrent to others who might be thinking of rioting. Unfortunately for him, the execution of the guilty men made things a thousand times worse, not because the citizens of Constantinople objected to the severity of the sentences, but because of the incompetence of the executioner, who made an appalling mess of his job.

The men who had been condemned to be beheaded were duly decapitated, and that was that; but the three men to be hanged were not despatched so easily. A gallows was set up in a public place in that quarter of the city known as Blachernae, not far from the spot where the great western wall met the Golden Horn, and a crowd of people assembled to watch them hanged, drawn there no doubt by the kind of morbid interest which always seems to attract spectators to executions. Amongst the crowd were some monks from a monastery, which stood in that part of the town, and which was dedicated to Saint Conon, a gardener who had been born in Nazareth and had been martyred for his faith during the Decian persecutions in the middle of the third century. Ropes were put around the wretched men's necks; the executioner stood back; the platform upon which they stood was suddenly withdrawn with a jerk, and all should have died as they fell and the nooses tightened. One indeed did so; but the other two fell to the ground, either because the ropes broke, or perhaps because the nooses had been badly tied and had come undone. There was a gasp from the crowd as the two men lay wriggling on the ground with their hands still tied behind their backs, unable to get to their feet again. But the hangman had not finished; he was not going to allow this initial failure to defeat him, and he pulled the men to their feet, forced them up on to the scaffold again, and once more put the ropes around their necks. Again he failed; as before they dropped to the ground, and the crowd roard its disapproval. Before he could try again, there were cries of 'To the church, to the church!', and the monks of Saint Conon rushed forward and took up the two criminals in their arms. With the crowd cheering them and threatening to hang the hangman if he interfered, they hurried the two condemned men in a state of collapse down to the Golden Horn, where they put them in a boat, and rowed them across to the other side; eventually they sought asylum in the Church of Saint Lawrence, and were at once granted sanctuary. One was a Green, the other a Blue.

Eudaemon the Prefect was told of what had happened, and immediately sent a detachment of soldiers to the church with orders to allow no one to enter or to leave the building; he did not dare order the arrest of the fugitives, while they remained within the safety of the house of God, especially since it happened to be a Sunday. News of the two men's almost miraculous escape from death and of their flight to the church spread like wildfire throughout the city, and a number of Blues and Greens rushed to their aid, determined to prevent their further arrest and to form a guard of honour around them; but they were not allowed by Eudaemon's soldiers to enter the building. While some of these self-appointed vigilantes remained to keep an eye on the progress of events, others rushed back to the Hippodrome, where they made a report to the leaders of the two factions. Tension in the city mounted dangerously high, but neither side dared make a move; the soldiers stayed where they were; the two men were fed and looked after by the priests of Saint Lawrence, and stalemate seemed to have been reached.

The Ides of January fell two days later on Tuesday the 13th. By long-established custom this was a day when chariot races were held in the Hippodrome, and the Emperor was expected to attend. The great stadium was even more crowded than usual; the seats were packed to capacity, and people were perched on anything and everything which provided a vantage point. From the start the atmosphere was tense and angry, and Justinian had not taken his seat for five minutes before the two official spokesmen for the Blues and the Greens, the Demarchs as they were called, one after the other began to beg him to pardon the two fugitives in the Church of Saint Lawrence. It was well understood that the Emperor was under no obligation to reply through his own spokesman, the Mandator, although he often did so; and on this occasion he chose to sit silently in the *kathisma* as though he had not heard the words addressed to him. He may have been advised by Eudaemon, the City Prefect, that it was essential to be firm and not to give way to popular pressure on behalf of the two condemned men on the grounds that, if rioters were once allowed to get away without retribution, worse riots would be sure to follow, especially since the capital was so full of unrest; or he may have decided on his own behalf not to respond to the appeals made to him. In any case, the Mandator remained in his place without saying a word.

The races were duly run, and the people cheered as usual, but even the excitement of the racing did not make them forget the two refugees in the Church of Saint Lawrence. At the end of each race, the Demarchs rose to their feet and demanded their release; the Prefect may have condemned them to death, but their double escape was a plain proof that God did not mean them to die. The Emperor was God's vicegerent on earth, and the Demarchs addressed him with proper respect as 'thrice August', wishing him a long life and a victorious one each time they stood up to address him, but his continued refusal to answer them created an ever greater atmosphere of frustration and anger as the races went by. The people were patient, however, and while there was still a chance of persuading Justinian to recognise the *fait accompli* of God's action on behalf of the two condemned men, the Demarchs continued to repeat their prayers for an imperial pardon. It was not until the twenty-second race that their patience at last ran out; there was still no word from the Emperor, and the day was nearly over; unless something was done before everyone went home, all the efforts made to save the two wretched fugitives from Eudaemon's police would have been wasted. Suddenly, instead of renewed pleas for their lives, the cry went up, 'Long live the humane Greens and Blues!' It was astonishing; seldom if ever had the names of the two factions been linked in this way. It could only mean that they had decided in advance that, if all else failed, they would act together to force the government to grant a pardon to the two men whose cause they had jointly espoused. Again and again, the cry went up, 'Long

67

live the humane Greens and Blues,' and each time more and more people in the crowd joined in, and the shouting grew noisier and more defiant. As Justinian left the *kathisma,* another watchword began to be heard: *'Nika! Nika, Nika!'* the crowd began to cry. The word meant 'conquer', and the rising which followed was to be known as the Nika revolt.

The mob wasted no time. Thousands of people streamed out of the Hippodrome and made for the Praetorium, where they demanded to be told by the Prefect what he intended to do to the two men awaiting their fate in the Church of Saint Lawrence; like Justinian, however, the Prefect refused to answer. But by this time a feeling of enormous and exhilarating excitement possessed the people of Constantinople; after months of anger and frustration at the way in which they had been treated by the government in general and by John of Cappadocia in particular, at last they were doing something to relieve their feelings and to show the Emperor that they would tolerate his ministers' misrule no longer. The blood of the crowd was up, and the people were not prepared to take the Prefect's silence for an answer; instead, they broke into the Praetorium, hoping to find Eudaemon somewhere inside and to force him to speak to them. They failed. Furious at this setback, they ran amok, releasing a number of people who were being kept in cells awaiting trial, killing the soldiers and officials who tried to resist them, and eventually setting the building on fire. Waiting only long enough to make sure that the flames had taken hold, they rushed in a growing frenzy of elation at their own success to the Palace itself, chanting *'Nika! Nika! Nika!'*

The Palace was well guarded, but blood had already been shed, and the Palace Guards, who were more decorative than they were belligerent, did not rush out to do battle with the rioters, but remained peaceably inside as the crowd set fire to the gatehouse. The Chalkê with its great bronze doors was burnt to the ground, and the flames spread northwards to the Senate House and the Church of the Holy Wisdom; before night had fallen both buildings were reduced to smoking heaps of rubble, while other fires raging nearby lighted up the sky over Constantinople with an angry red glow.

As the hours of darkness passed, the mob dispersed. Drunk with violence and tired out by the excitement of the day, everyone eventually went home to bed, and silence fell over the battered and smoking city. No doubt Justinian and his chief ministers in the Palace reassured each other that the worst was over; as on many previous occasions in the reigns of former Emperors, the people had had their say and shown the government the strength of their feelings; now things would return to normal, and the Emperor would take note of their grievances and do what he could to put things right, like the wise sovereign that he was. But though the fires had died down, the night air was still filled with the acrid smell of smoke, and when the citizens of Constantinople woke up in the morning, their minds were still filled with the bitter memories of past injustice and exploitation. It was Wednesday, 14 January, and the order went out from the Palace that the races should be renewed; but for once in their lives the Byzantines were no longer in the mood for chariot racing. They had tasted power, and they had no intention of being fobbed off in their quest for justice by another day's sport in the Circus. Instead they set fire to the baths of Zeuxippus on the west side of the Augusteum, which had escaped the previous evening, and once again the centre of the city was filled with the hiss and crackle of flames and the noise of crashing masonry and cheering people, as passions were rekindled after the short respite of the night.

Things were now so serious that Justinian decided that he had no alternative but to give way to the people's demands. They had crowded into the Hippodrome in even greater numbers than on the previous day, not to watch the races, and no longer merely to intercede for the two men whose lives were still at risk from the hangman, but to clamour for the dismissal of three of the Emperor's principal ministers. Eudaemon must go; they would no longer put up with him as Prefect of the City. Tribonian must go; they would no longer tolerate his open perversion of justice, or continue to watch him sell his verdicts to the highest bidder; what sort of justice was that? And last but not least the repulsive Praetorian Prefect of the East, John the Cappadocian, who had ruined so many people and committed so many acts of violence under a cloak of legality, must go too; they would no longer sit back and see good men made destitute by this monster of a man. Justinian let it be known that he agreed. All three would be dismissed from office immediately, and in their place he would appoint three men of well-known integrity, whom he named.

But it was too late. If it had been an ordinary riot over a political grievance, Justinian's agreement to the demands of the people, angry as they were, would almost certainly have quietened them, and that would have been the end of the matter. They would have triumphed, and they would have gone home happy to have had their way. Similar riots, if perhaps not quite such violent ones, had been settled often enough in the past by a judicious concession by the Emperor at the right moment. Indeed, even at this juncture the Blues and the Greens, who had started the trouble, would probably have been content with what they had won, if matters had been in their hands alone; but they were not. Behind the factions, the mass of disaffected and destitute people from the eastern provinces and elsewhere, who had flocked to the capital in search of work, were less easily pleased; and behind them again were some extremly dangerous men who had been waiting patiently for just such a moment as this. The Nika revolt was a godsend to the Senators and the large landowners who saw clearly that, if they could harness this outburst of popular discontent to their own purposes, there was a real chance of unseating the Emperor and ending his reign; and there was nothing they desired more fervently than that. The last thing they wanted to see at this stage was peace. So they did everything in their power to maintain and increase the momentum of the revolt; Justinian's concessions were greeted as signs of weakness, and the violence was redoubled. In fact, from this moment the riot took on all the characteristics of a popular revolution.

Revolutions need leaders, even if they are mere figureheads, whereas riots are usually the outcome of short periods of mob rule. No one knows who first suggested that it was time to put one of Anastasius' three nephews at the head of the popular revolt against Justinian, but it was probably one of the Senators or some other influential figure lurking in the background of the week's events. Unfortunately, two of these three brothers, Pompeius and Hypatius, were out of reach of the rebels, for they were in the Palace with Justinian in company with a number of other Patricians and officials, and the Palace was in a state of virtual siege. The third brother, Probus, was thought to be at home in his house in the city, and the mob went streaming away in a state of great excitement to find him and put him at their head, whether he wanted to lead them or not. But Probus was no fool; as soon as the violence had begun, he had suspected that events might take just such a course, and since he was not in the least eager to play such a dangerous role as the mob was likely to force on him, he had hurriedly left Constantinople for his country estate. The people found his house empty, barred, and shuttered. Frustrated and angry at being cheated of their figurehead, they burned it down in a fit of irrational spite, and returned to the Palace in an ugly mood.

By this time, Justinian was thoroughly alarmed, as well he might have been. But it was abundantly obvious to everyone in the Palace that order had to be restored somehow, and Justinian made up his mind to try to crush the insurgents by force. But the Palace Guards, while not yet prepared openly to disobey the Emperor's direct command, managed subtly to make it clear that they were unwilling to do anything to interfere with the natural course of events, though they were prepared to go on mounting guard on the Palace itself. They had no particular affection for Justinian personally, and they preferred to wait and see which way the wind would blow at the end of the day before they committed themselves too deeply. Their behaviour was a serious blow to the Emperor and his cause, and it might well have proved fatal to him, if there had not been others to whom, as luck would have it, he could turn for help in this moment of extreme crisis. Two generals, whose loyalty was not in doubt, Belisarius and a man named Mundus, happened to be in the city at the time, and each of them had a number of mercenary troops with him as a personal bodyguard. The men under the command of Belisarius were most of them Goths, totally devoted to their commander and completely without interest in the political issues which had caused the Nika revolt, while the troops around Mundus were recruits from a German tribe, the Heruls, who were equally devoted to their leader; and none of them had any particular affection for the people of Constantinople. In all, they probably amounted at the most to two thousand men, but they were much better than no men at all.

On Thursday morning, 15 January, Belisarius rode out of the Palace at the head of his Goths to crush the rebellion. There was a pitched battle in the streets close to the Augusteum, and at first the people got very much the worst of it; a number were killed, while the soldiers suffered very few casualties, and it looked for a time as though the forces of law and order were about to prevail, and that the revolt would be suppressed. But just when the fighting had reached its peak and the people were about to turn and run for the safety of their homes, some clergy from the Church of the Holy Wisdom took it into their heads to try to separate the combatants, and thus save lives; they appeared in procession carrying some of the holy relics, which they had managed to save from the fire two days previously, when their Church had been burnt down, and they tried to come between the fighters. But neither they nor their relics meant anything to Belisarius' Goths; some of the clergy were hurt, and some of their relics were rudely trodden in the dust. The sight of such sacrilege infuriated the rebels, who began to fight with renewed ferocity, while many people who had not dared to commit themselves to either side in the battle now joined Belisarius' opponents; they were no longer in any doubt where their sympathies and their duty lay, nor could they continue to stand aside while holy things were desecrated by pagan soldiers. Climbing up on to the roofs of the houses and to their top floors, the people of Constantinople bombarded Belisarius' men with anything and everything, from roof tiles to boiling water, which came to hand. Even the women of the city joined in, screaming at the Goths like wild cats and egging their men on to fight more fiercely, until eventually the disconcerted and greatly outnumbered soldiers were slowly forced to retreat to the comparative safety of the Palace, leaving the rebels triumphant and even more exasperated than before. Compromise of any sort was now out of the question.

During the next two days, Friday and Saturday, the citizens of Constantinople went on a rampage of violence, arson, and pillage. Anything and everything connected with the government became their target; they set fire to public buildings wherever they found them, and since there happened to be a strong north wind blowing, the flames spread with appalling rapidity through the dry wooden buildings of the city. The Church of the Holy Peace was burnt down, and so were those dedicated to Saint Theodore Sphoracius and Saint Aquilina. The hospitals of Eubulus and Sampson and the Baths of Alexander were totally destroyed, and fanned by the wind, which carried sheets of flame and showers of sparks up into the cold, grey January air, the fires spread to the Mesê and to some of the residential quarters of the city. The homes of unpopular officials were looted and burnt to the ground; old scores were settled, and though no one knows how many murders were committed during the course of these few anarchical days, it was thought that many people took advantage of the violence of the times to settle long-standing debts of hatred and to avenge old grievances. The Palace was in a state of siege, though Belisarius and his men sallied out every now and again, and when they did so, there was desultory fighting in the streets; but the people avoided another head-on collision with the Goths, waging guerilla war on them from the roof-tops and the windows of the houses instead, and then running for safety up one of the many side streets before their enemies could retaliate. As long as they followed these tactics, Belisarius could not hope to crush the rebellion; but since the rebels did not dare to attack the Palace as long as Belisarius and Mundus were there to defend it with their men, military stalemate was reached.

Meanwhile, inside the Palace the alarm was great. Justinian did not trust the Palace Guards, and he had justifiable grounds for strongly suspecting that many of the Senators and other courtiers, who had been caught there when the rebellion began, and who now surrounded him with bland faces and polite smiles, were inwardly praying for the victory of the rebels. As the days passed, he became more and more afraid that some sudden act of treachery by one of these secret enemies inside the Palace was the greatest danger which he faced, and on the evening of Saturday, 17 January, after a conference with his closest advisers, he decided to order them all to leave the Palace. The only exceptions which he was prepared to make were on behalf of men like John the Cappadocian, who was allowed to stay because he was bound to the Emperor both by loyalty and by common interest; Narses could stay with him too, and so, of course, could Belisarius and Mundus; but almost everyone else was ordered to leave. This general banishment included the two nephews of the Emperor Anastasius, Pompeius and Hypatius, of whose intentions Justinian was particularly suspicious, and when they begged him to allow them to stay, his suspicions grew even stronger, though they swore most solemnly that they were entirely loyal to him, the Emperor would have none of it, and ordered them to go. It was a bad blunder, for in forcing them to leave, he handed them over to the rebels who were only too eager to use them for their own purposes.

Justinian did not lack courage. On Sunday morning he went to the Hippodrome by the private way from the Palace, took his place in the *kathisma,* and made a personal appeal to the startled crowd who were gathered there to make peace. The news of the Emperor's appearance spread through the city almost as fast as the flames of the previous week, and a huge crowd soon gathered to hear what he had to say. Holding a copy of the Gospels in his hand, he swore that he would grant an amnesty to everyone concerned in the rioting and would listen to any demands the people cared to make, as soon as law and order had been re-established, and peace had been restored. But the majority of the crowd was hostile to him, whether egged on by the Senators or simply because many people who had suffered under John the Cappadocian were present, and there were cries of 'Swine!' and 'You are lying.' Others cried out, 'You'll keep your promise as you kept faith with Vitalian,' and the crowd roared its approval. Vitalian had been a rebel general, who had been enticed into the Palace where he had been murdered, and rumour had it that Justinian had been the instigator of the crime, though his complicity had never been proved. He tried to speak again, but the Mandator's voice was drowned by the baying of thousands of angry voices; there was no more he could do, and he left the *kathisma* to a torrent of jeers and derisory cheers. As he returned to the Palace, the news broke that the nephews of Anastasius had been freed, and the huge crowd in the Hippodrome surged off to Hypatius' house determined to make him Emperor in Justinian's place, whether he liked it or not.

He did not like it at all. Indeed, he had foreseen this moment, and it had been in an attempt to avoid it that he had begged Justinian not to eject him from the Palace on the previous evening. His wife Maria liked it even less than he did, imploring him in tears not to allow himself to be taken away by the mob to what she was sure would be his certain death. But the people would not take 'no' for an answer, and Hypatius was bundled out of the house, trembling and protesting his reluctance, by hundreds of jubilant supporters, who carried him off to the Forum of Constantine. His arrival was greeted with rapturous applause, and a golden chain, which someone was wearing as a necklace, was hastily commandeered and wound round his head like a diadem, while the crowd cried, 'Long live Hypatius!' As royalty was thus forced upon him, the wretched Hypatius was shaking like a leaf with fear, but as he saw the size of the crowd which was cheering him, and began to recognise a large number of Senators and other eminent people amongst his supporters, he began to recover his nerve, hoping against hope that things might turn out well after all.

Immediately after his 'coronation' there was a council of war to discuss the best course of action to follow; opinion was divided, some urging caution, while others wanted to strike while the iron was hot. One of the Senators, Origen by name, was strongly in favour of a waiting policy, arguing that time was on their side, and that since Justinian's resources were strictly limited, all that they had to do was to sit back until they ran out, and the Emperor would then have no alternative but to fly of his own accord. But the majority wanted to seize the initiative while the revolutionary fervour of the people was at its height; if they did not act now, passions would cool, and people would begin to get tired; some would go back to their homes and their families, and all Justinian would have to do then would be to let loose Belisarius' troops with orders to round up the rebels. Hypatius, who seems to have been a man who tended to veer from one extreme to the other, declared himself to be in favour of immediate action, and his willingness to act with decision delighted the mob. He was rushed off to the Hippodrome, where he was installed in the *kathisma* amidst scenes of wild enthusiasm. Thousands of people crowded into the arena to cheer their new Emperor and to heap insults and abuse on the absent heads of Justinian and Theodora.

To the little party of people who still remained in the Palace, the outlook could not have looked blacker. The cheering of the rebels in the Hippodrome could be heard like the noise of the sea in the distance; the Guards were sullen and aloof, obviously preparing to desert to the other side at the first convenient opportunity and only deterred from such a course by the presence of Belisarius' Goths and Mundus' Germans; and as the news was brought to the small group of men still loyal to the Emperor that the people had crowned Hypatius and were hailing him as their new sovereign, the despondency of Justinian's friends deepened and turned into something very like despair. A conference was called to consider the situation, but no one had anything constructive to suggest as a possible way out of the hopeless position into which the events of the previous week had somehow forced them all; a week ago Justinian had been the supreme and unchallenged ruler of the Roman world, Emperor and Autocrator; now there was hardly a housemaid or a footman in the Palace who would still do his bidding.

It was not a large conference. Both Justinian and Theodora were there; so were Belisarius and Mundus; John of Cappadocia and

Narses were there too, and no doubt there were others whose names have not been recorded. They met in gloomy silence. At last one of them had the courage to say what everyone else was thinking: the Emperor could still escape from the city by sea; it was not too late for that. It is not known who it was who was honest and brave enough openly to admit defeat, but whoever it was no one disagreed with him. Indeed, Belisarius, John the Cappadocian, and Justinian's other closest friends and colleagues took it in turns to urge him to go while the going was good; he could sail to Heraclea Pontica on the southern shore of the Black Sea, they advised him, where he would be safe for the time being, and if the situation improved, he could return as easily as he had departed to resume his rightful position in the Palace. Everyone must have known that, once he had fled the city, he would never come back; but it was a polite and face-saving fiction to suggest that one day he might do so. Justinian listened morosely to what his friends had to say to him; it was impossible to disagree with them; the rebellion had succeeded, and there was no longer any point in refusing to bow to the inevitable. No other course was open to him but flight.

It was at this point that Theodora, who had been a small and silent observer of the events of the afternoon, intervened for the first time; to everyone's surprise, when Justinian had finished speaking, she rose to her feet. Everyone fell silent, and all eyes were turned in her direction. 'My lords,' she said, 'the present occasion is too serious to allow me to follow the convention that a woman should not speak in a man's council. Those whose interests are threatened by extreme danger should think only of the wisest course of action, not of conventions. Now in my opinion, in the present crisis if ever, flight is not the right course, even if it should bring us to safety. It is impossible for a man, once he has been born into this world, not to die; but for one who has reigned it is intolerable to be exiled. May I never be deprived of this purple robe, and may I never see the day when those who meet me do not call me "Empress".' Turning to Justinian who, like the rest of those present, sat in stunned and sheepish silence, she said, 'If you wish to save yourself, my Lord, there is no difficulty. Over there is the sea, and there too are the ships. Yet reflect for a moment whether, when you have once escaped to a place of security, you will not prefer death to such safety. I agree with an old saying that the purple is a fair winding-sheet.' Theodora then sat down. It was magnificent.

Alone among the others, she was indomitable, and the men avoided each other's eyes in slightly ashamed embarrassment; but her words had a dramatic effect on them all, turning the tide of their despair and defeatism into one of determination to win whatever the cost might be. The decision was taken to stay and fight.

While this fateful conference was being held in the Palace, a curious and in its way equally fateful little incident was taking place in the Hippodrome. Hypatius, though now 'crowned' by the rebels and firmly seated on the Emperor's chair in the *kathisma* with a hundred thousand people wildly cheering him in the densely packed arena below and on the tiers of stone seats around it, was still sufficiently fearful of his chances of success to try to insure against failure by means of an ingenious little stratagem. He sent a message to Justinian, couched in the most respectful terms, to tell him that he, Hypatius, was only acting a part; moreover, he was a most unwilling actor, who longed more than anything for the collapse of the rebellion which, he ventured to suggest most humbly, the thrice-august Emperor might succeed in bringing about, if he attacked the great crowd of rebels now squeezed tightly into the Hippodrome. This message was entrusted to a man named Ephraem, who was ordered to make his way to the Palace as quickly and as secretly as possible and there to deliver it to Justinian himself. He set off at once, but on arrival he met an imperial secretary, Thomas by name, in one of the corridors of the place, who told him that both Justinian and Theodora had already set sail for the Black Sea and were no longer in the city. Whether this was a genuine mistake on the part of Thomas, who may have heard a rumour that the Emperor and Empress had fled, or whether he intended to deceive Ephraem for reasons of his own, we shall never know; it has been suggested that the man may have been disloyal to Justinian and unwilling to carry messages to him, but he may equally easily have believed what he told Ephraem to be the truth. At any rate, Ephraem, who had no reason at all not to believe Thomas, hurried back to the Hippodrome, where he rushed up to Hypatius in the *kathisma* in obvious excitement. 'Sire,' he cried, 'God wishes you to reign. Justinian has gone.' The news was immediately broken to the crowd, which went wild with delight, while Hypatius began at last to play the role of Emperor with confidence and even enjoyment. But both he and his supporters were very soon to be painfully disillusioned.

After Theodora had rallied her husband and his advisers, it had not taken long to make plans. The first thing they decided to do was to try to sow dissension in the crowd in the Hippodrome; this was in line with the traditional Roman policy of *divide et impera*. Narses ordered his eunuchs to mingle with the people there, and to do everything in their power to create a split between the Greens and the Blues. They were supplied with plenty of money in small change, which could be used in a tactful way to bribe those who were open to bribery, while their instructions were to remind the Blues of the favours they had received at Justinian's hands in the past, and at the same time to insinuate that Hypatius, like his uncle Anastasius before him, would be sure to favour the Greens. They were also told not to allow the Blues in the crowd to forget Theodora's well-known hatred of the Greens. While Narses' eunuchs were occupied on their mission of discord, Belisarius prepared to lead some of his men to the *kathisma* by way of the back entrance from the Palace and the spiral staircase, which opened into the royal box itself, and there to arrest or kill Hypatius on the spot; but the way led through apartments which were occupied by some Palace Guards, who sullenly refused to allow him and his men to pass. A fight between the Gothic troops loyal to Justinian and those still awaiting the outcome of the revolution before finally committing themselves to either side would have been fatal at this particular moment, and Belisarius marched his men back to the Palace again.

Since this first plan had failed, another was quickly adopted; Belisarius and Mundus mustered every man under their respective commands, told them what they had to do, and led them out of the Palace precinct over the burned rubble of the Chalkê. With considerable difficulty Belisarius then led his Goths as quietly and as stealthily as he could over the blackened ruins of the buildings around the Augusteum to the western entrance to the Hippodrome, while Mundus took his Germans as inconspicuously as possible to another gate at the other end of the arena; it was known as the Nekra Gate because, when there were casualties during the chariot races, the dead were carried out through it. There were not many people about, for everyone who could do so had crowded into the Hippodrome, and the streets were nearly deserted. The few who saw the soldiers moving in a dark, silent mass towards their objective were either too frightened or too incurious to realise what they were doing; they did not raise the alarm, and both Belisarius and Mundus arrived at their respective points of attack undetected and with their troops in perfect order and disciplined silence. On arrival, since there was no further advantage to be gained by concealment, Belisarius drew his men up openly in the portico of the Blues to the right of the *kathisma* in full view of the suddenly horrified crowd, which was taken completely by surprise. Many of the rebels were armed, but whereas on previous occasions they had come face to face with Belisarius' Goths in the city streets where they had had room to manoeuvre and to hide or escape if things got too hot for them, now they faced them in the desperately restricted and overcrowded arena of the Hippodrome; there were no side streets down which they could run, no roofs from which they could throw bricks or boiling water, and not an inch of room in which to manoeuvre. Huddled together in a dense and helpless mass like sheep, they looked in dismay at the grim ranks of Gothic soldiers, as they formed up in order of battle and coldly, efficiently, and unemotionally drew their swords.

When Belisarius gave the order to charge, the people who were nearest to the troops panicked; they tried to back away, but there was no room to retreat, and those closest to the approaching Goths ran into those immediately behind them in a struggling and confused heap of tangled human bodies; some fell to the ground, while others stumbled over them, screaming and fighting in a mad scramble to escape by way of the gates at the other end of the Hippodrome. But as the vast crowd stampeded, and Belisarius and his Goths began their bloody and merciless work of killing, the soldiers cutting and thrusting with the murderous skill of professionals, Mundus and his Germans burst into the arena through the Nekra Gate, and the terrified rebels found themselves trapped like sheep between two packs of wolves. A massacre followed.

At the height of the carnage, the Palace Guards hastily decided to back the winning side before it was too late, and let it be known that they would allow anyone, who wanted to do so, to make their way to the *kathisma* without further let or hindrance from them. Justinian immediately despatched a small party of armed men under the command of two of his nephews, Boraides and Justus by name, with orders to arrest Hypatius and anyone else they found with him. Bursting in through the back door, they seized the terrified usurper, who had watched the battle in the arena from his vantage point on the imperial throne with increasing horror and dismay as he realised the magnitude of the disaster he was witnessing; his brother Pompeius, who was with him, was arrested too. They were dragged trembling before Justinian, who greeted them with icy restraint. He demanded of Hypatius a reason for his treachery. Why had he allowed himself to be crowned by the rebels? Simply and solely, the wretched man replied, to lure the Emperor's enemies into the Hippodrome where they could be dealt with by Belisarius, as indeed he had tried to tell Justinian in his message. What message, asked Justinian; he had received no message. In any case, if Hypatius was so loyal to him, why had he waited so long before leading the rebels into a trap? There was no answer to that, and Hypatius was reduced to begging for his life, pleading in his own cause that he had not been a free agent, but had acted all along under compulsion. This at least was true, and Justinian, who was neither a vindictive man nor a cruel one by nature, was inclined to believe him and spare his life; but a gesture from Theodora, who had not been brought up in the ferociously realistic world of the Hippodrome for nothing, checked his kindly impulse. Even if they had been the puppets of events, the two brothers were too dangerous to be allowed to live, for there was always the possibility that they would be used again as the tools of future conspirators. Reluctantly, the Emperor condemned them to death, and they were taken away. He seldom condemned a political prisoner to death again, and nor did Theodora; the killing at this time sickened and disgusted them both.

Meanwhile, the slaughter in the Hippodrome had gone far enough, and as night fell Belisarius and Mundus ordered their men to put up their swords; it was time to stop. The soldiers were exhausted physically and emotionally, and the few rebels left in the place, who had not somehow managed to escape, and yet had not been killed, were almost out of their minds with terror. As the Goths and the Germans wearily formed up to return to their quarters, between thirty-five and forty thousand people lay dead, dying, or wounded in the Hippodrome; the sand of the arena was drenched with blood; bodies lay in heaps on the stone seats, and the night air was filled with groans and cries for help. Outside in the city, the scene can only be imagined. The news of the appalling disaster which had overtaken the rebels must have spread from street to street carried by frightened and often wounded men as they tried desperately to reach the safety of their homes again, hugging the shadows and skirting the piles of rubble from burned buildings. In tens of thousands of houses, too, men must have sat shaking and breathless, terrified out of their wits but profoundly thankful to be alive, while their wives or mothers tended their wounds, tearing blood-stained clothing away from torn flesh, washing sand and grit out of open wounds, bandaging mutilated limbs, and soothing raw nerves. No doubt some of them berated their husbands or sons, telling them in the fear and agonising relief of the moment that they were fools ever to have got muddled up with the rebellion in the first place, and that they deserved everything that they had got, while in other homes the women just wept and comforted their men as best they could. But in every home there must have been agreement about one thing: it was finished; despite all the enthusiasm and the cries of 'Nika! Nika! Nika!' the victory had not been theirs. Against all the odds, Justinian had won.

Rebellions are always bitter for the losers. At dawn the next morning, Hypatius and Pompeius were executed, and as the winter sun came up out of Asia across the Bosphorus and lit up the blackened ruins of Constantinople's churches and civic buildings, their bodies were thrown into the sea. In the Hippodrome hundreds of women, whose men had not returned during the night, searched for them, determined at least to give them a decent Christian burial; and behind the scenes the city's sanitary department unostentatiously prepared to clean up the unlovely mess of the last ten dirty days.

VI

ΘΕ
ΟΔΩ
ΡΑ
After the crushing of the Nika revolt, Theodora emerges from the shadows, which surround her childhood and youth, into the full light of history; for the first time it is possible to begin to see what sort of a person she really was. The account of her early years in Procopius' *Secret History* presents her in such a uniformly lurid light that its picture of her is inevitably a distorted one. She becomes easier to see after meeting Justinian, and she stands out in brilliant and dramatic relief at the height of the Nika crisis, when she rose to make the little speech which was destined to change the whole course of events; but what she did with herself during the rest of those dark and dangerous days we do not know. Once they were over, however, and the life of the Palace returned to normal, she begins to appear more and more frequently in the records of the time, and we can see her for the first time, not only in the round, so to speak, but also in the undramatic light of her ordinary everyday life.

It was a privileged life, and she loved every minute of it. When old Justin had died, she and Justinian moved from the Palace of Hormisdas into the Imperial Palace itself, where they were surrounded by every possible luxury and comfort. Theodora was just over thirty years old at the time of the Nika revolt, but she looked younger, and everyone agreed that she was still as ravishingly beautiful as ever. Since she was also intensely feminine, she had every intention of remaining both young and beautiful for as long as possible, and she took the greatest possible care of herself and her appearance. Before having breakfast in bed, she would rise and spend hours in her bath; and then she would sit for at least as long in front of her mirror making up her face and doing her hair with the help of two or three of her personal maids. She dressed superbly, and since Justinian loved to load her with jewellery, she seldom appeared unadorned by precious stones of one kind or another. In the celebrated portrait of her in the Church of San Vitale in Ravenna, where she is depicted as she must have looked as an older woman not long before she died, she is wearing a head-dress set with enormous pearls as well as some emeralds, sapphires, and stones which look like jasper; her ear-rings are two square emeralds set in gold with a pearl and sapphire pendant to each of them; her necklace is also of emeralds set in gold, as is a large brooch on her bosom; and her small shoulders seem to be covered with a silken cape embroidered with pearls and a dozen huge diamonds. Her toilet completed, she would emerge from the *gynaeceum*, cocooned by a silken bevy of attendants, looking as regal as any Roman Empress before her and twice as lovely as most. Her day's work would then begin, and the morning would be entirely devoted to it; but though she enjoyed working, she always retired to bed again in the afternoon for a siesta, for she loved sleeping, and she was determined to preserve her youthful appearance by taking ample rest. In this respect, she differed from Justinian, who grudged every moment he spent in sleep, and who allowed himself only a few frugal hours in bed each night, rising long before dawn to devote himself to his various pursuits; his work with Tribonian on Roman law engrossed him, he was fascinated by theology, and he nearly always had schemes for new buildings somewhere in the Empire, which needed his attention and approval. They had different tastes in food and drink too. Luxury did not attract Justinian; he ate little and drank less, being perfectly happy with a slice of bread and a salad for his supper. Theodora thoroughly enjoyed her food. As a child in the Hippodrome she had probably had to be content with whatever her mother was able to afford to put before her three hungry daughters, and that had probably been insufficient to satisfy the healthy appetite of a growing child; perhaps it was against this background of remembered hunger and a barely adequate diet that Theodora became celebrated for the epicurean meals she provided for herself and her guests. Nothing pleased her more than to entertain her friends and to give them such exquisite food that they would never forget it, and her taste in wine soon became a by-word in Byzantine society. She was both a gourmet by inclination and a superb hostess by natural gift, and her position as Justinian's consort gave her every opportunity to indulge this side of her nature, although she never allowed anyone to forget for a moment that she was the Empress; her insistence upon the proper social observances and etiquette did not grow less as the years went by, and she never became easily approachable.

But Theodora did not spend all her time enjoying herself; she was extremely active in the government of the Empire. After the Nika revolt was over, Justinian never forgot that he owed his victory to Belisarius, Mundus, Narses, and above all to Theodora. At the height of the crisis she had proved to be more politically astute and more resolute than all his other advisers put together, and without her intervention he would almost certainly have lost his throne. It was only fair that, since he had retained it by following her advice, he should share it with her now that things had returned to normal.

The Empress as such had no constitutional right to a part in the Emperor's authority, for he alone was the absolute ruler of the Roman world; but simply because he was absolute and an autocrat in the fullest sense of that word, he could choose to share his power with whomsoever he wished, and no one could stop him. One Byzantine historian summed up the situation by saying that 'in the time of Justinian, there was not a monarchy but a dual reign. His partner for life was not less, but perhaps even more powerful, than he was.' There was no precedent for this complete sharing of authority, and yet no one could possibly mistake the fact that it was indeed shared; on taking office, bishops, magistrates, generals, governors of provinces, ministers of the crown, and other high officials had to swear 'by Almighty God, by his only Son Jesus Christ, by the Holy Spirit, by the holy and glorious Mother of God, Mary-ever-Virgin, by the four Evangelists, by the holy archangels Michael and Gabriel to render loyal service to the most pious and holy sovereigns Justinian and Theodora, wife of his Imperial Majesty'. In fact, as time went by, Theodora began to play a larger part in the affairs of everyday government than did Justinian, and she did so for very good reasons.

The Emperor was immensely busy with other things during this time. The nine or ten years following the suppression of the Nika revolt were the most glorious of his reign; he was at peace with Persia, and thus he was free to undertake the great political task of his life: the restoration of the Roman Empire to its former glory. During this period his armies under Belisarius reconquered North Africa, Sicily, and Italy, and restored them to his dominion. Meanwhile, the great legal work which he had begun with the help of Tribonian was brought to a triumphant conclusion. Plainly, he could not have done all this if he had been burdened every day with the necessity of taking in person all the detailed decisions which were part and parcel of the central government of his enormous realm; so he left much of this to Theodora. She took up the reins of government into her capable little hands with enjoyment, for the work suited her perfectly, and she was eminently well-equipped to do the tasks which came her way; she was highly intelligent; she had an unerring judgement as far as people were concerned; and she thoroughly enjoyed power.

But she did not like Constantinople very much, and so she took every opportunity which presented itself to leave the city and to spend a few weeks or even months in the country. Justinian did not always accompany her, for custom dictated that the Emperor should reside most of the time in the Imperial Palace, but he went with her when he could. At Hieron, a small town on the Asiatic shore of the Bosphorus near the point where it joins the Black Sea, there was a palace which she loved, and so Justinian had it greatly enlarged and splendidly furnished for her. He transformed the town too, building a magnificent church there and dedicating it to the Mother of God, as well as building baths, market places, and elegantly colonnaded streets, where people could wander in the shade with their friends and enjoy the pleasures of city life away from the dust and the crowds of Constantinople. As the heat of summer approached Theodora would issue orders to her court to prepare to leave for Hieron, and on the appointed day she would sally forth from the Palace in great state, surrounded by as many as two or three thousand attendants of one kind or another—guards, eunuchs, ladies-in-waiting, court officials, and a host of servants—and would go with them in splendid procession to the Golden Horn, where she would embark upon the royal barge, and the others would go abroad a great flotilla of small craft to sail to Hieron; with pennants fluttering in the breeze against the blue Byzantine sky and bedecked with silks and brocades, awnings and cushions, this small armada would then sail northwards, while the gulls screamed overhead and parties of shearwaters flew up and down the Bosphorus low over the water beside the boats; they were believed to be the souls of the many sailors drowned there, and they put the members of Theodora's retinue in mind of their own mortality. On arrival she would hold court in Hieron until such time as she decided to return to the capital, and the numerous government officials, who were dependent upon her authority and her orders, had either to find some sort of accommodation there for the summer or to commute by boat from Constantinople, whether they liked it or not. Many of them did not like it at all; if they decided to stay there, and were lucky enough to find lodgings, few of them could afford to bring their families with them, and if they decided to sail to and from Constantinople up and down the Bosphorus each day, it was both inconvenient and expensive.

Another thing which made the journey highly unpopular was the presence in the Bosphorus at this time of a large and reputedly fierce whale, which terrified the people of Constantinople. How it got there is a mystery, but it certainly did so, and stories of the way in which, when some wretched little party in a boat were least expecting it, it would rear its vast bulk out of the water, snorting and blowing apparently with anger, and proceed to overturn the boat and drown its occupants, spread alarm everywhere. The whale became so famous that it was even given a name, Porphyry; it haunted the Bosphorus for about fifty years, until at last it was washed up and stranded in shallow water near the mouth of the Black Sea, where it died. To the awed astonishment of everyone who saw it, the dead beast was forty-five feet long and fifteen feet across, so it is perhaps no wonder that during its lifetime the fear and fame of Porphyry the whale spread far and wide. Whether it was really as dangerous as everyone believed is another matter; but, homicidal or not, Theodora's courtiers were terrified of it, and the Byzantine world heaved a sigh of relief when the whale died.

Her visits to Hieron were not Theodora's only excursions into the country. Shortly after the defeat of the Nika rebels, before the rubble of the city had been cleared or rebuilding had begun, she made a spectacular progress to the province of Bithynia across the Bosphorus, travelling in ostentatious state through Chrysopolis, the golden city, in a gilded carriage shaded by a purple silk canopy and drawn by four milk-white mules, to bathe in the hot sulphur springs at Pythia. On a later occasion she visited some celebrated monasteries on the snowy slopes of the mountain which had been named Mount Olympus centuries before by some Greeks, who had colonised Asia Minor, and who had seen in its massive outline against the sky something to remind them of the home of their gods in Greece. As usual, she was accompanied by a host of guards and attendants, and she even took with her a popular preacher, a man named John who was the bishop of Tella, who was charged to tell the crowds which gathered to listen to him that the Empress would do everything in her power to endow their shrines and help their monasteries. She probably enjoyed herself thoroughly on these trips, but her triumphal progress was not undertaken for pleasure alone; it was intended to be a demonstration of the splendour and the power of the throne, unshaken by recent events, and as such it was an extremely astute political action on her part. If there were people in Bithynia whose faith in the stability of Justinian's government had been shaken by rumours, during the dark days of the Nika rebellion, that the Emperor had come within a hair's breadth of losing his crown, the sight of Theodora in all her power and glory, serene and radiant, was enough to restore their confidence.

When she returned to Constantinople, she and Justinian set about supervising the rebuilding of the city. He had always had a passion for building, which Theodora seems to have encouraged and shared; for even before the Nika revolt they had commissioned some splendid buildings, of which perhaps the best known is the Church of Saint Sergius and Saint Bacchus, two early Christian martyrs who had been killed during the persecution of Christians in Syria in the first few years of the fourth century. It still stands, and the Emperor's initials, intertwined with those of Theodora in the form of a monogram, can still be seen at the top of some of the columns there; there is also a moulding running all round the rotunda with an inscription describing Theodora's charitable works in the city. But it was the destruction of the city centre by fire during the Nika revolt which gave Justinian a chance to realise his architectural ambitions and dreams; tragic and destructive as the fires had been, they provided a golden opportunity to a man like Justinian to indulge his obsessional taste for building. Moreover, if the centre of the city had to be burnt to the ground, it could hardly have been destroyed at a better moment, for there happened to be an architect of genius alive at the time and known to Justinian. His name was Anthemius, and he came from a small town, Tralles, not far from Ephesus in the Roman province of Asia. The son of a doctor, he and his four brothers all made names for themselves in learned professions of one kind or another; Anthemius was a mathematician as well as an architect, and after the Nika revolt

Justinian gave him the task of rebuilding the Church of the Holy Wisdom on a scale worthy of the greatest Christian city in the world. In cooperation with an engineer of almost as great a genius as his own, Isidore of Miletus, Anthemius designed and built the great church which every visitor to Istanbul sees today; although it has suffered during the centuries, especially when it was turned into a mosque and its mosaics were either destroyed or covered with plaster, it is still one of the world's greatest buildings.

Meanwhile, the political power which Justinian gave to Theodora made it possible for her to put some of her most cherished ideas into practice. She had never forgotten the kindness with which she had been treated by the Christians of Egypt, all of whom were of the Monophysite party in the church, and the opinions which she had learned from them, when her fortunes had been at their lowest ebb, shaped and formed her religious outlook once and for all; she remained a devoted supporter of their cause for the rest of her life. Indeed, as the restoration of the Roman Empire to its former glory and extent was Justinian's life-work, so she regarded the restoration of the fortunes of the much persecuted Christians who were wedded to Monophysite doctrines as her life-work. She had begun to intercede on their behalf as soon as she had married Justinian, and before the Nika revolt she had succeeded in materially changing their lot. She did not try at first to persuade her husband that their persecution was wrong in itself, but rather that it simply had not worked. In Egypt the Monophysites had proved to be unassailable, as Justinian very well knew; and even in Syria, where monasteries had been closed by force and often with great barbarity, where bishops and priests had been murdered or hounded into the deserts of the region, and where monks and nuns had been subjected to repulsive indignities by imperial troops, despite their sufferings the vast majority of the people had remained obstinately loyal to the Monophysite cause. In fact, his uncle Justin's policy had failed. Justinian had listened and he had been impressed; for much of what she said was undeniably true. In the end, he had allowed himself to be persuaded that the only thing to do was to call the whole persecution off, and after they had been married a short time, he issued the necessary orders. Theodora had won the first round.

The effect throughout the eastern provinces was immediate, and everyone knew that they owed the sudden ending of the nightmare to their new Empress. Families heaved sighs of grateful relief; exiled bishops returned to their sees to be greeted by crowds of cheering people; priests returned to their cures, and monks and nuns to their monasteries, many of which were in ruins; but the years of horror were over, and God and Theodora were to be praised for the victory they had won over their Orthodox persecutors. Nor was it only in the eastern provinces that the effects of the new religious policy were felt. For the first time for years Christians with Monophysite opinions reappeared openly in Constantinople, even in the Imperial Palace itself, where they were greeted with great respect and exaggerated deference by the Empress. As time went by, more and more Monophysites were drawn to the capital by the prospect of Theodora's protection and favour, and none of them was disappointed. She made over the Palace of Hormisdas, where she and Justinian had lived together in the old days, to a number of Monophysite monks so that, to the righteous indignation and extreme annoyance of members of the Orthodox party, a monastery full of heretics was established within the precincts of the Imperial Palace at the very centre of the Byzantine world. But their annoyance was nothing to their anger and alarm when the Emperor himself began to show signs of favour towards these hated and heretical newcomers. There was nothing they could do about it, however, but bide their time with as good a grace as they could manage; and in fact there was worse to come.

Theodora persuaded Justinian that nothing but good could possibly come from a series of meetings between him and the leaders of the Monophysite party in the church; the right way to restore peace and unity both to the Church and to the Empire was by discussion, not by persecution, she told him. The result was that various eminent Monophysite churchmen were invited to Constantinople to meet the Emperor. Not surprisingly, after years of vigorous persecution, this invitation was greeted with some suspicion. Theodora was eager to persuade Severus, the deposed Patriarch of Antioch, who had been her tutor in Alexandria, to come to the conference; she had fallen under his spell in Egypt, and he seemed to her to be the man most likely to convince Justinian of the justice of the cause which was so close to her own heart, for he was a man of great distinction. Even his opponents had to admit that he excelled almost equally in faith, learning, eloquence, and courage. He had the kind of mind which might justly be called great, for he was conciliatory rather than contentious in debate, and he avoided sterile argument for argument's sake which so often passed for theological discussion in Byzantine circles.

Justinian agreed to see Severus, and a most courteous invitation to come to Constantinople as the guest of the Emperor and the Empress was despatched to him, but the old man was as suspicious of Justinian's motives as some of the other invited guests; the imperial change of heart seemed to him to be altogether too sudden, even taking Theodora's influence into account, and Severus begged to be excused on the grounds of his great age. Theodora was disappointed but not discouraged; if Severus would not come, some of his disciples must do so in his place, and Justinian must preside over a theological conference, during which members of the Orthodox party and Monophysites from Egypt and Syria should seek for unity and agreement. So others were invited, and a conference was duly convened in Constantinople, where it sat for a number of weeks; but to the bitter disappointment of the Empress unity was by no means reached. She was realistic enough, however, to recognise that she had been over-optimistic, to say the least, to hope for such an ideal outcome, and the failure of her first attempt to reconcile the two religious factions in the church in no way lessened her determination to go on trying; it would have taken much more than one set-back to divert Theodora from her course. Meanwhile, the fact that the two opposing sides had actually sat down together and exchanged views without coming to blows was, in itself, a considerable achievement, and this encouraged her not to give up hope.

In her relationships with some of the people involved in the great religious disputes of the day, Theodora revealed most clearly an aspect of her nature which it is hard for us to understand today; for while no one could have been a greater stickler for etiquette than Theodora in her everyday life in court and elsewhere, when it came to meeting people who were accounted holy by the standards of her own day she held them in such reverence that she was prepared to accept almost any snub or rudeness from them without a murmur. The men whom every Byzantine citizen judged to be the holiest of all men were those who had renounced the pleasures of this world for the austerities of the monastic life; half-starved anchorites, ragged monks from the hills of Syria or the deserts of Egypt, stylites or pillar saints, who lived for years sitting or standing on the tops of columns, and other ascetics were universally admired, and their way of life was often described as being 'the life of the angels'; they were 'citizens of heaven', who had been raised by prayer and fasting above the cares of this world into direct communion with God. So Theodora was not unique in adopting an attitude of deep respect and reverence for such people; she would not have been a good Byzantine if she had not treated holy men in a completely different way from that in which she treated everyone else. Even so, the lengths to which she allowed some of them to go without the smallest remonstrance were astonishing. The behaviour of the anchorite, Maras, was a case in point.

He was a remarkable man, singularly unattractive by modern standards, but hugely respected and admired in his own day. Born in Syria, he did not renounce the world until he was nearly thirty years old, but then he did so with great suddenness on his wedding day, announcing with obliging Freudian candour that he preferred God's light and easy yoke to the 'lethal captivity of bodily union' with a woman. Whatever the lady who was to have been his wife may have thought at the time, she was lucky to have escaped a life of conjugal bliss with Maras, or so it seems in retrospect; for he had not been in the monastery of his choice for long before he became known for his extreme asceticism and for the lengths to which he was prepared to go to mortify his flesh. Perhaps, if he had married, his wife could have put up with his taste for austerity, but a less amiable side of his character would almost certainly have made him a difficult husband; for, if he was hard on himself, he was at least as hard, if not harder, on everyone else with whom he happened to come into contact, quite regardless of whom they might chance to be. But so great was the respect paid by the Byzantines to ascetics that his fame soon spread, and eventually Theodora summoned the holy man to Constantinople, so that she might profit from his sanctity.

She and Justinian received him with deep reverence, but Emperors and Empresses meant nothing to Maras, who had renounced the world with all its pomps and vanities, and he was violently rude to both of them before storming out of the Palace without allowing either of them to say a word in reply. Theodora was deeply impressed; plainly, only a man of exceptional holiness could behave in such a magnificently other-worldly way, and it was her obvious duty to do everything she could for him. She invited him to be her guest in the Imperial Palace. He refused. She sent him a large sum of money, and begged him to use it to help the poor. He returned to the Palace, burst into the room where Theodora awaited him, and taking handfuls of gold coins out of the bag in which they had been presented to him, he threw them in her face, to the horror of her ladies-in-waiting, while she protected herself with raised arms from this golden assault and battery; only when the bag was empty did he deign to leave the room. But even this performance did not upset the Empress. On the contrary, she wrote him a humble little letter of apology for having dared to expose him to temptation, and begged him to allow her at least to help him by sending him a little food from time to time. He replied haughtily that she could offer him nothing which could be of any use to him at all 'except the fear of the Lord, if you are capable of it'. He then retired to a remote spot just outside the city in order to be further away from the Empress, and there he lived in a rudimentary tent.

But Theodora's offer of gold, even though he had refused it, was still destined to have its consequence, for news of it spread; and one night he was attacked by a gang of men who threatened to kill him, if he did not give them the money which had been presented to him by the Empress. He assured them that he had no money, and asked them to leave him in peace. 'If I wanted money, I should not live here,' he pointed out reasonably enough; but the thieves did not believe him, and one of them struck him with his stick. It was an unwise thing to do, for if Maras was a spiritual athlete, he was in equally good physical training; dodging the blow, he threw his assailant to the ground, grabbed his stick, and attacked the other six men in the gang, eventually knocking them all unconscious; he then tied them up, removed their weapons, and waited until they should recover consciousness. When they had all done so, he said, 'I asked you to leave me in peace, my sons, and I'm sorry you didn't listen to me. Now do me the favour of remaining peacefully where you are until morning, and by then I hope you will have made up your minds never again to attack a poor man.' This incident made Maras even more famous than before and deepened Theodora's admiration for him. Eventually she persuaded him to allow her to build him a monastery, where he lived as intransigently as ever until he died of the plague in 542. His death was regarded as a national disaster, and on Justinian's and Theodora's orders he was given a state funeral.

Not all the 'citizens of heaven' were as disagreeable as Maras, but this made little difference to Theodora; she loved them all, and her generosity and kindness to them was enormous. Nothing pleased her more than to be able to found monasteries, hospitals, and orphanages, in which they could do their work of mercy. She built churches, almshouses, homes for old people, places of retreat, and shelters for the very poor and the homeless; she bought a villa at Derkos in Thrace for a certain Theodosius, who succeeded Timothy as Patriarch of Alexandria, but who was later forced to retire; similarly, she bought a large estate in the suburb of Constantinople known as Sykae, the modern Galata, on the northern shore of the Golden Horn, for a truculent monk named Zooras, so that he might found a monastery there; her gifts to religious houses were endless and immensely generous; and she took a close personal interest in the building of the Church of the Holy Apostles which, in its day, must have been as magnificent as the Church of the Holy Wisdom, if not quite so vast. Nothing is left of it now, but Saint Mark's in Venice, which is a copy of it though not an exact copy, still gives some idea of its vanished splendour.

Above all, of course, she played her part in the worshipping life of the church. As Empress, she could hardly have avoided doing so, for protocol demanded that she should be present on all great religious occasions, but there is no reason to suppose that she found this aspect of her imperial duties in any way irksome; on the contrary, she prayed every morning, and seldom missed an opportunity to attend the holy liturgy. Regularly on the numerous major feasts of the Orthodox Church she went in splendid procession, dressed in purple and gold and accompanied by an imperial escort, to one or other of the great churches of Constantinople: to the Holy Wisdom or to the Holy Apostles, to Saint Sergius and Saint Bacchus, or to the Mother of God in Blachernae close to the Golden Horn, where she would sit surrounded by her ladies, while the liturgy of Saint John Chrysostom wound its endless and sonorous way to its divine climax.

On other occasions, she would visit some church or other, and there approach the altar with candles in her hands to kneel in prayer before a jewelled reliquary, for the city was rich in relics. Indeed, as the years had gone by, it had become the repository for an astonishing collection of deeply revered objects ranging from the Wood of the Cross, the Crown of Thorns, the Lance, the Seamless Coat, and the Nails of Christ's passion, through such things as the girdle once worn by the Mother of God and the hair of John the

Baptist, to an abundance of relics of the saints and other holy men. Daniel's body had been brought to the city by Constantine's mother Helena; the bodies of Saint Timothy, Saint Andrew, and Saint Luke had arrived a little later; they had soon been joined by those of Samuel and Isaiah; and in Justinian and Theodora's day the mortal remains of Saint Anne arrived to swell this stiff and silent company of august corpses.

Sometimes, too, Theodora would attend the consecration of a new church, visit a monastery to ask for the prayers of some much-revered monk far gone in the love and knowledge of God, go to the Holy Wisdom to give thanks for a victory, or don full mourning to hear a litany of penitence for whatever sins had brought the wrath of God down on the city in the form of an earthquake, an epidemic, or some other natural disaster. Religious practices were as much part of her life and that of every Byzantine, and the need of them as completely unquestioned, as regular meals are an unquestioned part of the lives of most people today, and for much the same reason; everyone knew that you could not live without them. For without them you would be cut off from the source of life and would wither away.

But if religion was an integral part of her life and the Monophysite cause her lifelong passion, she had another passion: she was a feminist. She fought tirelessly and at times ruthlessly to improve the lot of women; no trouble was too great for her to take on their behalf, no battle too fierce for her to enter, if it would help members of her own sex to lead a better life than that which they had enjoyed hitherto, and no quarter or mercy could be expected from the Empress by anyone she caught oppressing or exploiting women or denying them their rights as human beings.

Needless to say, there were plenty of candidates for her compassion, for although women played a much more independent role in Byzantine society than they did in some other civilisations of the ancient world, it was still basically a patriarchal society in which men were the dominant sex. Indeed, as Theodora had good reason to know, the lot of women in certain professions and walks of life was made even harder by being subject to various legal disabilities. This she was determined to change, and with memories of her own past as the spur, one of the first things she did on achieving power was to launch a determined attack on the legal status of girls and women who chose the stage as a career. By law they were so closely

94

bound, both to their profession and to the man who employed them, that it was very difficult to change their way of life once they had embarked on it; they were also debarred from marrying people of more exalted station than their own, as Theodora had discovered, though the old Emperor Justin had at least changed that. Theodora determined to change the law which forced other disabilities upon girls on the stage, and there are records of 227 actresses in Constantinople alone taking advantage of their new freedom to abandon the stage once and for all, as soon as the Empress's new legislation made it possible.

This was not all. Justinian's first edicts are full of traces of Theodora's determination to better the lot of members of her own sex; there is an edict making it possible for the first time for a daughter to have an equal right to inherit with a son; another ensures that a wife's dowry should become her property again after the death of her husband; and yet another changes the status of the children of female slaves in such a way that they do not automatically become slaves themselves. But she reserved her most determined attack for the men who made a fortune out of prostitution. Byzantine society tolerated two social evils, slavery and poverty, which between them left many women and girls at the mercy of any man's sexual whim, and they had no redress. Inevitably this encouraged some people to cater commercially for such whims in the great cities of the Byzantine world, and the result was that there were very few tastes which could not be satisfied in the brothels of places like Constantinople, where there was a perennial demand for young prostitutes. One of the easiest ways to get rich quickly was to join the ranks of the enterprising pimps who made it their business to procure young girls and then to sell them to the owners of the bawdy houses which were to be found in all big cities. They travelled round the provinces openly buying teenage girls and sometimes children as young as ten years old from their parents, who were often glad to sell them for a few gold coins, so deep was their own poverty; the sale of a daughter made one less mouth to feed, and the pitiful little sum of money they received in exchange probably helped to pay off some small but crippling debt, which they could never have settled without such a windfall. In return, they were assured that their daughter would have a marvellous opportunity to better herself in the capital or some other big city, which she would never enjoy if she stayed at home; life would be easy; she would be dressed in fine clothes, and in a few years she would probably be rich enough to return home and keep her parents in luxury in their old age.

The truth was very different. The girls were sold at a handsome profit to bawds and whoremasters in the big cities throughout the Empire, where they were housed in miserable conditions and kept in a state of virtual slavery. Out of touch with their families and friends, cut off from the outside world, and forced to submit to whatever took the sexual fancy of their customers, they led the most miserable of lives, and most of them soon lost all hope. Since every girl on arrival was made to sign a written contract, by which she traded her liberty for her keep (though few of them had any idea what they were doing when they made their pathetic little marks on the documents presented to them), they stood no chance at all of being released until they were either too old or too worn out to be of any further use to the man who owned the brothel, whereupon they were thrown into the street to fend for themselves as best they could. Occasionally it happened that a customer would be so sorry for one of the girls he met there that he would offer to marry her in order to rescue her from her miserable existence; but even when that happened, and it must have been a rare occurrence, more often than not her employer would refuse to release her, and because she had signed a contract with him, he was within his legal rights to do so.

Perhaps with memories of her own youthful experience in mind, Theodora set out to abolish this whole repulsive commerce in young girls. She had made a beginning before the Nika revolt, but it was not a trade which could be banished overnight, and it was not until four years later that she made her final and decisive move. On 14 November, 535, she caused an edict to be issued which made the activities of pimps a crime, and which banished all brothel-keepers from the capital and from every other major city throughout the Roman world. 'We have set up magistrates to punish robbers and thieves,' the imperial edict ran; 'are we not even more strictly bound to prosecute the robbers of honour and the thieves of chastity?' But she was determined to be scrupulously fair to those whose means of livelihood she was destroying, even though their trade was a loathsome one, so she let it be known that she was prepared to buy the girls back from their employers for the same amount of money as they had paid for them in the first place; the brothel-keepers were required to state on oath what they had given for each girl in their service, and they were told that they would then be compensated by the same sum of money at the expense of the Empress. The average price proved to be five *nomismata*, which was about the same as ten pounds sterling at present values, and this Theodora paid from her privy purse. Meanwhile, she had converted a palace on the Asiatic shore of the Bosphorus not far from the Black Sea into a convent named *Metanoia* or Repentance, and here the girls whom she rescued from the bawdy houses of Constantinople were looked after, while they were helped to begin new lives. Theodora's enemies were persistent people, however, and they managed to turn even this humane enterprise against her by spreading rumours that she had forced many girls against their will to give up their lives as prostitutes, and that some of those who were sent to the *Metanoia* threw themselves from the top-floor windows of the building rather than endure such an unwelcome reformation.

There was probably more substance in another charge brought against her by her enemies, who accused her of being so bigoted a feminist that she treated women with unfair favoritism at the expense of men. It was well-known, they said, that the Empress was always prepared to champion members of her own sex, whether they were in the right or not; so that wives who were divorced for adultery or some other perfectly legitimate reason only had to appeal to Theodora and to bring counter-accusations against their husbands, and they could be sure that either she would compel their husbands to take them back, or she would force the unfortunate men to pay double the legal alimony which was due to them. Sometimes, it was said, she even had a husband thrown into prison and whipped because he refused to do exactly as she told him, so that husbands everywhere learned to put up with almost anything their wives did rather than risk falling foul of the Empress. These sound like stories told by men, but even if they are exaggerated, there is probably some truth in them; she was ferociously loyal to her friends and to those whose causes she espoused and not always over-nice in the ways in which she treated her adversaries. When a somewhat pompous old Patrician of great age and illustrious family, to whom some of her friends owed money, appealed to her to make them pay their debts, she publicly mocked the old man, and sent him away with a flea in his ear. On another occasion, a young man named Saturninus, who had married a girl from her *entourage*, fell foul of her by talking slightingly in public about his new wife; the news reached Theodora that he was openly complaining that, when he had taken his bride to bed on his wedding night, he had discovered that she was no virgin. Theodora was furious, and ordered some of her men to teach Saturninus a lesson in manners; accordingly, they waylaid the young man, 'hoisted him aloft as one would a schoolboy', and gave him a sound beating to deter him from gossiping in the future.

But if Theodora was a feminist, she could be extremely fierce to those women who, in her opinion, brought her own sex into disrepute; and although she was prepared to defend any woman whom she thought to be unjustly accused, she was also a stickler for the precepts of conventional morality and a passionate defender of the sanctity of marriage. Two young women of noble blood, the daughters of a Consul and the offspring of generations of consular and senatorial ancestors, who had married young, were both widowed at an early age. This was a state of affairs which, understandably, they found difficult to endure, and like many others at the time they saw no reason why they should put up for ever with this unwanted chastity; but the way in which they openly consoled themselves for the loss of their husbands with other men became a minor scandal in Byzantine society, and one which did not please the Empress. Theodora summoned the erring sisters to her presence, and told them firmly that they must remarry at once rather than continue to set a bad example to others by their promiscuity. Remarriage as such would probably have been highly acceptable to the two young widows, if they had been allowed to choose their husbands, but they were not to be allowed to do any such thing; the Empress had already chosen new husbands for them, and they were peremptorily ordered to marry two men of extremely humble birth, whom they hardly knew, and did not like. Tears and arguments made not the slightest difference, and in the end the two young women were reduced to taking sanctuary in the Church of the Holy Wisdom in an attempt to avoid being married against their will. Theodora, however, was adamant, and bided her time. In due course the sisters got bored, and decided that even marriage to unsuitable husbands was better than being cooped up in the Cathedral for life with no husbands at all; so they duly emerged, and obediently married the men chosen for them by the Empress. It is only fair to add that, once she had got her way, Theodora showered the two bridegrooms with honours, thus making what amends she could to the injured sisters for the indignity of their marriages.

She proved equally obdurate in her support of the sanctity of marriage on a much later occasion, after the lost provinces in north Africa had been reconquered by Belisarius and recovered for the Empire from the Vandals, who had overrun the whole area during the previous century. When the fighting was over and peace had been restored to the provinces of Mauritania, Numidia, and Africa, Belisarius was withdrawn, and a Patrician named Areobindus, who had married a niece of Justinian's, was appointed Master of Soldiers there. He was a timid man with no military experience, and he soon found himself out of his depth in the murky and still turbulent waters of north African politics. The natives of the place, the Moors and the Berbers, were hostile both to the Vandals and to their new masters, the Byzantines, while the Vandals were smarting under their defeat and only superficially pacified. They soon took the measure of Areobindus, and it was not long before a military revolt was engineered by a Roman General of Vandal origin, who persuaded the Moors to support him; the rebels attacked the Palace in Carthage where Areobindus lived, the guards defended it, and blood was shed. Areobindus was scared out of his wits, and promptly lost his nerve; he fled for safety to a fortified monastery near the harbour, from which retreat he was tempted to emerge only by a promise of safe conduct to Constantinople. Trembling and accompanied by the bishop of Carthage holding a copy of the Gospels in his hand, Areobindus presented himself to the successful rebel General, who greeted him with great respect and entertained him to supper, explaining as he did so that the boat, which was to take him home to the Bosphorus, was being made ready for him. Once the meal was over, however, his host made some excuse or other to leave the room, soldiers entered in his stead, and Areobindus was unceremoniously murdered.

But the Vandal triumph did not last very long. There were a great many people left in the city and in the province who hated both the Vandals and the Moors, and there was also a large body of Byzantine troops in the place who, in order to save their lives, had pretended to acquiesce in the murder of their commander and to submit to the successful rebels, but who were secretly loyal to Justinian. They were led by the commander of an Armenian regiment, a man named Artabanes, who had already achieved distinction in the army, and who now became the master-mind in a conspiracy to assassinate the leader of the rebels. The rebel General was first lulled into a false sense of security by Artabanes who, like most of his countrymen, was urbanity itself when he chose to be diplomatic, and then, a month after the murder of Areobindus, the Vandal in his turn was invited to a banquet as the guest of Artabanes. He came surrounded by soldiers, but they were relieved of their side-arms before going into dinner, as custom dictated, and when he was comfortably drunk, Artabanes duly murdered him. A fight broke out at once between his followers and Artabanes' men, but the rebels had been taken by surprise, and they were exterminated.

When the news reached Constantinople, Justinian was delighted, and immediately appointed Artabanes as Master of Soldiers in the place of the murdered Areobindus. The Armenian was handsome, brave as a lion, generous by nature, and extremely well-born, being related to the Arsacid kings of Armenia, and Justinian's niece, whose name was Praejecta, was overwhelmed with gratitude to him, not only for avenging the death of her husband, but also for rescuing her from an extremely difficult position; for as the niece of the Emperor she had been a very valuable hostage in the hands of the rebels. The young widow was a pretty girl, and Artabanes promptly fell in love with her. The lady in her turn was delighted by his attentions, and before long she promised to marry him. It appeared to be a most suitable match, and when she returned to Constantinople and told her uncle the news of her engagement, Justinian immediately recalled Artabanes and greeted him with every sign of affection and approval, promoting him to be Commander of the Militia, Commander of the foreign contingent of the Guard, and Consul. Beneficence could hardly go farther; but just when the sun of imperial favour was shining most brightly upon the dashing Artabanes, and both his marriage to Praejecta and the brilliance of his future career seemed to be assured, a most unexpected and unwelcome figure from the past arrived in Constantinople. Apparently Artabanes had entirely forgotten that long ago, somewhere in Armenia, he had already been married. The marriage had not lasted longer than a few months; he had never heard from his wife since they had parted; and it was all so long ago that he had had no idea for years whether she was alive or dead. In fact, however, she was very much alive, and somehow she had got wind of her husband's good fortune; so, just when the final touches were being put to the plans for his marriage to the Emperor's niece, she appeared in the capital like some spectre from the past to claim her conjugal rights. She found an immediate supporter in the Empress. Artabanes, Praejecta, and even Justinian himself argued with her that the best course was for Artabanes to obtain a speedy divorce from the wife of his youth; it was only a recognition of the truth that theirs had never been a true marriage, or that, at best, it had totally broken down years ago; but Theodora was inflexible. The bonds of matrimony were sacred, and she forced Artabanes to go back to his legal wife. Then, to make doubly sure that that was the end of the matter, she arranged for Praejecta to marry a nephew of the rebel Hypatius, who had been executed after the Nika revolt, thus effectively removing her from the marriage market and at the same time binding a dynastically dangerous young man to her own family by the ties of marriage. It was typical of her political astuteness as well as of her views about marriage, though even she could not have foreseen that Artabanes would be so antagonised by the whole affair that after her death he would join a conspiracy against the life of Justinian: a conspiracy, incidentally, which failed.

But Theodora was a complex character, and her reactions were seldom wholly consistent or simply predictable; she gave ample proof of her genuine belief in the sanctity of marriage, but there were also occasions when it suited her to protect someone from the consequences of some illicit love affair or other, and then she did not hesitate to do so, especially if that person was a woman. Sometimes it was her feminism which proved stronger than her principles, and sometimes it was her politics. In the case of Antonina, the wife of Belisarius, it seems to have been a bit of both. Since their relationship was destined to be of great moment in Theodora's life, it is important to understand why these two women became so close and dependent upon one another. Antonina, like Theodora herself, had been born in the Hippo-drome, had endured the same sort of poverty during her childhood as the daughters of Acacius the bear-keeper, and like them had led an early life of easy and uncertain virtue. While she was still very young, she had met a man of her own class, with whom she had lived as man and wife, though whether they were ever married is unknown, and she had had a number of children by him, including a son named Photius; at least, it is always assumed that the children of her youth were his, though if she was as promiscuous at this time as many of the sources hint, their paternity must have been open to question. Little else is known of her early years, though it is believed that her father was a charioteer, and it is certain that the man with whom she consorted died soon after the birth of her children, leaving her without a protector in the harsh world of the Hippodrome. Somehow or other, however, she had then met Belisarius, and although by this time she had passed her prime physically, he had fallen hopelessly in love with her, and had married her. He doted on her for the rest of his life with such a total devotion—such a blind infatuation—that his contemporaries unhesitatingly attributed it to magic; Antonina must have bewitched him; plainly she had given him love potions, they believed, for otherwise no man could have remained so ridiculously and passionately in love with his wife for so long. He loved her to distraction, taking her with him everywhere on his campaigns to Africa, to the eastern frontier, and to Italy, and letting her into all his secrets, both military and political. Even his closest friends could not understand his extraordinary devotion to the charioteer's daughter, especially since she was by no means a dewy little rosebud by this time, but by any reckoning rather more than slightly overblown. If Belisarius had been a middle-aged lover and Antonina a ravishing young creature half his age, his behaviour might have been more easily understood by the Byzantine world; but in fact it was the other way round. She must have been at least forty when Justinian came to the throne, and thus she could not have been less than five years older than her husband, and she may even have been as much as ten years his senior; yet he behaved like a schoolboy suffering from a serious attack of calf-love. It was incomprehensible, especially as everyone except Belisarius knew very well that she was deceiving him with a lover; for unlike the Empress, during her time in the Hippodrome Antonina seems to have acquired a taste for sexual adventures, and when she married Belisarius, she did not mend her ways.

How many lovers she took over the years no one knows, but there was one with whom she had a particularly turgid, persistent, and scandalous affair. His name was Theodosius; he was half Antonina's age; and he was a proselyte to the Christian faith. Indeed, Antonina and Belisarius had sponsored him at his baptism, and she stood as his godmother, while Belisarius became his godfather. Not content with this, they became so fond of the young man that they decided to adopt him, and thus he became legally their son. However, none of this deterred Antonina from taking a much warmer interest in him as time went by than was either usual or proper in a godmother, let alone in a mother for her adopted son; she had no scruples at all as far as her love affairs were concerned, and she did not hesitate to seduce him when she got the chance. At first, she behaved discreetly enough not to arouse anyone's suspicions, but prudence was foreign to her nature, and it was not long before she threw discretion to the winds and began to flaunt her relationship with him in everybody's face. All her servants knew what was going on; they could not have failed to do so, for she took Theodosius to her room quite openly as long as Belisarius was out of the way; her friends soon discovered what was happening, and only her husband remained in ignorance of the truth. Even Antonina did not want to rouse his anger unnecessarily, and she took reasonable precautions to keep him in the dark. But when the family was in Carthage during the war of reconquest in north Africa, she began to get careless, and Belisarius surprised the lovers in a hopelessly compromising situation in a room in the basement of the palace in which they were living at the time. The state of their clothing left no room for reasonable doubt about what they had been doing together, and naturally enough Belisarius flew into a towering rage. But Antonina was equal to the occasion; although she and her lover were half naked, she poured derision on the idea that they had been misbehaving, and told her husband that they had been in the process of hiding some of the most valuable pieces of booty captured in his recent campaign so that Justinian should not get his hands on them. What better place was there in which to hide treasures of this kind than in a basement room in the palace, she asked him; and how could he possibly imagine that she would do what he was suggesting with her own adopted son? How she explained their near-nudity is not known. Almost incredibly, Belisarius believed her; his rage subsided, and everything returned to normal.

Having succeeded in gulling her husband so easily, from that moment Antonina hardly tried any longer to hide the true state of affairs from the rest of the world. When Belisarius moved from Africa to Sicily with orders to wrest it from the Goths by diplomatic means if possible but by force if necessary, Antonina and Theodosius remained behind until the island had been safely reconquered, and then joined him there. On arrival, Antonina persuaded her husband to appoint Theodosius domestic bursar of their household; unable to refuse her anything, obligingly he did as he was asked, thus making it even easier for the lovers to carry on their illicit affair than it had been in the past. They lived together so openly and brazenly that their affair created a major scandal throughout the island, both amongst the natives of the place and also amongst Belisarius's fellow officers, who were devoted to him and appalled at Antonina's behaviour. No one dared say anything, however, for Belisarius was so besotted with her and so totally blind to what was going on that everyone suspected that he would refuse to listen to any complaint against her, however well attested it might be. They were reluctant, too, to offend Antonina, for they feared that she would not be over-scrupulous in revenging herself on anyone who had the temerity to whisper anything unpleasant, however true it might be, in her husband's ear. So everyone kept silent; or, rather, most people did so, and their wisdom was soon proved by the fate which overtook three people who were rash enough not to follow their cautious example.

A chambermaid named Macedonia, who had a grudge against her mistress, decided to tell Belisarius the true state of affairs, and she took two household slaves along with her as witnesses to support her story. Before breaking her news however, she made Belisarius promise that, whatever she told him, he would keep the source of his information secret and never reveal her name to anyone. Belisarius duly promised, heard her story, and fell into a rage. He cross-questioned Macedonia and the two slaves, but all three swore that their story was true, and he was quite unable to shake them or to find any inconsistencies in what they said; everything fitted together perfectly, and each detailed piece of evidence corroborated the rest. Convinced at last that they were telling the truth, he dismissed them and stormed off to order the immediate arrest of Theodosius, fully intending to put him to death. But some of the other servants in his household, who had got wind of what was happening, were so frightened of what Antonina would do if her lover was molested that they thought it wiser to warn the young man of the danger in which he stood rather than to wait upon events. Theodosius, who was deeply alarmed, managed to smuggle

A head of marble, thought to be Theodora.
Courtesy Castello Sforzesco, Milan.

A head, also thought to be Theodora,
discovered near Nish.

The church of Alaham in Syria, built in Justinian's reign.
Courtesy M. Babey, Basil.

The church of S. Vitale in Ravenna containing mosaics of Theodora and Justinian. Courtesy Scala.

A copy of a Justinian gold medallion commemorating a
victory over the Vandals in 534. Courtesy Michael Holford.

A mosaic of Justinian flanked on his left by Archbishop Maximian
and possibly Belisarius on his right, with assorted courtiers.
In S. Vitale, Ravenna. Courtesy Scala.

A mosaic in S. Appollinare Nuovo, originally of Theodoric and altered to fit Justinian. Courtesy Scala.

himself on to a boat and leave the island before Belisarius's men could apprehend him, and having once escaped he did not stop until he reached Ephesus nearly a thousand miles away on the coast of Asia Minor, where he took refuge in the great Church of Saint John. But he really need not have bothered; for, as soon as Antonina heard the news, she sought out her husband, and once again by some extraordinary alchemy of her own she had no difficulty at all in persuading him that she was the victim of an atrocious slander. How she explained Theodosius's flight, if he was innocent of the charges brought against him by the three servants, heaven alone knows; but she did so. She was, she told him, entirely innocent; moreover she was astonished and hurt that he should have so readily believed such a pack of lies about her; the least he could do in reparation was to tell her the names of her accusers. Despite his solemn promise to poor Macedonia, Belisarius, who was putty in his wife's hands, betrayed her identity and that of the two slaves, and all three had their tongues cut out by Antonina's orders before being sewn into sacks and thrown into the sea. Theodosius was then recalled from Ephesus to be beside his mistress once again, and everyone congratulated themselves on having been wise enough to hold their tongues in the past; at least they still had tongues in their heads to hold, which was more than could be said of the three dead servants.

But Antonina over-reached herself in the end, and Theodora had to come to her rescue. The first crisis came when Theodosius, perhaps alarmed by the risks he ran each time that another indiscretion on the part of his mistress led to yet another row with Belisarius, perhaps also slightly exhausted by her insatiable physical demands upon him, or even perhaps a little bored with her ageing charms, ran away from her and entered a monastery. Antonina was desolate; she wore mourning, refused to see any of her friends, and spent much of her time in tears; whether they were tears of grief, anger, or frustration is a matter for speculation. She even had the effrontery to complain to Belisarius himself of the intolerable loss of her faithful, affectionate, and charming godson, and to beg him to get the young man back. So insistently did she work on her gullible husband that in the end she prevailed upon him to go to Justinian and tell him that he himself could not do without the services of his much-loved adopted son. The Emperor eventually issued the necessary orders, and Theodosius was duly wrenched out of the peace of his monastery and returned to the hungry bosom of his mistress, while Belisarius obligingly left the lovers alone in Constantinople, and went to take command of the imperial army on the Persian frontier. Once again, Antonina threw caution to the winds, and her relationship with her godson became an open scandal; she almost ate her young lover, and moreover she did so virtually in public.

But she had counted without the intervention of a bitter and determined enemy. Photius, her own son by the man with whom she had lived in the Hippodrome, had become progressively disgusted by his mother's behaviour. He was fond of Belisarius, who had always treated him generously and well, and the sight of him being duped and humiliated again and again in the face of the world sickened and revolted him; but there was little that he could do about it, while Antonina stayed close to her husband's side. When she stayed behind in Constantinople, however, and Belisarius departed to take command of the army in the East, Photius, who went with him, had unimpeded access to his step-father, who listened in growing anger to what Antonina's son had to say to him. As to Photius himself, he had watched too many previous attempts to open Belisarius's eyes to the truth about his wife to be under any illusion about the difficulty of his task; but Antonina was not there to defend herself, and he had accumulated so much evidence of her guilt that it would have been enough to open the eyes of a dead man. Moreover, he was Antonina's son and thus the last man likely to invent the detailed story which he put before Belisarius, who concluded very reluctantly and after some time that he was hearing the truth at last about his wife's persistent and open adultery with Theodosius. Black with rage, he made a solemn pact with Photius to revenge himself upon the guilty pair, if it was the last thing that he did; though even at this moment of his greatest fury and disillusionment, he told his step-son that he still loved Antonina. 'As long as I can punish the man who has defiled my house, I shall do her no harm,' he said. The two men took no immediate action, but waited for a propitious moment. It came when Antonina, having sent Theodosius to Ephesus for some reason, decided to join her husband again for a little while on the eastern frontier. For the first time in her life, when she arrived, he greeted her with a stony face. Without even allowing her to speak, he ordered some of his men to arrest her and put her in close confinement, and when she protested, he told her that he had a good mind to kill her. While Belisarius was working himself up into paroxysms of rage and screaming at his deeply shocked and alarmed wife, Photius interrogated one of Antonina's eunuchs, and having dragged the secret of Theodosius's whereabouts out of the terrified man, he hurried to Ephesus. On arrival, he called on the local bishop, and with his connivance he proceeded to kidnap the trembling lover from the Church of Saint John where, once more, he had taken sanctuary on hearing of the arrival of Photius. He pleaded pathetically that to take a man by force from a place of sanctuary was against both the law of God and the law of the land, and he was right; but his pleas were ignored, and he was carried off captive to a remote castle in the Taurus mountains in Cilicia near the border with Syria.

Meanwhile, however, although Belisarius kept Antonina under close guard, she managed to despatch one of her servants to Constantinople with a message for the Empress begging for her help, and Theodora was in no mood to sit by while her *protégée* was punished by Belisarius. She persuaded Justinian to order him to release Antonina at once and to treat her with the respect due to her position, while she herself had Photius arrested and thrown into a dungeon in the Imperial Palace, where he was questioned about the whereabouts of Theodosius. He refused to answer, and it is said that Theodora then gave orders for him to be tortured until he replied, but this may be an invention of her enemies. Torture or no torture, Photius continued to say nothing; but his courage did him little good, for somehow or other Theodora discovered where the young man was imprisoned, and immediately sent some of her men to release him. Theodosius was again restored to Antonina's arms, and Belisarius was forced to watch impotently as his plans for revenge crumbled before his eyes. But even this humiliation did not kill his love for her, and it was not long before Theodora had stage-managed a reconciliation between them. Presumably, Antonina succeeded once again in convincing her almost infinitely convincible husband that she was as pure as the driven snow and entirely innocent of adultery with Theodosius; otherwise even Belisarius would have been unlikely to have allowed his adopted son back into the bosom of the family as if nothing had happened. As for poor Photius, he languished for years in Theodora's dungeon, or so it was said, and when at last he was released, he was so determined never again to meddle in his mother's affairs that he went to Jerusalem and entered a monastery there.

The story illustrates once again the complexity of Theodora's character. Her open condonation of Antonina's affair with Theodosius was wholly inconsistent with her usually rigid views on the sanctity of marriage; but it was consistent with her feminism, and it suited her political book. For by binding Antonina to herself in gratitude and complete loyalty she gained a very real measure of control over Belisarius by way of his wife, and this was important to her. If there was one thing which mattered to her more than anything else, it was the safety of her husband's throne; even her worst enemies, Procopius included, never accused her of infidelity to Justinian, with whose destiny and fortunes her own were intimately linked; his interest was her interest, and it was paramount in her mind, as she showed beyond doubt during the Nika revolt. She was totally loyal to him. After the crushing of the great rebellion, the only man who could possibly be regarded as a potential rival to the Emperor was Belisarius. As a soldier he had proved himself to be almost invincible, waging Justinian's wars and reconquering north Africa, Sicily, and eventually Italy for him; his troops adored him, and were willing to follow him anywhere; he was the idol of the people of Constantinople and of the Byzantine world at large; and since he was fond of money, and the booty from his various campaigns was enormous, he became immensely rich as the years of conquest went by. All this made him the kind of man who had both the power and the popular support to make a bid for the throne, if he should ever wish to do so, and this worried Theodora; but what made matters worse, worrying her even more, was an incident during the war in Italy, where his popularity spread even to the Goths whom he was fighting there. Their admiration for him as a soldier became so great that, at one point, they offered to submit to him on one condition: namely, that he would become their king. With uncharacteristic guile, he pretended to accept their offer; but he did so only as a trick to persuade them to allow his army into Ravenna, which he had been besieging for some time. Once the city was safely in his hands, he told the Goths that he had never had any intention of usurping the position of his master the Emperor in Constantinople, and when they complained of his perfidy, he defended his action as a legitimate *ruse de guerre*. But when the news reached the Imperial Palace, both Justinian and

Theodora were alarmed; if the Goths could offer Belisarius a throne in Italy, there might well be other people in other places who were planning to offer him other thrones. So it is not surprising that Theodora was determined to bind his wife to herself with steel cords of obligation and self-interest. As long as Antonina owed her own safety to the protection of the Empress, Theodora knew that she could count on her absolute loyalty; and as long as she could do that, she knew that she would have nothing to fear from her doting husband. So she did everything in her power to help Antonina in her affair with Theodosius and thus to gain the most useful of allies. In fact, Belisarius was the soul of loyalty; once he had taken the oath of allegiance to Justinian, it never occurred to him to plot against the throne or even to covet it. So all Theodora's precautions turned out to be unnecessary as far as he was concerned. Nevertheless her sway over Antonina proved far from useless to her. She had other enemies, and an agent as devoted, intelligent, and unscrupulous as Antonina was an invaluable asset to her; for in addition to all her other complex characteristics, Theodora was a patient, skilful, and determined political schemer and a past-mistress of intrigue.

John of Cappadocia was one of many people who found out too late and to their cost how expert the Empress was in the undercover world of secret plotting and counter-plotting, and just how useful Antonina could be to her in its dark and dangerous corridors. Theodora had always hated the Cappadocian, for he had never bothered to treat her with even common politeness, let alone to flatter her; on the contrary, he had behaved as arrogantly and boorishly to her as he was accustomed to behave with everyone else, and she had been delighted with the rest of the Byzantine world when he had fallen from power during the Nika revolt. But after the rebels had been crushed, Justinian had not felt himself irrevocably bound by a promise, which had been extorted from him by force, to dismiss John, and after a decent interval he reinstated him in his old office; indeed, he went further, making him a Consul and raising him to the rank of Patrician. It is possible that Theodora tried to dissuade her husband from doing this, but if so she failed. The reason was almost certainly Justinian's increasingly urgent need of money to pay for Belisarius' conquests; as long as the Byzantine armies were engaged in the magnificent but ruinously expensive business of regaining the provinces which had been lost to the

Goths and Vandals in the West, he needed a great deal of money, and John was the one man who could be guaranteed to find it for him somehow.

Unfortunately for the ordinary Byzantine tax-payer, John's fall from power and short-lived disgrace had failed to teach him manners, and as soon as he was back in office he began to behave as over-bearingly and as brutishly as ever. He was coarse by nature, and the way in which he flaunted his animal appetites in the faces of his less ostentatious fellow citizens earned him both their disgust and their contempt. He loved good food, vintage wines, and exotic dishes; it was said at the time that the shellfish of the Black Sea grew wings so that they might escape the people whom he sent to collect them for his omnivorous maw; but he was a gross feeder rather than an epicure, and there were few evenings when he did not get hopelessly drunk, while many days ended with him being violently sick all over the floor or over his neighbours at dinner before being carried unconscious to bed. Outside his own house, he was carried around the streets of the city in an ornate litter accompanied by bevies of young women and girls wearing transparent dresses, which left nothing to the imagination, and shocked even the hardened citizens of Constantinople, who were far from easily embarrassed. But despite all his ostentation and vulgarity and the excesses in which he indulged, he amply justified Justinian's trust in him as a raiser of money for the imperial treasury; for, just as in the past, he proved to be indefatigable, intelligent, efficient, and completely unscrupulous at his job, and the money rolled in. To the Emperor therefore he could do no wrong, and Theodora was forced to bide her time. This did not worry her unduly; she was good at it.

Eventually, like all men of his ilk, John over-played his hand, and presented her with precisely the opportunity for which she had patiently waited for years, while at the same time provoking her beyond endurance. Like many of his contemporaries, especially those with as little education as he had received, he was a superstitious man. He believed implicitly in omens; he dabbled in magic of various kinds; he consulted fortune-tellers, and believed everything they told him; and he flirted with whatever occult practice happened to be fashionable at the time. As a result, all the charlatans in town battened on him like leeches, exploiting his credulity and feeding his vanity by flattering him and extolling his extraordinary psychic powers. One professional diviner of the future went as far as to tell him that one day he would 'inherit the mantle of Augustus' and wear the imperial purple; it was written in the stars, he assured him. John believed him. Trembling with excitement and bursting with pride, from that moment he could think of nothing but becoming Emperor. He did not know whether the prophecy meant that he would inherit the throne when Justinian died, or that he would somehow supplant him; but he was no fool, and he realised that the road to the throne was bound to be both difficult and dangerous, by whichever route he might reach it, and he did not talk openly about the revelation which had been vouchsafed to him by the fortune-teller. But he did begin to create a political party devoted to his own person by the simple expedient of buying the loyalty of all those whose support was for sale, and since he was immensely rich and could afford to pay handsomely for a man's allegiance, there were plenty of takers. He began to travel extensively in the provinces too, seeking popularity there by remitting the taxes of those who were prepared to pledge him their support in return, though he was careful not to tell them precisely what his political plans were; and once again there were plenty of recruits, who were glad enough to escape some of the crushing burden of taxes imposed on them in exchange for a few vague promises of support for the repulsive Cappadocian.

Up to this point John had behaved fairly discreetly, and had run little risk; but then he did something which was both extremely foolish and lethally dangerous. From the beginning he had recognised that his most redoubtable opponent would be Theodora, for he was under no illusions about either her intelligence or her power, and he knew that, before his prophecy could be fulfilled, somehow the Empress would have to be disarmed as a political force. He decided to try to do this by doing everything he possibly could to turn Justinian against her; he planned an elaborate campaign of cleverly disguised calumny and malicious rumour, and he made sure that the Emperor should hear the slanderous stories which were circulating about her. He hoped in this way to deprive her of the source of her power, which was her husband's devotion and trust; but it was an appalling miscalculation, for it grossly under-estimated both Justinian's deep and genuine love for his wife and Theodora's formidable capacity to look after herself.

She was very soon told about what was going on, for she had informants everywhere. She and the eunuch Narses had grown more and more fond of each other as time had gone by, and Theodora was as close to him as she was to Antonina. Since his corps of eunuchs was devoted to him, and he was devoted to the Empress, at his instigation they became the nucleus of what was virtually an unofficial private secret service, reporting everything they heard—gossip, scandal, rumour, tittle-tattle, and hard fact—to Narses, who passed the information to Theodora. In addition to the eunuchs, most of her own ladies-in-waiting and her personal maids were also devoted to her, and they too acted as her eyes and ears wherever they went. Her feminism, too, had won her a host of friends; the capital was filled with women whom she had helped, and who were eager to show their gratitude by keeping her informed of anything which might affect her interests one way or another, so they also swelled the ranks of her unofficial agents. Lastly, since everyone knew that the quickest way to preferment of any kind was through the Empress, people were not lacking in every walk of life who, in the hope of currying favour, hurried to her or to Narses with whatever titbit of information happened to come their way; and for years Theodora had shown herself extremely generous to anyone who had brought her news of any kind, even if it was of no particular use to her, precisely in order to encourage them to go on keeping their eyes and ears open in her interest.

The consequence was that no one had ever been served by a more formidable or better informed intelligence service than Theodora, and John the Cappadocian's activities did not escape her attention for more than a few weeks. The first thing which she was told was that he appeared to be trying to form a political party devoted to his own interest, and this was a little puzzling; he was already Prefect of the City, Consul, Patrician, and as close to the Emperor as any man could very well get, so why should he want a party of personal supporters? It was inexplicable. But not long afterwards, news of the fortune-teller's prediction reached her, and all became clear. How it reached her it is impossible to say; perhaps John had talked too freely when he was drunk, or perhaps the fortune-teller himself had made a good story of the Cappadocian's gullibility and of how profitable it had been to him. At any rate, Theodora was told the whole story. At first, she could hardly believe that this gross creature could seriously be aspiring to the throne, but when the source of the malicious stories about herself, which had suddenly begun to circulate in great numbers, was also traced to John, she could no longer refuse to believe that his intentions were treacherous; for if he was not planning some sort of treachery, why should he be trying so hard to poison Justinian's mind against her?

From the moment when Theodora discovered the truth, she determined to ruin him however long it might take her to do so, and whatever means she might have to employ in the process, and from then on a state of undeclared war existed between her and John, even if at first he did not realise that this was so. But he was no fool, and it was not long before he guessed that Theodora must have discovered what was afoot, for her whole attitude towards him, even though it had never been friendly, had subtly but decisively changed. This greatly alarmed him, as well it might have done, and he began to take meticulous precautions to protect himself. He surrounded himself with armed guards; he double-checked the locks on every door into his house each evening; he ordered his servants to search for assassins in every dark corner and under every bed in the place at regular intervals throughout the night; and he trembled like a leaf at every unexpected noise. But like a child who is frightened of the dark, as soon as the dawn broke and the sun rose over the steel-grey waters of the Bosphorus, touching their wrinkled surface with gold, his self-confidence came flooding back. He remembered how indispensable his services were to the Emperor, and the dark shadow of Theodora retreated until the evening. He need not fear her. He was quite capable of looking after himself.

But John counted without the subtlety and persistence of Theodora's powers of intrigue. She did not dream of doing anything as foolish as to lift a finger against him precipitately; at first, she did not even complain to Justinian of his slanders against her. All she allowed herself to do at this stage was to try to make her husband see how much genuine suffering the Cappadocian was causing, and had always caused, to the ordinary people of the Empire, how much he was hated, and how deep and dangerous was the resulting unrest; in other words, she appealed to the Emperor's political sense, his passion for law and order, and his concern for the welfare of his subjects to open his eyes to the true nature of his minister; but she was unsuccessful. Justinian could not bring himself to do without an official, of whom even his worst enemies said that he was the most able administrator of his time. Later on, she tried to play subtly upon her husband's fear of treachery, not accusing John of anything, but hinting that he was getting dangerously powerful, but once again Justinian would not listen. He seemed to be incapable of breaking the habits of a lifetime; for years he had trusted John, and he was not going to start distrusting him now. He had even grown to be fond of the man, and he remained obstinately deaf to his wife's warnings. Theodora was forced to turn elsewhere.

She turned to Antonina. She could not have made a more skilful move; for Antonina was totally devoted to her, and she loathed John of Cappadocia. She knew how jealous he was of her husband, for he did not try to hide his envy of Belisarius' popularity, and he hated him for it. If John ever got the opportunity to say something coarse, unpleasant, or scathing about him, he took it, and Antonina's affair with her godson had given him ample opportunity to be both offensive and obscene. Antonina was not prepared either to tolerate or to forgive him for this; she might be regularly unfaithful to her husband, but no one else was allowed to take liberties with him or show him the slightest disrespect. So she had already become the Cappadocian's enemy long before Theodora enlisted her aid in her campaign to destroy him, and this fact alone would have made the Empress's move a shrewd one; but Antonina was also a very intelligent woman with a flair for intrigue which made her almost Theodora's equal in the murky business of political conspiracy, and this made Theodora's move even more dangerous from John's point of view. Separately, each woman was a highly dangerous enemy; together they were deadly. The plot which they eventually hatched against John was no less deadly, for they decided to attack him in his one amiably weak spot, where he was most vulnerable.

The Cappadocian had a daughter, whose name was Euphemia. She was his only child, and he doted on her, lavishing his whole affection on her; she was his pride and joy. While he was away in the provinces on business, Antonina set out to get to know the girl and to gain her confidence. It was easy enough to make the first approach, and soon she began to visit her daily, flattering her as skilfully as she had for years flattered her husband in order the better to deceive him, and worming her way into her teenage affections. Euphemia, who was still extremely young and inexperienced for her age, soon fell under the spell of the older woman, and it was not long before Antonina could do more or less as she liked with her. Pretending that it was a great relief to have found someone to whom she could unburden herself of all her cares and worries, she led the girl to believe that there were no secrets which she would not share with her, and she set out to fascinate her with stories of the private lives of people who moved in court circles, their loves, their foibles, their guilty secrets, and their hidden fears, while Euphemia listened goggle-eyed and with rapt attention. She had never heard such things before in her life, for her father, like many men with crude and lecherous tastes of their own, had brought her up in almost monastic seclusion, so determined was he that she should retain her innocence.

When Antonina considered the moment to be ripe, one day when they were chatting together alone, she began to speak of her own husband's discontent. Euphemia could have no idea, she told the wide-eyed girl, how bitter and sick at heart Belisarius really was. Having conquered north Africa, Sicily, and Italy, bringing two kings captive to Constantinople in the process and a vast amount of booty and money with them, the loyal and victorious general had received nothing but ingratitude and suspicion from Justinian and Theodora. It was indiscreet to say so, Antonina went on to say in a carefully hushed voice, but between friends it was impossible not to admit that the Emperor and Empress were cruel and unjust. Euphemia, who had been taught by her father to loathe Theodora and to fear her as his sworn enemy, listened to these highly dangerous words with a naïve lack of suspicion, and then obligingly asked the question for which Antonina had been skilfully angling. 'But with the army behind him, why on earth does your husband put up with such treatment?' she inquired innocently. A military rebellion, Antonina told her with a grave face, would never succeed without a powerful political ally in the capital. Of course, if Euphemia's father or some other really powerful minister in the government were privy to such a thing, then with the help of God there would probably be no difficulty in succeeding.

That a girl as young as Euphemia should rise to such a bait dangled over her nose by as expert an angler as Antonina is not surprising, but that such an old shark as John the Cappadocian should have taken the lure is much more difficult to understand. But the fact seems to be that Euphemia told her father about her conversation with Antonina, as she was intended to do, and that he swallowed the bait. Perhaps he was so obsessed with dreams of power and so sure that the fortune-teller's prophecy could not be wrong that, far from arousing his suspicions, his daughter's news simply raised his hopes to new and dizzy heights. For with Belisarius behind him his long-cherished dream of ascending the throne, which was at present inconveniently occupied by Justinian, entered the realm of immediate practical politics for the first time. So it was with excitement rather than with suspicion or foreboding that he asked Euphemia to arrange a meeting between him and Antonina at the first possible opportunity. Realising that she had hooked her fish, Antonina, like the good fisherwoman she was, decided to play him carefully rather than risk losing him by a show of over-eagerness, which might arouse his suspicions; so she promptly refused to meet him. She told Euphemia to inform her father that, since the city was swarming with spies and informers, most of them in the pay of the Empress, a meeting between the wife of the supreme commander of the army and a minister of the crown as important as John could hardly go unnoticed; to make an assignation with him in Constantinople was to play too dangerous a game, and one at which she was unwilling to try her hand. Her caution pleased and impressed the Cappadocian, so that, when she sent him word that in a few days' time she was going to rejoin her husband in Syria, and offered to meet him outside the city at some point along her route, he eagerly agreed. Belisarius owned a villa not far from Chalcedon on the Asiatic side of the Bosphorus at a small place named Rufinianae, and Antonina informed John that she would stay there for a couple of nights after leaving the capital. If he could find a plausible excuse to leave the city, she would meet him there in the privacy of her little rural retreat, where they could talk freely and without fear. John was delighted once again by her cautiousness, and immediately wrote to fix a day on which to meet her there. Meanwhile Theodora, who had been informed all along of the progress of events, told Justinian everything.

At first, he would not believe her. The Cappadocian had become part of his life; it seemed impossible that he could be a traitor. It was only with difficulty that he could be persuaded to send two of his most trusted servants, Narses the eunuch and Marcellus the captain of the guard, to Belisarius' villa on the appointed day with orders to arrest the Cappadocian if they became sure of his treasonable intentions, and to kill him if he resisted arrest. Even then, when the die was cast, Justinian seems to have been reluctant to believe in John's treachery for it was rumoured after the event that, in a last gesture of affection, the Emperor had tried to warn his favourite, indirectly and in a roundabout way, not to keep his appointment with Antonina. Probably Justinian did no such thing, but if he did so, the Cappadocian must have failed to understand; for he kept his appointment with her, waiting until after dark to set out on his journey across the Bosphorus, and travelling by night to Rufinianae, where Antonina, Narses, and Marcellus were impatiently awaiting his arrival. He took an escort of armed men with him as a personal bodyguard; he made his way as stealthily as possible in order not to be seen or recognised on the way; and he took care to see that he was not followed. When at last he arrived at the villa, Antonina, who was greatly relieved to see him, greeted him, and led him into the garden as the safest place in which to discuss their business together. With Narses and Marcellus carefully hidden on one side of an ornamental hedge and some of their men concealed elsewhere within calling distance, she conducted her unsuspecting victim to a bench on the other side of the hedge, where she led him on in conversation until he promised faithfully to do everything in his power to support a military revolt against the Emperor. Narses and Marcellus had heard enough. They emerged from their hiding-place, and told John that he was under arrest for high treason. This was easily said, but the Cappadocian was a man of enormous strength, and he drew his sword. Narses and Marcellus hurriedly called their men out of hiding, and John bellowed for his bodyguard. Antonina prudently removed herself from the scene, and there was a fight, during which Marcellus was wounded, and John managed to escape. He hurried back to Constantinople as fast as he could and on arrival he went straight to the Church of the Holy Wisdom, where he demanded sanctuary.

His panic was his undoing, for by his flight he virtually admitted his guilt. If he had had the presence of mind and the nerve to go straight to Justinian on arrival in the capital, there to brazen it out before him, perhaps by protesting that he had only been doing his best to protect the Emperor from what he had genuinely believed to be the treachery of Belisarius and his wife by posing as their ally, he might have got away with it. As it was, however, he left the field open to Theodora, who was quick to take advantage of her hard-won opportunity to do what she had longed to do for years:

namely, to ruin him. John was deprived of all his offices and banished to Cyzicus in the Asiatic province of Mysia, where he was effectively prevented from ever casting covetous eyes on the throne again by being forcibly ordained deacon; since ordained men could never become Emperors by constitutional law, it was a move intended to scotch John's unruly ambitions once and for all. His fortune was confiscated as a matter of course, but Justinian allowed him to keep enough money to live in comparative comfort in his enforced retirement, even though this lenience did not please Theodora. But John did not long enjoy it.

While a man named Peter Barsymes who, according to Procopius, was as big a crook as John himself took his place and his job in Constantinople, the Cappadocian began his time of exile in Cyzicus. The bishop of the place, a man named Eusebius, was extremely unpopular with the people of his see; they had laid complaints against him in the capital on more than one occasion, but the Emperor had done nothing about their grievances, and the bishop had continued in office. Feeling against him had continued to increase in intensity, and not long after John the Cappadocian's arrival in the city, some young men belonging to the circus factions murdered Eusebius in the market-place. John was known to be one of his enemies, and people suspected that he had been privy to the crime, if not an accessory to it. Some Senators were sent from Constantinople to investigate the murder and to punish those responsible for it, if their identity could be established; during the investigation which followed, John's complicity was not proved, but nevertheless he was found guilty of being an accessory. It was said that the members of the commission of inquiry were under secret orders from Theodora to punish John, whether he was guilty or not, though this may not have been true; they may genuinely have believed in his complicity in the crime. In any case, he was stripped and beaten like a common criminal, and then shipped to Egypt with neither money nor belongings and wearing nothing but a rough cloak. On the voyage he was forced to earn his bread by begging in the sea ports at which the vessel called, and when he reached Egypt he was thrown into prison at Antinoopolis.

Theodora's enemies claimed that even after all this she was still not satisfied with her revenge, but that she continued to wait for yet another opportunity to make John suffer. It came, they alleged, some years later, when somehow or other two of the young men who had been involved in the murder of bishop Eusebius fell into her hands. She brought great pressure to bear on them to make them accuse the Cappadocian of taking an actual physical part in the killing, but though one of them yielded to her pressure, the other refused to do so, even though he was tortured; so once again she was cheated of her desire, for the evidence of one of them would be of no avail if the other denied its truth. It is not a very plausible story, and it was probably an invention of her enemies, although it is just possible that it is true. What is certain is that John remained in prison in Egypt until after Theodora's death, when Justinian allowed him to return to the capital. At first, he still dreamed of being restored to high office, but this was not to be. Reduced to great poverty, eventually he decided to take his ordination seriously, even though it had been forced upon him; he was already a deacon, and now he sought to be ordained priest. At the ordination ceremony, however, he found himself without a decent cassock, and was forced to borrow one from a monk who was standing by. It transpired later that the monk's name was Augustus, and it was not long before some wit realised that, at long last, the fortune-teller's prophecy had come true: the mantle of Augustus had indeed fallen on John.

Theodora's battle of wits with the Cappadocian and her eventual victory prove beyond doubt that she was a formidable and at times unscrupulous political opponent; but how unscrupulous was she? To what lengths was she prepared to go to achieve her own ends? It is a difficult question to answer. Procopius tells a number of stories, in which he accuses her of some appalling crimes, but as always his anecdotes are highly suspect, for a number of reasons. For one thing, they are not corroborated by other contemporary historians, and, for another, they bear once again the unmistakable stamp of his own neurotic and obsessional desire to blacken her name, in this case by adding tales of sexual atrocities to his earlier tales of her sexual perversity and insatiability. For instance, he tells two stories of how she falsely accused people, against whom she had grudges, of illegal homosexual acts. One, he says, was a young man named Vasianus, who had been rude to her, and whom she was therefore determined to destroy; she brought a charge of sodomy against him, and without bothering with the formality of a trial, she had him mutilated and emasculated. The other was a member of the Greens named Diogenes, against whom a similar charge was brought by two young boys in his employment, who had been egged on, according to Procopius, by the Empress, although in this case he does not even say why Theodora is supposed to have disliked the accused man. However, he was duly brought to trial, but although she tried to tamper with one of the witnesses by having him tortured, Diogenes was finally acquitted. Neither story inspires much confidence, and nor does another in which the same historian describes with relish how the governor of Cilicia Secunda, a man named Callinicus, who had had two murderers executed by due process of law, was impaled on their grave by order of the Empress for no better reason than that the two criminals had been Blues whom she favoured.

But his nastiest and most damaging story about her alleged crimes deserves a little more attention. It concerns a singularly attractive character who rejoiced, if that is the right word, in the name of Amalasuntha. She was the only daughter of the greatest of the Gothic kings of Italy, Theoderic, who did so much to embellish Ravenna, where she was brought up and given a Roman education. When her father died, she could not inherit the throne herself, for Gothic law did not allow women to do so, but she became Regent during the minority of her son, who succeeded his grandfather on the throne. She had all the virtues; she was good-looking, intelligent, brave, and inspired with a deep and genuine longing to civilise her own Gothic countrymen by welding them together into one nation at peace with the native Italians. To this end, she entered into a friendly alliance with Justinian, and did what she could to educate the Goths in the more civilised ways of the Romans; but this policy was anathema to many of her own people, who despised the Romans as effete and unmanly, and she became violently unpopular. Her son was a weakling, who died young, and after his death she was seized and imprisoned on an island in Lake Bolsena in Tuscany by a cousin who succeeded the dead boy on the throne. Attempts were made to keep Justinian in ignorance of the imprisonment of his ally, but one of his agents in Italy, a senior soldier named Peter, heard of it, and hastened to tell the Emperor the truth. Justinian immediately wrote to Amalasuntha, assuring her of his protection, and telling Peter to inform the new Gothic king that he intended to support his ally, even if it meant going to war to do so. But before his letter could be delivered, Amalasuntha was murdered—strangled, it was said, in her bath—by some Goths who had a grudge against her.

This would have been the end of the matter if Procopius had not added a postscript to the story; Theodora, he said in his *Secret History*, was the real villain of the piece, for the murder had been committed at her instigation and by her orders. She had written to Peter, he alleged, telling him to procure Amalasuntha's death, because she viewed with alarm the possibility that the Gothic princess would seek refuge in Constantinople and there capture the affections of her husband. Some historians have taken this accusation seriously; they have seen nothing in Theodora's character to make the idea of her complicity in the murder incredible as such, and it must be admitted that she did some ruthless things in her time, though whether she ever descended to murder is another matter. But if the story's credibility is to be judged by the credibility of the motive attributed to Theodora, then it must be rejected out of hand; for the idea that she should have had the woman murdered because she was afraid that Justinian, who had never even met her, was about to fall in love with her, is more than enough to stretch credulity to breaking point. The one thing Theodora never had cause to worry about was her husband's fidelity; every record of the time speaks of his devotion to her; he was hopelessly in love with her all his life. The truth is probably much simpler; it is not only possible but probable that Amalasuntha was indeed murdered by some of her own people who had reasons of their own to hate her, as was believed at the time, and like much else in Procopius' *Secret History* the story of her complicity in the crime must be dismissed as a malicious libel. Evidence, if it exists, of how unscrupulous Theodora was prepared to be must be sought elsewhere. Since her passions were most deeply engaged in her lifelong struggle on behalf of the Monophysite party in the church against their Orthodox opponents, it is in the records compiled by a number of reputable contemporary historians of her well-documented battle of wits with Popes and Patriarchs that we must look for confirmation or contradiction of Procopius' highly uncomplimentary estimate of her character.

VII

Θ έ
Ο Δ ύ
Ρ Α

If the first conference arranged by Theodora between representative churchmen of the Orthodox party and leading Monophysite Christians, which has already been described, failed to bring the two sides together in perfect agreement, it bore considerable fruit nevertheless. The ending of the persecution and the semi-official recognition of the Monophysites implicit in their invitation to the conference in Constantinople and their welcome by the Emperor gave them a new status and confidence, which soon had results. In the eastern provinces, they quickly regained the ground which they had lost during the time of persecution, and began to increase in numbers everywhere, proving once again the truth of the saying that 'the blood of the martyrs is the seed of the church'. Many people had behaved with astonishing courage and faithfulness under the sufferings imposed on them by imperial commissioners and Orthodox bishops alike, preferring to die rather than renounce their own particular brand of faith; others had suffered banishment or imprisonment; monks had watched their laboriously and lovingly built monasteries wantonly destroyed, their springs dammed or diverted, their wells poisoned, and the few fruit trees, which they had managed to plant in the inhospitable soil of the Syrian mountains or elsewhere where they lived, rooted up; but few had changed sides. As always under persecution, there had been some apostates who, by collaborating with the enemy, had earned the bitter contempt of those who had remained faithful, and now that the worst was over, they were treated as social outcasts by everyone; even the Orthodox minority despised them. As for the ordinary man in the street, who had watched the struggle from as inconspicuous a vantage point as possible, keeping his head well down in an attempt to avoid trouble, his admiration for those who had suffered and endured knew no bounds, and when the danger finally passed, thousands joined the Monophysites. It was said that the popular preacher, John of Tella, who had accompanied Theodora on her progress through Bithynia after the Nika revolt, converted nearly 170,000 people to the Monophysite party in the church in a matter of months; everywhere their cause prospered as it had never prospered before. Even in the capital they made converts, as more and more of them preached and ministered openly in the city, and the people of Constantinople who, like Theodora, were fascinated by holy men, flocked to hear those of the newcomers who had made reputations for themselves during the persecution by their courage or their feats of endurance.

As time went by too, the leaders of the Monophysites lost the suspicion with which they had greeted Justinian's first overtures; they began to believe that the old days of ill-will were truly over, and that they could safely profess their faith wherever they wished. Many of them, who had not dared to do so before, now came to Constantinople, partly at least out of curiosity, and partly to see their guardian angel, the Empress, who had wrought such a miraculous transformation in their fortunes. Theodora greeted them all in the Imperial Palace, and made the most eminent of them her guests. Peter, the bishop of Apamea in Syria Secunda, who had been banished from his diocese during the persecution and had sought refuge with Severus in Egypt, came with a staff of monks and priests, and was lodged in the Palace of Hormisdas; Zooras, the tiny but fanatical Monophysite monk, who was later to prove too much even for Justinian's tolerant and even temper, was warmly welcomed; Jacob Baradaeus, an astonishing man who had been put into a monastery at the age of two by his parents, and who had acquired a widespread reputation not only for great sanctity but also for his ability to work miracles, was given a furnished house by Theodora, where he lived in total seclusion and practised an austere asceticism; the Sheikh Harith ibn Jabala, who was head of the Christian Arabs, all of whom were staunchly Monophysite, came to pay his respects; John of Egypt, Constantius of Laodicea, and many others were drawn to the capital by the sun of Theodora's favour during this great revival of Monophysite fortunes for which she had worked so hard.

But it was the arrival of her old mentor, Severus, who had been persuaded to change his mind and accept the Empress' invitation to come to Constantinople after all, which delighted her most. She was overjoyed too, when Justinian proved to be as deeply impressed by the old man as she could have hoped him to be. Needless to say, however, this invasion of the capital by leaders of the Monophysite party in the church deeply disturbed members of the Orthodox party, whose fears grew as they watched their triumphant rivals, assisted by the Empress, going from strength to strength. The Imperial Palace was full of them, and it was not long before the influence over Justinian of Severus, the old Monophysite Patriarch of Antioch, seemed to be almost as great as it had always been over Theodora. Monophysite priests openly proselytised and baptised in the churches and in an increasing number of private houses in the city and its suburbs; everyone flocked to hear Zooras preach fiery and uncompromising sermons in the monastery which Theodora had built for him at Sykae on the other side of the Golden Horn, and there to marvel at his austerities; in court circles (where until recently it had been as much as a man's job was worth even to mention the Monophysites), Patricians, Senators, and Consuls vied with each other in their admiration for these impressive visitors from Syria and Egypt, and tried to emulate their austere ways; a chief minister of state named Theodore gave away his entire fortune to the poor, and joined the Monophysites in a life of total poverty, while an aristocrat named Tribonius retired to one of their monasteries, where he spent the rest of his life in prayer except for a few hours a day when he ministered to the needs of the poor. In fact, the Monophysites became fashionable, and the *beau monde* buzzed round them like bees round the flowers in a garden.

Then on 5 June 535, a decisive event took place. Epiphanius, who had been Patriarch of Constantinople for sixteen years, and who had both married and crowned Justinian and Theodora, died. His death took everyone by surprise, for he died suddenly, and from the point of view of the Orthodox party he could scarcely have chosen a worse moment at which to do so. The Monophysites were at the height of their newly won popularity and power; the Court was dominated by Severus; and the Empress was not one to miss the golden opportunity presented to her by the death of Epiphanius to further the cause of those to whom she had been devoted for so long. So the supporters of Orthodoxy waited anxiously to hear the name of the man who would become their new archbishop, knowing that the appointment was in Justinian's hands but fearing that those hands would be guided by Theodora; there was nothing they dreaded more than the prospect of a new archbishop chosen by the Empress from the ranks of her Monophysite friends. They were not kept in suspense for very long, for the Emperor wasted no time in choosing a man for the job, and they were both surprised and greatly relieved to hear that he had chosen a well-known and deeply respected bishop named Anthimus to fill the vacant archiepiscopal throne.

For a number of years, Anthimus had been bishop of Trebizond on the southern shore of the Black Sea, where he had won a reputation for himself as a man of wide learning, humility, and contempt for the pleasures of this world; his people had loved him, and his Orthodoxy had never been open to question as far as anyone knew. Needless to say, this greatly reassured the worried citizens of Constantinople, who turned out in force to cheer him as he was made archbishop in the Church of the Holy Wisdom. Theodora alone knew that for years he had been a secret sympathiser with the Monophysites; even Justinian may not have known the truth. It was only after he had been enthroned and installed in the Patriarch's chair that people began to wonder whether he was as rigidly Orthodox as they would have wished, and as they had hitherto assumed; for one of the first things that he did after entering his new office was to sally forth on his ass and ride to the Imperial Palace to pay his respects to Severus, whom he had long considered in secret to be one of the great doctors of the church. It was a small thing in itself, but there were people in Constantinople with nostrils which had been trained for years to pick up even the faintest scent of heresy with the sensitivity of a secret policeman in a Communist country detecting a whiff of bourgeois reaction, and their new Patriarch's visit to the old heretic disturbed them.

The accession of Anthimus to the Patriarchal throne of Constantinople was the first major victory won by Theodora. There were five great metropolitan sees in the Christian world, each with its Patriarch, and Constantinople ranked second in seniority to Rome itself. The other three were Alexandria, Antioch, and Jerusalem, of which the first two were already firmly controlled by Monophysites, while Peter, the Patriarch of Jerusalem, although a staunch member of the Orthodox party himself, was forced by the number of people in his jurisdiction who sympathised with the Monophysite cause to follow a policy of moderation. So the capture of Constantinople decisively altered the balance of power against the Orthodox, and left the Popes of Rome in a position of weakness to which they were not accustomed. As it happened, however, this alignment of the two sides was not destined to last very long, for shortly after the enthronement of Anthimus in the capital, the Patriarch Timothy of Alexandria, who had welcomed Theodora with such kindness some years previously, died after a short illness, leaving his see vacant and once again upsetting the balance of power. It was a blow to the hopes of the Empress and the Monophysite party and a cause of great rejoicing to Orthodox Christians, who saw the hand of God in the timely death of the arch-heretic, and it greatly raised their hopes. By this time they realised that they had been fooled by the Empress over the appointment of Anthimus, and they were determined to do everything they possibly could to fill the vacant throne of Alexandria with a man of their own persuasion, and thus avenge the defeat they had suffered in Constantinople; though they realised that this would be difficult. Undaunted by the obstacles in the way of victory, Orthodox men and women everywhere prayed long and earnestly for an Orthodox successor to the dead heretic; pulpits rang with calls to the faithful to pray without ceasing for a successful outcome to the struggle which was bound to ensue over the vacant see; the monks known as the Sleepless Ones, who were well known for their unbending Orthodoxy, let it be known that although some were always at prayer—hence their name—those on active duty, so to speak, would be reinforced until the right appointment was made; and Constantinople took on the aspect of a city in the grip of a major political crisis, which, of course, it was. For other pulpits vibrated to the thunder of Monophysite preachers like Maras, Zooras, and John of Tella urging their supporters to pray even harder than the hosts of Midian who were encamped all around them in all their Orthodox militancy.

Meanwhile Theodora, who had dearly loved Timothy, and who mourned his death as that of her spiritual father, had no intention of allowing Egypt, the heart-land of Monophysitism, to be lost to the cause which she had espoused, if she could help it, and she set about choosing a successor to the dead man who would tread in his footsteps and be faithful to his principles. It has often been said that Theodora was not really interested in peace and reconciliation in the church but only in the triumph of the Monophysite party, of which she was as bigoted and fanatical a member as any Orthodox bigot and fanatic of the opposite side, but her choice of a man to succeed Timothy goes some way to contradicting this accusation; for she chose a gentle and irenic man, Theodosius by name, in preference to a certain Gaianus, who was the choice of a large selection of the people of Alexandria itself. They were both convinced Monophysites, but where Theodosius was a man of moderation, Gaianus was an intolerant fanatic.

Whether she had any difficulty in persuading Justinian to nominate Theodosius is not known, but it is unlikely; by this time she seems to have won him to her own point of view in ecclesiastical matters, even if only for an experimental period during which he would be able to see how well or badly her policies worked in practice. At any rate, Theodosius was duly nominated by the Emperor; his name was put forward to the electoral college of bishops and priests in Alexandria whose job it was to ratify the Emperor's choice by duly electing his nominee, and that should have been the end of the matter. But, as though the split in the church between the Orthodox party and the Monophysites was not enough to bedevil ecclesiastical affairs, the Monophysites themselves were split into two parties known as the Corrupticolae and the Phantasiasts; the Corrupticolae were comparatively moderate in their opinions, while the Phantasiasts were extremists. When Theodosius' name came before the electoral college, those members of it who were also Corrupticolae voted for him, and since they were in the majority, he was duly elected; but the minority who were all members of the Phantasiasts defiantly refused to elect Justinian's man, and elected Gaianus instead. Their action created a situation without precedent, but it was one which, on the whole, delighted the people of Alexandria, who were traditionally impatient of the control exercised over them by the government in Constantinople, which they regarded as an upstart city which should never have gained pre-eminence over such an ancient and noble city as their own. Ecclesiastically, the relationship between the two places was even worse, for Alexandria had been senior to Constantinople as a diocese for centuries, and the Alexandrians had never accepted the higher status suddenly conferred on the Patriarchs of Constantinople in the fourth century. So any excuse for a show of independence was welcome to the Alexandrians, and a chance to demonstrate their religious independence of Constantinople was most welcome of all. In fact, the people of Alexandria were informed with much the same kind of spirit of resistance to the central authority in the capital of the Empire as inspires the Basques of Spain to defy Madrid, or that which drives the Czechoslovaks passively to resist the domination of Soviet Russia today. So the refusal of the members of the Phantasiast party to nominate the man of the Emperor's choice delighted them, and they flocked to the support of Gaianus, egging him on to seize the Patriarchal throne regardless of the wishes of Constantinople.

This was not as difficult as might be imagined, for it was customary in Alexandria for the dead archbishop's successor, whoever he might be, to enter into his inheritance in a most peculiar manner. It was his duty publicly to watch over the corpse of his predecessor, and in due course, while prayers were said for the gift of the Holy Spirit, he had to take the dead man's hand in his own, and place it on his own head; having done this, he removed the dead man's pallium, which was the most important part of his insignia of office, while more prayers were said, and placed it around his own neck; and when this somewhat macabre ceremony was completed with due solemnity, he was regarded as being the dead man's legitimate successor with all the authority of his office. All this Gaianus did, protected from interference by a large crowd of his supporters, who then escorted him triumphantly to the Patriarchal residence through streets packed with thousands of the citizens of Alexandria, who greeted him rapturously as their new father in God. But when the news reached Constantinople, Theodora was furious. She had no intention of allowing Gaianus and his Phantasiasts to enjoy their ephemeral victory, and she sent Narses to Alexandria with orders to arrest Gaianus and to put down any opposition he might encounter in the process. Theodosius was then to be consecrated bishop, and enthroned as the legitimate Patriarch.

It was a dangerous operation, for it could easily have stirred up a hornets' nest of opposition to Constantinople, not only in Alexandria itself, but in Egypt generally, and this could have been disastrous; the Empire depended for much of its corn on Egypt, and most of it was shipped to Constantinople and the other great ports of the Byzantine world through the docks of Alexandria; so any interruption in this traffic had always been greatly feared by the imperial government. Indeed, it had been for this reason that the Monophysites of Egypt had been exempted from the general persecution of the sect in the immediate past. But it would have been equally dangerous to ignore Gaianus and pretend that the whole thing had never happened; for if the Alexandrians were allowed to defy the authority of the Emperor with impunity on one occasion, they would certainly defy it again and again in the future, whenever they chose to do so. So, when Narses sailed for Egypt, he took with him a considerable body of troops; Theodora was taking no chances. Events proved her wisdom, for when the eunuch reached Alexandria the city rose against him in violent protest, determined to protect Gaianus from arrest. There were battles in the streets; even the women of the city took part, hurling things at the imperial soldiers from the flat roofs of the houses; but by a combination of firmness when attacked and diplomacy behind the scenes, Narses managed to contain the fighting to a comparatively small section of the city, where the fanatical hard core of Gaianus' supporters entrenched themselves and resisted all attempts to dislodge them. In the end, after several days of fierce attack and counter-attack, when stalemate seemed to have been reached, Narses was forced to burn them out by setting that part of the city on fire. This settled the matter; the imperial troops prevailed, and Theodosius was duly made archbishop of Alexandria, while Gaianus was taken back to Constantinople in chains to be confined to a monastery there. None of these stirring events brought any comfort to the Orthodox party. Severus was Patriarch of Antioch, Anthimus Patriarch of Constantinople, and now Theodosius was Patriarch of Alexandria; and all of them were Monophysites. The Empress seemed to have triumphed.

It is difficult not to feel sorry for Theodora's opponents; they had been outwitted, outmanoeuvred, and outclassed at every turn, and they had suffered a series of crushing defeats during the course of a suprisingly short period of time. In less than ten years from the day that she and Justinian had been crowned in the Church of the Holy Wisdom, the Empress had rescued the Monophysites from bitter persecution, and in the process she had turned the tables on the Orthodox party so completely that they were now in the political wilderness, while the Monophysites had captured most of the key positions of real power. But if it is hard not to feel sorry for them, by their ungracious behaviour they themselves did everything in their power to make it as easy as possible to withdraw all sympathy from them; for they took the series of defeats they had suffered neither humbly nor charitably. Sure of their own rectitude, they denounced their successful rivals as godless heretics, venting their spleen in particular on leading Monophysites who lived in the capital or who were staying there; Severus was a pagan in league with the devil, who practised black magic in his spare time; Peter of Apamea was an immoral pig 'having his stomach for God' and regularly patronising prostitutes; Zooras was off his head, a dangerous madman; and Anthimus the new Patriarch was a wolf in sheep's clothing, a sly and deceitful hypocrite, a liar and dissembler. But Justinian, to whom the angry Orthodox churchmen poured out their bitter and uncharitable complaints, took no notice of them, and they were forced to watch helplessly as their rivals went from strength to strength under the protection of the Empress. But just when everything seemed to point to the ultimate triumph of the Monophysite party, a wholly unexpected visitor arrived in the city and turned the tables on them.

On 19 February 536 Pope Agapetus reached Constantinople and presented himself to the Emperor and Empress, not primarily as the Pope of Rome, but as the ambassador of the Gothic king of Italy, Theodahad, with whom Justinian had recently broken off all diplomatic relations in protest at the murder of Amalasuntha. War had not followed immediately upon the lady's death, but it was impending, and the Pope had been sent to Constantinople in a surprise move to try to preserve the peace, if it was still possible to do so. He was a Roman by birth, the son of a priest named Gordianus, and he had not been Pope for more than nine months. He was already an old man, and he was not destined to live for very much longer; but neither his age nor the novelty of his position as Pope deterred him from acting with initiative, courage, and determination during his short term of office. On arrival in Constantinople he was received with the greatest respect in the Imperial Palace, where he was lodged in the apartments reserved for the Emperor's most honoured guests. After a few days of polite formalities, however, relations between Justinian and the Italian Pontiff became increasingly strained. Discussions about the political crisis in Italy were begun, but it soon appeared that Agapetus was more interested in the recent defeats suffered by Orthodox churchmen at the hands of the victorious Monophysites than in averting war in Italy between the Goths and the Emperor's army under the command of Belisarius. Justinian was not at all pleased by his guest's interest in things which he considered to be none of the Pope's business, and when Agapetus flatly refused to pay his respects to the new Patriarch, Anthimus, because he suspected him of being tainted by heresy, Justinian lost all patience with him. 'Do as I tell you,' he ordered the old man, 'or I shall send you into exile.' Theodora did her best to repair the breach between the two men by being as charming to her guest as she could, but she was just as determined as Justinian to force Agapetus to be civil to Anthimus. She resorted to subtler methods of persuasion, even offering the obstinate Italian financial rewards for his cooperation, but she had no greater success than her husband. The Pope proved to be both adamant and tiresomely incorruptible.

To understand the uncompromising stance adopted by Agapetus and the other Popes of the time in what they considered to be matters of heresy, it is not enough to invoke the divine authority which was believed to be vested in the successors of Saint Peter; the political situation in Italy after the collapse of the Empire in the West must also be understood. For more than two centuries the country had been overrun and devastated by barbarian invasions. At first, these had not caused as much material damage as might be imagined, for the Goths, who had swept down through the long-civilised and immensely rich countryside of France and thence over the Alps down through the old heart-lands of ancient Rome, had not been bent on destroying the Empire but rather on securing a share of its riches and a chance to learn something of its civilised way of life. So, even though wave upon wave of barbarians had passed through the country, and there had been battles in which people had been killed and cities had been sacked, most of the time the life of the indigenous Romans had gone on much as usual. After the first Gothic incursions in the third century and just before the much greater irruptions which were to come, Paulinus, a member of an immensely rich and noble Roman family living on his estates in Aquitaine in the last quarter of the fourth century, still sent to Rome for his tennis balls; and even after the invaders had crushed all military opposition by the Romans, and had set up their own petty kingdoms throughout the lands which had formed the western half of the Empire, life did not change all that much. For the Gothic kings were determined to show themselves to be more Roman than the Romans themselves, adopting their ways, dressing like Roman Emperors, patronising the arts, and doing their best to ape the more civilised people, whom they had conquered, in all things. But though they copied their Roman subjects, they despised them too, for centuries of comfort had made them soft; they might be more civilised than their German conquerors, but in other ways they were unmanly, cowardly, and contemptible to Gothic eyes.

Meanwhile, of course, the native Romans harboured some equally ambivalent feelings towards their conquerors. The psychological shock of the invasions had been enormous, for they had destroyed the universally accepted myth of the invincibility of Roman arms, and the eventual fall of Rome itself to Alaric and his Goths in A.D. 410 had been like the drying up of the sea or the disappearance of the moon; the impossible, the unthinkable, the inconceivable had suddenly and incredibly happened. For a time people simply refused to believe it. For centuries the city had dominated the earth; it was synonymous with civilisation, law, earthly power, and historical continuity. Now that it had gone down under the black tide of barbarism, time seemed to be out of joint, and the world had lost its moorings; people did not know where or to whom to turn for hope or for guidance.

Gregory the Great, though he lived a little later than the period of this book, was the spokesman of more than his own immediate time when he cried in despair, 'Where is the Senate? Where is the people? The bones are all dissolved, the flesh is consumed, all the pomp of the dignities of this world is gone . . . For the Senate is no more, and the people has perished, yet sorrow and sighing are multiplied daily among the few that are left. Rome is, as it were, already burning and empty. But what need is there to speak of men when, as the work of ruin spreads, we see the very buildings perishing?' It was the voice of the dark ages in the West.

But in the chaos of the times, when nothing seemed permanent, one institution did remain; the church stood like a rock, while all else collapsed around it. The last of the Roman Emperors might leave Rome and seek safety in the marshy fastness of Ravenna, cowering there while Italy was overrun and Rome was subdued, but the Popes never left the city; and when there were no more Emperors in the West, it was upon the Popes that the mantle of their imperial authority fell. Gothic kings came and went, ruling or misruling, and the Roman people tolerated them, because they had no alternative; but it was to the Popes of Rome that they turned for faith, for hope, for leadership, and for an identity which would lend some sort of significance to their lives and salvage some sort of self-respect and proper pride out of their ruins.

The Popes varied very much as men, and some were better Pontiffs than others, but they were Romans themselves, and they understood the needs of their people; they stood up to the Gothic kings with courage and dignity; they defended the people wherever and whenever they could; and above all they defended the faith by which the people lived: defended it with obstinate, unbending tenacity and rock-like intransigence against all-comers. It was here that their strength lay, for although the great majority of the Goths were Christians, they were Arians, denying the eternal divinity of Christ, and this doctrine had been roundly condemned as heretical by the church at the Council of Nicaea in 325. Faithful as always to the decisions of the Oecumenical Councils of the Holy Catholic Church, which God, after all, had promised to lead into all truth, and which could not therefore be mistaken when it came together in a properly convened Council and made its mind up on matters of truth and falsehood, the Popes did not hesitate to tell their Gothic masters that as Arians they were in gross error; they were heretics; their immortal souls were in terrible danger; in fact, they were wrong. They told the Goths this with great courage, unflagging persistence, and unquestioning confidence in their own knowledge of the truth, if seldom with much humility or charity. Their staunchly Catholic fellow countrymen might have lost most of their pride as Romans; they might have to endure a life of subjection to barbarian rulers; and their farms might be burned or their cities destroyed during the wars which swept over their homes; but at least they were totally superior to their conquerors in their Catholicism. The truth was theirs, the Gospel was theirs, and therefore in God's good time the future would be theirs too, for they had it on the highest authority that neither death nor hell would be able to prevail against the church which was led by the successors of Saint Peter in Rome.

With this background, it is not surprising that Agapetus, who was as much a product of his age as any other Roman living in the West in those dark days, should have proved so uncompromising. Justinian's flirtation with the Monophysites must have appalled him; it was bad enough that the western Emperors should have first abandoned the eternal city to the tender mercies of barbarian conquerors, and then simply faded out of history, leaving the burden of protecting the Roman people from the errors of their Gothic masters to the successors of Saint Peter, but that the Emperor in Constantinople, who claimed to be appointed by God as vicegerent of Christ on earth, should blithely compromise himself with heretics, who were in gross error about the very nature of Christ himself, was infinitely worse.

Being an honest and outspoken man of integrity and courage, no doubt Agapetus told Justinian all this in no uncertain terms and at considerable length, for it is known that they had long and frequent discussions together. No doubt, too, Justinian listened with deepening gloom to the Pope's blunt words, for he must have realised that, unless he could change the old man's mind, his whole elaborate, costly, and carefully planned policy in Italy and the West, which was just about to enter its final and crucial phase, would be utterly ruined. All that was needed to make military success in Italy impossible was for the Pope to return to Rome and there to tell the people not to cooperate with Belisarius and his army, on the grounds that the heretical Gothic devil they all knew so well was better than the Monophysite devils in imperial uniforms whom they did not know. What must have made these conversations with Agapetus even more depressing for the Emperor was the fact that he was far too intelligent not to see the force of the Pope's arguments; anyone in the same situation as Agapetus would have argued in the same way.

So Justinian was forced to consider the possibility of a complete *volte face* in his recent religious policy towards the Monophysites. It has usually been assumed, either that he did not tell Theodora that he was considering such a change, or that, if he did so, she fought the idea tooth and nail; but there is no evidence of this. In fact, it is much more likely that he discussed the whole thing with her at length, for it is known that he consulted her in everything. Her feelings can easily be imagined, for the possibility of losing all that she had gained would have been a bitter pill to swallow, especially when her victory had seemed to be so complete until the arrival of this tiresome bishop from Rome. But Theodora was both a highly intelligent woman and also a political realist; indeed, she was more of a realist in this respect than her husband, and if Justinian realised that he could not possibly jeopardise his whole military adventure in the West by bitterly antagonising the very people whom Belisarius was supposed to be rescuing from the barbarous and heretical Goths, Theodora would certainly have recognised the political impossibility of such a course quite as clearly as he did. It must have been perfectly plain to her that, if Justinian was forced to choose between losing the war in Italy on the one hand and withdrawing his favour for the time being from the Monophysites, he had no alternative but to choose the latter course. In the long term, the Monophysite provinces in the East might well prove to be more important to the survival of the Empire than Italy; but in the short term, the reconquest of Italy had to take precedence of all else. The Empire was too deeply committed to turn back now, and Theodora would have been the first person to accept the fact, however unpalatable it might have been. The worst, however, had not yet come to the worst, and for the time being Justinian temporised. He no longer tried to bully Agapetus into paying his respects to those whom he suspected of heresy, but he did not succumb to the old man's demand that he be allowed to depose and excommunicate all leading Monophysites in the city. An uneasy stalemate was reached.

It was broken by the Pope's insistence that at least he should be allowed to confront and confound the diminutive monk Zooras. Justinian tried to dissuade him from doing so; the monk, he told Agapetus, was no respecter of persons, and he could not answer for the consequences if the two men should meet, for despite his small stature Zooras was a man of savage manners when aroused. But Agapetus was adamant, and in the end Justinian agreed to arrange a confrontation between the two opponents. A time was arranged for the meeting, and a messenger was despatched to the monastery in Sykae with orders from the Emperor to fetch Zooras to the Imperial Palace; but when the imperial courier arrived, he found the doors locked and barred against him. Zooras, who had been warned of the Pope's intention, told the Emperor's emissary that, since it was Lent, he was forbidden by divine law to interrupt his devotions for anyone's sake, even that of the Emperor, let alone that of his visitor from Rome.

'I have nothing further to say to you,' he told the discomfited messenger. 'If the Emperor wishes to use force to make me obey, that is his business.'

Justinian was furious. He had not wanted to interfere with Zooras in the first place, but the aggressive little man's open defiance enraged him. He promptly sent an officer of the Imperial

Guard with about a dozen men to arrest Zooras and bring him by force to the Palace. They duly set out, but when they reached the Golden Horn and summoned a boat to take them across to Sykae on the other side, a sudden gust of wind caught the vessel as it was approaching the quay and threw it on the shore. It was retrieved, and the men embarked and began their journey, but once again disaster overtook them; it was a heavy, thundery day with a leaden sky, and just when they were about to reach the further shore a violent little squall blew up, whipping the water into a miniature cauldron and carrying their boat back into the main channel before they could reach the land. The officer lost his temper, swore at the boatmen for their incompetence, and ordered them to take to their oars and row the boat to land. No sooner had they begun to do so, however, than the boat was struck by lightning, and although no one was hurt, the terrified occupants of the boat gave up the unequal struggle, and sailed back to Constantinople as fast as they could. The officer then hurried back to the Palace to tell a dumbfounded Justinian that God was against him, and that he had better leave Zooras alone.

The story spread rapidly throughout the city, and everyone concluded that the Monophysites were under the protection of divine providence; even some impeccably Orthodox churchmen gloomily came to the same conclusion.

But if providence had had a hand in protecting the insubordinate monk from the Emperor's displeasure and the *odium theologicum* of the Pope, it was erratic in its favours, and it did not do much to protect the Patriarch Anthimus from either the one or the other. For shortly after the abortive attempt to summon Zooras to the Palace, Justinian decided that he had no alternative but to agree with Agapetus and meet his demands; a rupture with Rome at this particular moment would be worse politically than another period of strife with the Monophysites, however undesirable that might be, and however disappointing to Theodora it was bound to be.

So it came about that the people of Constantinople woke up one morning in March 536, to find that their new Patriarch, who had not yet been in office for a year, was to be deposed. They greeted the news with excitement, for there was nothing they enjoyed more than political drama in high places. Later when they learned that Menas, the staunchly Orthodox superior of the great monastery of Saint Sampson in Constantinople, was to be consecrated in a few days' time by Pope Agapetus, the news triggered off an explosion of delight, which revealed only too clearly the hidden strength of the Orthodox party. It had probably never been in any permanent danger from Theodora's Monophysites, whose sudden run of quick political victories had mesmerised the Orthodox party into forgetting its own numerical superiority; some of the Greens tended to support the Monophysites, but on the whole the people of Constantinople were solidly Orthodox. Predictably, the Monophysites behaved as badly in defeat as their enemies had, when they themselves had been in the ascendant; they openly reviled Justinian for his treachery, but it was for the Pope that they reserved their most pungent insults and abuse. But so fickle was providence that it now changed sides again, withdrawing its protection from the leading actor in this whole series of dramatic moves and counter-moves: less than a month after the deposition of Anthimus on 21 April, when he was about to set sail for Italy, Pope Agapetus died.

His death plunged Constantinople into an immediate crisis. The Monophysites celebrated his demise with such unseemly and riotous rejoicing that every Orthodox churchman in the place was enraged, and it looked as if there would be fighting in the streets between the two rival ecclesiastical factions. But at this dangerous and critical moment, the new Patriarch Menas acted with firmness and decision. While Justinian gave orders to increase the number of troops in the city, Menas called a council to confirm the deposition of Anthimus and to bring Zooras, Peter of Apamena, Severus, and the other leading Monophysites to trial for their heretical beliefs. He worked quickly, and on 2 May, ten days after the death of the Pope, a sufficient number of bishops had been brought together under the chairmanship of Menas himself to constitute a valid council qualified to do what was required of it.

The first item on the agenda was the deposition and trial of Anthimus, and the assembled bishops duly met and summoned the accused man to appear before them to answer the charges which were to be brought against him, though no one expected him to be able to do so successfully; the bishops were confident of their own rectitude, and the outcome of the trial was a forgone conclusion. But their confidence was badly shaken, and their carefully arranged programme rudely upset, when it transpired that Anthimus could not be found. The city was searched with the utmost thoroughness;

monasteries suspected of Monophysite tendencies were ransacked for the missing archbishop; churches where he might have sought sanctuary were turned inside out; the homes of known sympathisers of the Monophysite cause were minutely investigated by parties of police who went through them with meticulous care; with the Emperor's permission, even the official buildings and the servants' quarters in the Imperial Palace were opened to the searchers, who were eventually reduced to interrogating children in the streets of the city as to whether they had seen the missing man; but the gentle and learned old man from Trebizond, who had been Patriarch for less than a year, had disappeared as completely as if the earth had opened and swallowed him. But it was not the earth which had swallowed Anthimus; it was the *gynaeceum* in the Imperial Palace itself, where Theodora had made him her guest, and hidden him from all prying eyes, including even those of her husband. Protected by the Empress and her devoted staff of women and eunuchs, no one discovered his whereabouts until after Theodora's death years later, when to the world's astonishment he turned up once again, looking older and even more gentle than before, and beaming in a vague and amiable way at the surprise he was causing.

At the time, however, both the manner of his disappearance and his whereabouts remained a mystery, though the fact that he had vanished had to be accepted eventually by the members of the council which had been called to condemn him. Strictly, they should not have taken any further action against him, for he had a legal right to defend himself, and this he could not do if he was absent; but the bishops, though ruffled and annoyed, had no intention of allowing a mere technicality of this kind to stop them from passing their predetermined judgement on him. His deposition was confirmed, he was convicted of heresy, and he was anathematised. So were Severus, Peter of Apamea, and Zooras.

Theodora, who had perforce to bow to events, did everything in her power to protect her friends in their defeat, just as she had protected Anthimus. She helped Severus to return to Egypt, where he died in peace three years later, and she persuaded Zooras, who remained truculent to the bitter end, to accept exile to a monastery in Thrace about thirty miles west of the capital, where she promised him that he would be safe. But for the time being she could do no more; until the furious gale of reaction, which was blowing across the Byzantine world, had spent its force, she had no alternative to sitting back and watching the progress of the storm.

The persecution of the Monophysites was renewed in Syria, and even in Egypt they were not left alone this time; Theodosius, the Patriarch of Alexandria, whose appointment she herself had secured and enforced, was deposed and replaced by a monk named Paul, who was so savagely Orthodox that he let loose a reign of terror over the Monophysites throughout his archdiocese.

But Theodora was not a woman to sit down for long under defeat without planning a counter-attack, and the death of Agapetus presented her with just the kind of opportunity for revenge which suited both her audacity and her skill as an intriguer. So while the triumphant champions of Orthodoxy were trumpeting their anathemas in Constantinople and despatching their bloody minions to light the fires of persecution once again all over the eastern provinces of the Empire, she sat down in the Imperial Palace and sought a way of putting a man of her own choice upon the vacant apostolic throne of Saint Peter in Rome. She might have just lost a battle, but she had by no means lost the war.

VIII

ΘΕ
ΟΔΥ
Ρ Α

Before describing Theodora's attempt to capture the see of Rome, it is worth looking for a moment at another series of events which she set in motion at this time, for they were typical, both of one of the most terrible aspects of her day and age, and also of one of its more splendid characteristics, and they were destined to have lasting consequences.

When the renewed persecution of the Monophysites reached its height, it began to look as if they would be either exterminated or at best reduced to an insignificant faction, so fiercely were they being harried and hounded throughout Syria, Mesopotamia, and Egypt. It was at this juncture that Theodora sent for the Syrian monk, Jacob Baradaeus.

Jacob had been forced to leave the house which she had originally given him, and he was living as a recluse in a monastery in the capital. As has been said already, he was a remarkable man who, as a result of a vow by his parents, had been put into a monastery near a town named Nisibis, which was close to his birthplace in Mesopotamia, at the age of two. There he was trained in Greek and Syriac literature as well as in the strictest asceticism, and as he grew to manhood he became celebrated both for his learning and for the severity of his self-discipline. On the death of his parents, he inherited a large fortune and two slaves, whom he set free, making over his whole inheritance to them as a gift. As time went by, both his learning and his austerity were eclipsed by the fame of his powers of healing, and sick people flocked to him from all over the eastern provinces seeking cures for their various diseases; some even came to see him from as far away as Persia, so widely did stories of his miraculous powers spread, while it was said that others were healed at a distance without actually coming to see him at all. He was about forty years old when Theodora summoned him to the Imperial Palace, and he was not at all the same kind of man as most of the other ascetic monks whom she had welcomed to the capital, and sheltered from the animosity of their Orthodox opponents. He was courteous, quiet in manner, and softly spoken; since he never intended to do anyone any harm, he never suspected ill-will in others, and his genuinely simple, innocent, and loving disposition was in marked contrast to the ferocious sectarianism and savage belligerence of many of the people around him. But those who mistook his gentleness for softness were greatly mistaken; he was as tough as nails, completely unafraid of anyone or anything, inexhaustible physically, and able to survive for weeks on a diet which most people would have regarded as inadequate to provide the bare necessities of life for a dog.

Theodora summoned Jacob Baradaeus as a result of a visit which she had received from the Sheikh Harith ibn Jabala, a Ghassanid king of a small buffer state on the borders of the Empire, who came to tell her of the desperate plight of his Christian Arabs. They were Monophysites like most of the other Christians in that part of the world, and they were suffering terrible things at the hands of the imperial Commissioners, who had been sent east to extirpate all heretics; unless something was done at once, the Sheikh told the Empress, he feared that this renewed harassment might succeed in its objective. What the hard-pressed people of the eastern provinces needed above all was a new bishop to ordain men to replace the priests, who had been arrested or even in some instances martyred by their Orthodox oppressors; for with no bishops left and virtually no priests either, the Monophysite Christians were like sheep without shepherds. If a bishop could be found who was willing to go to the eastern provinces and face the very real dangers which would inevitably surround him day and night once his presence became known to the authorities there, who would hunt him unmercifully like a wild beast, plainly he would have to be a man of very special quality endowed with some very special virtues: courage, cool-headedness, pertinacity, and that elusive and sometimes dangerous gift known as leadership. How it ever occurred to Theodora that the monastic recluse, Jacob Baradaeus, might be the man to fit this exacting bill no one will ever know; but it did occur to her, and it was an inspired choice on her part. For in addition to the virtues already mentioned, all of which he possessed in abundance, Jacob Baradaeus spoke both Syriac and Greek like a native, he had the physique and stamina of an Olympic athlete, and he turned out to be a master of disguise; indeed, the name 'Baradaeus' was a nickname meaning 'rags' or 'tatters', and he got it because he spent so many years disguised as the poorest of beggars, totally deceiving the authorities in the process, that he became affectionately known as Jacob Baradaeus: old Jacob ragbag, in fact.

Jacob listened to Theodora, and agreed to undertake the task. She was delighted, and immediately arranged for him to be secretly consecrated bishop by one of the Monophysite bishops who were living in what amounted to captivity in various places near the capital; it is not known whether it was Severus, Peter of Apamea, or Theodosius of Alexandria who actually consecrated him, but within a few days of his meeting with the Empress he was made nominal bishop of Edessa, the modern Urfa in eastern Turkey, though everyone knew that he would probably never be able to take possession of his see, which was already in the possession of an Orthodox bishop; but that did not unduly matter, for he was also given the roving commission of a Monophysite metropolitan and an oecumenical authority.

Disguised as a beggar, he then travelled east on foot through the whole of Asia Minor to Syria, Mesopotamia, and the adjacent provinces, where he began to exercise one of the most remarkable ministries in the history of the Christian church. Everywhere he went, he sought out his persecuted fellow Christians of the Monophysite party, raising their hopes and spirits for the first time for months, loving them, curing their diseases, baptising their children, celebrating the holy mysteries of the Eucharist in their houses and abandoned churches, and ordaining men to the priesthood. The effect on their morale was immediate and sensational, and it was not long before the Orthodox authorities discovered what was going on. They mounted a vast man-hunt for Jacob Baradaeus, offering a huge reward for any information which might lead to his capture, but not a soul was prepared to breathe a word which might betray him. He became a sort of legend, and though the authorities searched for him for years, they never caught him. It is said that on one occasion some soldiers, who had somehow got wind of his presence in their vicinity, actually met him on the road, dressed as always in indescribably ragged and tattered clothes and looking as though he smelled to high heaven;

taking him for a tramp or a beggar and keeping their distance, they questioned him roughly as to whether he knew where the bishop of Edessa was; when he replied truthfully that he believed he was somewhere in the neighbourhood, they let him go on his way without suspecting for a moment that they had been ta..ing to the man for whom they had been searching for so long.

During the course of his extraordinary ministry, Jacob Baradaeus travelled hundreds of thousands of miles, mostly on foot, through deserts and across mountain ranges; he endured intense heat and extreme cold, slept where he could, and lived in the constant knowledge that he was being hunted. During the course of his travels he became known and loved from the borders of Persia south to Arabia and Egypt and west through Mesopotamia, Armenia, Syria, and the whole of Asia Minor to the Asiatic shore of the Bosphorus, and everywhere he went he built up the persecuted Monophysite Christian church. It is said that he ordained 80,000 men to the priesthood, and consecrated 89 bishops and 2 Patriarchs. So firmly did he build the church, which he loved and served, that it still exists today throughout Syria and Egypt, and bears his name: the Jacobite church. Inevitably, he became the subject of hundreds of stories which, if unlikely to be true in literal fact, are vehicles of a symbolic truth which is both deeper and more important than factual reminiscence: the dead were raised to life, the blind were restored to sight, rain was given when the land was parched, and the city of Edessa was saved from destruction by the prayers of Jacob Baradaeus, who happened to be there during the time of its greatest danger.

Meanwhile, in Constantinople Theodora was preparing to take the war to the enemy's camp by capturing the innermost citadel of Orthodoxy in Rome. Her aim was to put a man upon the pontifical throne there who would make peace with the Monophysites and reinstate all those deposed by Menas and his council. In effect, this meant choosing as successor to Pope Agapetus a man who was either a Monophysite himself or at the very least a sympathiser and friend of their cause. There is no doubt that she must have discussed this with Justinian, for she could not have acted as she subsequently did, if he had withheld his consent to it, let alone if he had never heard of the project. Probably she discussed her plan with him fully from the moment when it first occurred to her, just as, a few weeks earlier, he had discussed with her the possibility of making a change in his religious policy under pressure from Agapetus. But Justinian's agreement to Theodora's scheme is superficially more difficult to understand, for by natural instinct he was Orthodox, and the prospect of a Monophysite Pope would not normally have appealed to him; but probably what attracted him was the possibility of putting an end to the great division of the church into two hostile camps, which was bound to continue as long as half the church was governed by Orthodox churchmen and the other half by their opponents. A Monophysite on the chair of Saint Peter could be expected to come to terms with his fellow Monophysites in the East, and Justinian probably reckoned that the sacrifice of his own slight personal preference for Orthodoxy would be a small price to pay for the ecclesiastical unity for which he so much longed, even if that unity was achieved under Monophysite auspices; so he gave Theodora his consent to her plans.

She wasted no time in putting them into effect. Her first task was to find the right man to succeed the dead Pope, and as it happened she did not have to look far afield; for when Pope Agapetus had arrived in Constantinople, he had been welcomed to the capital by a deacon named Vigilius, who was the papal nuncio in the city appointed by his predecessor. Vigilius was a member of a well-known Roman family, and his ancestry was illustrious; the son of a man named John, who had been a Consul, many of his forbears had been Senators, while others had served with distinction in other walks of life. He himself was a man of unlimited ambition, whose main aim in life was self-advancement, and he loved money. Before Theodora met him, he had already tried to prepare the way to the pontifical throne in Rome for himself by persuading Boniface II to nominate him as his successor, and this Boniface had done; but when the time came, his hopes had come to nothing because of the open hostility of the Roman Clergy to his candidacy, and his bid for the papacy had failed. Being the man he was, he had paid assiduous court to Theodora from the moment of his arrival in Constantinople, for it was second nature to him to curry favour where favour might one day be useful, and it was to Vigilius that Theodora now turned. Normally, she was such a very shrewd judge of character that she probably had some idea of what sort of man he was, for even his vices fitted him well for the part she wanted him to play; his ambition would guarantee his cooperation, and his thirst for self-aggrandisement would ensure that he raised no conscientious objections to her plan. But plainly she did not know just what an unprincipled and vacillating man he was; he had no morals at all, either good or bad, and as for firmness of either character or resolve, he was about as steady as a wisp of straw in a high wind. Ever ready to enter into slightly shady and highly secret deals if he thought that they were in his own interest, he was equally ready to abandon them the moment it proved convenient to do so. He trimmed and prevaricated throughout his whole life, and even those historians who have done their best to find something good to say about him have had to admit that he was a miserable creature. But none of this did Theodora yet know.

Having summoned Vigilius to her presence, the Empress offered him the succession to Pope Agapetus on condition that once he was firmly seated on Saint Peter's chair he would faithfully support her own ecclesiastical politics; he must renounce the doctrines of Chalcedon, and he must restore Anthimus to his patriarchal throne in Constantinople; finally, he must write to all other leading Monophysites to tell them of his agreement with their doctrines, and thus restore peace to the church. Vigilius leapt at the chance of an alliance with Theodora, and agreed at once; he would have happily murdered his grandmother for less. Theodora then despatched him to Rome with a letter to Belisarius and another to Antonina, in which she gave precise orders as to what should be done to make him Pope. She had wasted no time in launching her counter-attack.

But when Vigilius arrived in Rome, he suffered a shattering blow to his hopes. A new Pope had already been elected by the electoral college of bishops, consecrated, and enthroned; Saint Peter's chair was no longer unoccupied. This was highly irregular for, as Emperor, Justinian should at least have been told before anyone was elevated to the vacant throne, even if he was not invited to approve of the man chosen for the position. But what had happened was that, when the death of Agapetus was reported to the Gothic king of Italy, Theodahad, who had sent the old man to Constantinople as his ambassador in the first place on a peace-making mission, he had made up his mind to put someone into the dead man's place before Justinian could interfere or prefer a candidate of his own. If war should break out between his own Goths and Justinian's army under Belisarius, Theodahad was determined that the new Pope should be a man of his own choosing and not someone in the pocket of the Byzantine Emperor. So he had hastily selected a sub-deacon named Silverius, and had forced the electoral college in Rome to confirm his choice, whereupon in June 536, some bishops had consecrated him as their new Pontiff, while Gothic soldiers had stood around to make sure that they obeyed orders.

Silverius was the son of Pope Hormisdas, born before his father had entered the priesthood, and he inherited some of his father's firmness and strength of character. No one has ever needed those qualities more than he did, for he had not been Pope for more than a few days before he found himself in a most unenviable position. Almost immediately after he had been consecrated, the Gothic king Theodahad died. This left Silverius in the most dangerous situation; his patron was dead; he had not had time to win either the support or the affection of the Italian church, of which he had just been made head by force; and he had been elevated to the papal throne without the knowledge or the agreement of the Byzantine Emperor, whose troops had recently captured Naples, and who were now at war with the Goths. Silverius was no fool, and he realised that his position was extremely precarious; as a result, he determined to do something as soon as he possibly could to win Justinian's approval before he incurred his wrath. So he sent a messenger to Belisarius with a letter, in which he invited him to come to Rome as soon as possible, promising to do everything in his power to help him enter the city with his army. On 9 December 536, Belisarius arrived below the walls of Rome, and faithful to his promise Pope Silverius threw open the gates of the city to Justinian's troops, who marched in and occupied it at once.

When the news of these events reached Theodora, she was not amused. Her plan to have Vigilius made Pope had failed, and this was a bitter blow to her; but she was not someone to allow a single reverse to stop her trying to achieve her end another way. Her first thought was that, if she could not put a Pope of her own choosing on to Saint Peter's chair, she would have to try to use the man already on it, even though he was someone else's choice. So she wrote to Silverius, congratulated him on his elevation, and asked him as tactfully as possible if he would be good enough to restore Anthimus to the Patriarchal throne of Constantinople; but he brusquely refused. The tone of his letter left Theodora in no doubt that she would be unable to win him to her side as an ally, and so with her usual realism she decided to treat him as an enemy. She wrote to Belisarius ordering him to depose Silverius and to put Vigilius in his place, even if he had to use force to do so. Belisarius was too good-natured and generous a man to be anything but distressed by the thought of carrying out such repugnant orders, for Silverius had been good to him, keeping his bargain and opening the gates of Rome to his men, and the last thing he wanted to do was to repay his faithfulness with brutality; so he played for time. Antonina, however, was less bothered by such humane scruples than her husband, and she had little difficulty in persuading him to do as Theodora ordered.

But as it happened, before either of them could do anything, more urgent matters engaged their attention; the Goths under the leadership of Theodahad's successor besieged Rome, encompassing the city with a large army. Belisarius had only about five thousand men under his command, and the situation was grave. The citizens of Rome dreaded the horrors of a siege by the barbarians more even than its occupation, and rumours of treason on the part of some people who had not been at all pleased to see the Byzantines arrive in the first place were rife. So Belisarius had other things to think about than the deposition of Pope Silverius. But he was not allowed to forget him for long, for after a week or two of the siege someone brought him some letters, which purported to be messages from the Pope to the new Gothic king offering to throw open the gates of Rome to his troops: to be more precise, offering to throw open the Asinarian Gate, which was next door to the Lateran Palace in which Silverius lived. Although his proximity to this particular entrance to the city lent a certain superficial plausibility to the letters, apparently the fact that they were forgeries was so obvious for other reasons that Belisarius refused to take them seriously, let alone take any action against the Pope on their account. Instead, with Antonina's rather surprising agreement he decided to make one more attempt to coax Silverius into cooperating with the Empress instead of fighting her and putting his entire future at risk by his continued stubbornness. So the two men met and talked for over an hour, but with admirable courage Silverius refused to compromise; he would have liked to make his peace with the Empress, but he was not prepared to do so at the expense of his own deepest beliefs, and he could not do what Theodora asked him to do with integrity. Belisarius bowed to the inevitable, and as the obedient servant of the Empress he began to make plans to depose him.

The news that someone had tried falsely to accuse him of a treasonable plot to throw open the Asinarian Gate to the Goths was not long in reaching Pope Silverius, and he prudently decided to move from the Lateran Palace near the walls of the city to a house on the Avantine Hill, which was miles from any gate, and where he would therefore be less open to suspicion. There Belisarius sent for him, ordering him to come to the Pincian Palace, where he himself had made his headquarters, but promising him safe conduct on his way home. By this time there was a good deal of alarm in papal circles, for it was obvious that some sort of plot was being hatched against Silverius, and his friends strongly advised him not to obey Belisarius' summons; they did not trust these Byzantines, who claimed to be Romans but who spoke almost nothing but Greek, and who had brought down another siege upon the city by their unwanted presence. But Silverius decided to do as he was told, and he went to the Pincian Palace, where he had another long discussion with Belisarius; once again, however, the two men reached no agreement, though Belisarius was as good as his word, and the Pope was allowed to return unmolested to his own residence.

Deadlock seemed to have been reached, and when a few days later Silverius received yet another summons to Belisarius' headquarters, his friends were even more alarmed than before, and Silverius himself was uncertain whether to obey or not. At first he refused to do so, but later he changed his mind, perhaps realising that Belisarius could easily resort to force if he wished, and having said his prayers he made his way up the Pincian Hill, accompanied by a large retinue, to the Palace. There is an eye-witness account of what happened when he arrived; he was separated from those who had come with him, and ushered by himself into an inner room, where he found Antonina reclining on a couch with Belisarius seated on the floor at her feet, while a number of servants were standing around the room.

'Well, my Lord Pope,' said Antonina without rising from her bed, 'what have we and the people of Rome done that you should be so eager to hand us all over to the Goths?'

History does not relate what Silverius replied, if indeed he spoke at all. His pallium was removed; he was stripped of his pontifical vestments, and he was forcibly dressed in the habit of a monk. Then, as he was removed from the room under guard, one of

Belisarius' staff went outside and announced to the Pope's horrified retinue that he had been deposed and banished to a monastery. The next day, 29 March 537, Vigilius was made Pope in Silverius' stead, while the Byzantine army stood round menacingly to make sure that the ceremony was obediently carried out by the bishops who had been hastily collected and ordered to perform it.

The unfortunate Silverius was sent under close arrest to the small province of Lycia in southern Asia Minor; he was destined never to see Rome again. The story of his movements after arriving in his place of exile is complex and murky. At first, he was confined somewhere in the diocese of Patara, where the local bishop discovered his presence, and was horrified to hear his tale of deposition and abduction. Being a man of courage, the bishop of Patara wrote to Justinian complaining bitterly of the injustice done to the rightful Pope by one of the Emperor's most senior officers, and surprisingly his letter had an immediate effect. Justinian issued orders that Silverius should be returned to Rome, where the case against him should be reopened, and the truth of the charges of treason brought against him should be re-examined; if he had not been guilty of offering help to the Goths, then he should be restored to his former position as Pope.

Whether Justinian expected or intended these orders to be obeyed to the letter or not will never be known. He must have been aware of Theodora's part in the deposition of Silverius, and it is difficult to believe that he had not been told that the Pope had been arraigned on a trumped-up charge of treason; it is just possible, however, that he had been led to believe that Silverius really was a traitor, and that therefore he issued orders for a new trial in good faith. In the event, however, they were totally ignored, for when Vigilius heard of them, he became understandably terrified. If Silverius was brought back to Rome, exonerated, and replaced on Saint Peter's chair, what was to become of Vigilius himself? So he ran to Antonina, and between them they made absolutely sure that Silverius should never reach Rome. Instead, and presumably with the connivance of Belisarius, he was taken as a prisoner to the small island of Pontia in the Tyrrhenian Sea sixty miles due west of Naples. There, less than a year later, he died. His earliest biographer said of his exile and death that, having been 'sustained with the bread of affliction and the water of necessity, he weakened and died'. It is not clear whether this means that he died of a broken heart or of physical starvation. Procopius hints at dark and terrible things being done to him by one of Antonina's manservants and at Theodora's complicity in his murder, but he does no more than hint; he does not go on to describe what happened or to produce any evidence for a charge of murder. This has not prevented some people from repeating it, however, for there is no denying that the death of the unlucky Silverius was most opportune from Theodora's point of view; it left Vigilius without a rival, and to all appearances she had now triumphed as completely in Rome as she had recently been defeated in Constantinople. With the new Pope as her obedient puppet, it looked as though she would be able to do as she liked in ecclesiastical matters at long last.

But Vigilius begged for time. Of course, he would keep his promises to the Empress, he told her, but he was sure that she would see the necessity of moving slowly and tactfully towards their common goal. There was no point in unnecessarily arousing the hostility of the Orthodox party in Rome, especially as the vast majority of the clergy and people of the city were passionately and rigidly Catholic and anti-Monophysite. Reluctantly, Theodora agreed, for it was impossible to deny that Vigilius had a strong case; over-hasty action at this juncture might have provoked a revolt against the new Pope, and thus have robbed her of her victory. Patience was a virtue which, though not natural to her, she had cultivated over the years as a politician, and she saw the prudence of Vigilius' caution. But the weeks passed into months, the months into years, and still the Pope procrastinated. It was never quite the right moment for him to keep his side of the bargain. His apologists have argued that his prolonged refusal to keep his promises to Theodora was due to his strength of character, not to its weakness; by true conviction he was staunchly Orthodox, they have argued, and though he may have made a bargain with her in a moment of weakness, as soon as he became Pope he realised the error of his ways, repudiated the compact with the Empress, and reverted to a sturdy defence of the truth. But his subsequent actions make this very difficult to believe, and there is a much simpler explanation of his behaviour; he was under greater pressure from the Catholic clergy and people of Italy not to compromise with heresy than he was from Theodora to keep his promises to her, and as usual he bent pliantly to the force of the strongest and the prevailing wind. To understand the dilemma in which he found himself, it is necessary to look for a moment at the war which was being waged in Italy.

It was not going well; at least, it was not moving quickly towards a victory one way or the other. The years immediately following Vigilius' consecration as Pope were years during which each army attacked, and was then counter-attacked; advanced, and retreated again; laid siege to city after city, was forced to lift the siege, and eventually laid siege to the same cities all over again. The siege of Milan was typical of the rest, if more terrible than any of the others. The year after Silverius was deposed to make way for Vigilius, Belisarius sent a small force to occupy Milan; he did this in fulfilment of a promise to the archbishop of Milan, who had begged him to rescue the people of the city from the Goths. His troops entered the place without difficulty, but as soon as the Goths heard the news, they descended upon Milan in considerable force and laid siege to it. Belisarius' men were so few in number that they could not possibly defend the city without assistance, and so all able-bodied Milanese males were pressed into service to help man the city walls. Meanwhile, on hearing what had happened, Belisarius despatched a large army to their relief; the imperial troops marched north as fast as they could, but on arrival they were shocked to find a much larger army of Goths laying siege to the city. Afraid to engage this superior host of barbarians, Belisarius' men encamped on the southern bank of the Po, and waited on events. The General in command of the Imperial troops inside the city sent a message to plead their urgent need of speedy relief, and he was promised immediate aid; but nothing was done. After what amounted under the circumstances to a criminal delay, word was eventually sent to Belisarius asking for reinforcements, and once more Belisarius acted at once; he ordered a large force, which was in the neighbouring province of Aemilia, to hasten to Milan. But again delay followed delay; one of the commanders of the relieving force fell ill, and another refused to move without first getting confirmation of his orders; finally, when they did at last move, they discovered on arrival that there were not enough boats to transport so large an army across the river Po.

While this saga of ineptitude and mismanagement was unfolding, the people of Milan were starving. When the supply of dogs and mice in the city ran out, the Goths, who were kept informed by their spies of the plight of the inhabitants, sent envoys to invite the

General in command of the garrison to capitulate on condition that he and all his soldiers should have their lives spared. The commander was prepared to agree to these terms as long as the lives of the inhabitants of the city were spared too; but the Goths, who were extremely angry with the Milanese for inviting Belisarius to send his troops to the city in the first place, flatly refused to spare them. The commander did not want to save himself and his men at the expense of the civilian population, and he refused the Goths' terms; but his men were reduced to such straits by the sufferings they had endured during the siege that they forced his hand, insisting that he should accept the offer of the Gothic commander, and arguing that it was better to save some lives than none at all. So the handful of exhausted imperial soldiers were allowed to march out of the city unmolested into an honourable captivity; the full fury and barbarity of the Goths then fell upon the people of Milan, and there followed a bloody massacre on an appalling scale. Then as now, it was the richest and most populous city in Italy, and if the records of the time are accurate, it must have had a population of about half a million when the siege began. All the adult males were slaughtered; all women and girls were dragged off into slavery; and the city itself was first looted and then razed to the ground. Amongst the dead was Vigilius' brother, Reparatus. He was the Praetorian Prefect of Italy, but this did not save him; he was cut in pieces and thrown to the dogs. Cerventinus, another brother, escaped, taking the news of the disaster to Constantinople, where he was welcomed by Justinian. One modern historian has said that, 'in the long series of deliberate inhumanities recorded in the annals of mankind, the colossal massacre of Milan is one of the most flagrant . . . It gives the true measure of the instincts of the Ostrogoths, claimed by some to have been the most promising of the German invaders of the Empire.'

Caught up as helpless spectators of the war between Justinian's men and their barbarous opponents, the people who suffered most were the ordinary people of Italy. Even those who were luckier than the Milanese suffered terrible things; their lands were ravaged by both sides but particularly by the Goths, who were forced to live off the land in the absence of any organised commissariat. But even though the Imperial soldiers were supplied with food from Sicily, they were not averse to a little looting when the opportunity arose, and after a year or two of war there was hardly a place where the armies had not passed and passed again, robbing as they went until there was nothing left to rob. Houses stood empty and bare; agriculture ceased in the provinces, and everywhere people were dying of hunger and disease. It was said that in the country around Ancona alone fifty thousand peasants and small farmers died. Everywhere people were emaciated, grey with hunger and under-nourishment, their eyes deeply sunk in their heads; some were reduced to a diet of roots and acorns, and scattered over the countryside were the corpses of others who had died while they tried to tear up a few handfuls of grass with hands too weak for the task. There was no one to bury them, but the crows, the half-starved farm dogs, and the wild foxes found little on them to satisfy their own hunger. Perhaps the worst story was that of two women, who lived in a lonely house near Rimini, where they offered a night's lodging to anyone who happened to pass by. One after another, over a number of weeks, seventeen unsuspecting guests accepted their hospitality, only to be killed in their sleep and subsequently eaten by their ghoulish hostesses. There is no telling how long their cannibalism might have continued, if their eighteenth guest had not woken in the nick of time to save himself; having forced the two women to confess, he killed them in disgust, and told his story to a horrified world.

During these desperate years, even more than in less terrible times, the thing which kept the people of Italy from total despair was their Christian faith, and Vigilius would have had to have been as insensitive as a stone not to have realised it, living in the midst of them as he did, and seeing the plight to which they had been reduced by the war; indeed, he shared their suffering to a certain degree, for if he did not starve, he mourned the loss of his brother. It must have been perfectly clear to him that if he was suddenly to do what Theodora was constantly demanding, openly giving his blessing to the Monophysites and thus implicitly denying the superiority and even the truth of the Orthodox faith, of which hitherto the men who had held his office had been the chief defenders, the blow to all those who looked to him as the shepherd and bishop of their souls would have been shattering. In fact, for once in his life his motives for procrastinating and refusing to keep the promises he had made to the Empress were entirely creditable, for they were rooted and grounded in compassion for his fellow men in their present distress. As it happened, to do nothing was also the line of least resistance, for Theodora was a long way away in Constantinople, while the fiercely Orthodox clergy and people of Catholic Italy were all around him; so once again by acting as he did, he was also bending to the prevailing wind, while writing long and unctuous letters to Theodora defending himself and promising to act as soon as the war was at an end and all its horrors were forgotten. But plausible, persuasive, and even reasonable as Vigilius' arguments for inaction undoubtedly were, as time passed she became more and more sure that he had no intention of ever honouring his promises to her. He had satisfied his own ambition; he was firmly installed in the chair of Saint Peter, and he had no desire to risk being unseated by offending the Italians. Somehow she would have to force him to keep his side of the bargain, or he would never do so.

It was a bitter pill for Theodora to swallow, and as the full realisation of his ingratitude and treachery filled her mind, she became more and more angry. If anyone had told her at that moment, when she was in her most resentful mood, that shortly she would almost have forgotten Vigilius and all his miserable doings, she certainly would not have believed it. Yet just about two years after the massacre of Milan, a disaster of such terrible magnitude struck the Byzantine world that even the horrors of the war in Italy paled into insignificance and were forgotten. It was, as one historian has said, 'one of those immense but rare calamities in the presence of which human beings can only succumb helpless and resourceless'. Despite its enormity, however, catastrophe came to the Byzantine Empire so gently and quietly that at first no one noticed its terrible arrival.

IX

At the eastern edge of the Nile delta, where cultivated land gives way to desert, close to the Mediterranean coast, there are two large mounds. They mark the site of the ancient city of Pelusium. In Byzantine days it was a busy little port standing at the mouth of the most easterly branch of the Nile, though later this part of the river silted up, and the city died. Here in the spring of 542 a very small creature was unwittingly imported into Egypt, probably by boat by way of the harbour, though it is possible that it travelled down the Nile by felucca. No one noticed its arrival, which was not surprising, for it was less than a millimetre long; and no one at that time had given it the name, *Xenopsylla Cheopsis*, which it bears today. Instead, everyone knew it simply as a flea. But it was no ordinary flea, for it carried in its stomach a cargo of blood containing a large number of bacteria belonging to the species *pasteurella pestis*, the bacillus which, when injected into the bloodstream of a human being, causes bubonic plague. The flea which brought the plague to Pelusium in 542 probably travelled in the warm fur of a black rat, and the rat had probably come from Ethiopia, where the plague was already raging. Where the disease had originated before invading the land of the Ethiopians is a matter for conjecture; presumably, then as now, it was endemic to western Arabia and to parts of central Africa where *pasteurella pestis* may linger on for centuries in some remote fastness far from all human habitation in the veins of some warm-blooded animals and in the stomachs of fleas. Then, perhaps every four or five hundred years or so, something happens to disturb the rats, the squirrels, the jerboas, or the other small rodents upon which the fleas live; there are floods, or there is a drought, or the food supply runs out, and the rodents are forced to move from their home-lands to keep alive. Like some invading army, thousands of them spread out, taking with them on their backs tens of thousands of fleas, each carrying its lethal cargo of *pasteurella pestis,* and when they reach the habitations of men it is never long before the plague begins to claim its first victims.

So it happened that in the spring of 542, a few weeks after the plague had begun to rage in Ethiopia, some rats with fleas on their backs somehow reached the little Egyptian port of Pelusium, presumably by ship, and the plague got a toe-hold inside the Byzantine Empire. People soon began to die, for the cities of the Byzantine world might have been specially designed to suit the life-style of the black rat. They usually had sewers of a sort, but they were rudimentary except in the largest places like Alexandria, Antioch, and Constantinople, and in some small towns sewage was either thrown into the streets, where eventually rain washed some of it away, or it was taken in buckets and thrown away in great heaps outside the city walls. There is a description of the outskirts of one such Byzantine town, piled high with human excrement and dung from the streets, and littered with the corpses of domestic animals—cats, dogs, asses, and mules—which had been thrown there when they died, and left to rot; but no doubt in cities as large as Constantinople much of the daily output of garbage was dumped in open spaces in the city itself, for people could hardly have been expected to carry their rubbish a mile or more every day to reach the city walls or the sea-shores. The resulting mounds of refuse must not only have attracted the usual noisy and aggressive flocks of scavenging birds—gulls and crows and black kites—as well as stray dogs and mangy cats, but must also have provided ideal homes for a large population of rats. It only needed one rat to arrive in such a city with its bloodstream full of *pasteurella pestis* and with a few fleas filling their stomachs from the fountains of its doomed body, and no power on earth could prevent an outbreak of the plague from sweeping through the crowded and insanitary streets and narrow alleys in which most people lived. Even the rich, who lived in more spacious surroundings, were not immune, for their personal hygiene was not always over-scrupulous, and in any case they could not avoid meeting people in the streets and elsewhere during the course of their ordinary lives, when the cleanest of people might easily catch a flea from a less well-washed neighbour. Moreover, it must never be forgotten that no one knew how the disease was spread; the discovery that the flea, which infests rats, is the villain of the piece is entirely modern. As late as the last decade of the nineteenth century, one of the most learned English doctors of late Victorian times concluded positively that the plague was the result of contact with dead bodies: 'cadaveric poisoning', he called it.

The Byzantines had no idea how the disease attacked a man, or why it attacked some people and left others alone, and not knowing in what direction to look for danger, they had no means of trying to avoid infection. The best they could do was to avoid all contact with their fellow men, and even that did not work; for if their place of refuge from other people harboured a rat with a flea or two on its back, they died just the same. It was as if the world was being attacked by an invisible poisonous gas; death seemed to be in the very air that men breathed, and there was nowhere for anyone to turn for safety.

From Pelusium the plague spread slowly but inexorably to Alexandria and the other cities of Egypt. Soon it broke out in Palestine and began to spread northwards to Syria and Mesopotamia, and the borders of Asia Minor. Like a man watching gangrene spread from his toes through his feet and up his legs towards his body, the people of Constantinople waited in appalled fascination and helpless fear as the plague turned westwards in their own direction; obscenely it crawled across Cappadocia and Cilicia through Galatia and Phrygia and Paphlagonia, and everywhere it went people died like flies in city after city, until at last it reached Bithynia and the Asiatic shore of the Bosphorus. Everyone knew that only a miracle could stop it from leaping across the narrow waterway which separated the continents of Asia and Europe; and in fact there was to be no miracle. In May it broke out in Constantinople, where it raged for four black months. If it was not more deadly, it seems to have been more destructive than the epidemics which ravaged Athens in the days of Pericles and Rome in the reign of Marcus Aurelius, for it was more widespread than they had been; by the time that it had run its course, there was not a hamlet from the borders of Persia through the entire length and breadth of the Empire to the Adriatic coast, nor a town between the deserts of north Africa in the south and the Danube in the north, which had not been visited by it. In fact, it spread beyond the borders of the Byzantine world, making its way north from Sicily and Italy, which it reached by sea, up through France to the Atlantic coast; even then it did not stop, for it crossed the Channel to England, where it was known as the 'plague of Cadwallader's time', and thence it moved to Ireland, which it laid waste a hundred years after it had first broken out in Ethiopia. Everywhere people waited helplessly for it to reach them. Those who could do so fled from the towns into the country, though their flight seldom did them any good, for the disease followed them wherever they went. Fear hung in the air like mist, and ordinary everyday life ground to a halt; work stopped; labourers and artisans abandoned their trades; and in many towns where the luxuries of civilised life were there for the taking, and the shops were still stocked with perfume, silk, jewellery, ivory furniture, vintage wines, Persian carpets, and the masterpieces of the goldsmiths' and silversmiths' art, people starved to death for lack of food. No one dared bring supplies from the country into infected areas, and when people from the towns, driven by hunger and desperation, made forays into the country in search of something to eat, they were greeted with showers of stones by the terrified country people. Every man became an angel of death to his neighbour. In its passage the plague probably killed as many people as did the Black Death in the same countries eight hundred years later in the fourteenth century, and it may have killed more.

Procopius was in Constantinople during the epidemic, and he has left a detailed description of the disease. Hallucinations often preceded an attack; later, people were seized by a sudden fever, but it

... was of such a mild kind, when it first began, that neither to the sick themselves nor to a physician who touched them would it give rise to any thought of danger [Procopius wrote]. But on the same day in some cases, in others on the next day, and in the rest not many days later a bubonic swelling developed . . . Up to this point the disease followed much the same course in all who caught it; but from then on there were marked differences . . . Some fell into a deep coma, while others became violently delirious, though both types of patient suffered the same physical symptoms of the disease. Those in a coma recognised no one, sleeping the whole time, and if anyone was nursing them, they would eat without waking; but if there was no one to care for them, they soon died from lack of food and water. Those who became delirious, however, suffered from insomnia and were victims of delusions; they suspected everyone of trying to destroy them; they became frantic, rushing off in headlong flight, crying out at the tops of their voices, so that those who were doing their best to look after them were in a state of constant exhaustion and had a most difficult time . . . Surprisingly, neither the physicians nor the other people who were in regular contact with the sick and the dead seemed to catch the disease more easily than anyone else, for contrary to all expectation many of those who looked after the sick as well as those whose job it was to bury the dead survived without ever catching it themselves.

But if the unpredictability of the disease, attacking some people in one way and others in a totally different way, while leaving certain people severely alone even though they were in constant contact with it, interested and puzzled Procopius, the terrible manner in which it killed its victims filled him with horror and disgust.

In those cases where people neither fell into a coma nor became delirious [he noticed] the bubonic swelling often became putrid or gangrenous, and the sufferer, no longer able to bear the pain, died. One would have thought that in all such cases, much the same would have been true, but since some of the patients were out of their minds by this time, they were impervious to pain, having lost all sense of feeling . . . Death came in some instances immediately, in others after many days, while with some the body broke out with black pustules about the size of a lentil, and these did not survive one day but died at once. Many also vomited blood without any apparent reason, and this brought death at once. But I can say this, too, that the best physicians said that many would die, who unexpectedly recovered completely soon afterwards, and declared that many others would recover who died almost immediately . . . In the case of pregnant women, death was certain once they had caught the disease; for some died of miscarriage, while others died with their babies at the time of birth. However, they say that three women survived, though their babies died, and that one woman died during the birth of her child which survived. In those cases where the bubonic swelling grew to an unusual size before bursting and discharging pus, the sufferer soon recovered and lived, for the acute condition of the swelling was relieved this way; and this proved to be a general sign of returning health. But with some people, one or other of their thighs withered, while with others who survived their tongues were damaged, so that they either lisped or spoke incoherently and with difficulty for the rest of their lives.

The number of people who died that summer in Constantinople alone was hideous. At first, the deaths in the city were not much more numerous than usual for the time of year, and people began to hope that reports from elsewhere of whole cities being almost wiped out had been exaggerated; but as the infection spread through the crowded streets of the most populous place on earth, the number of fatalities grew. It was not long before 5,000 people were dying every day, and only a little later, when the epidemic was at its height, 10,000 deaths was the daily total according to Procopius. Another historian, John of Ephesus, who was also in Constantinople when it was at its worst, said that on the worst day of all 16,000 people died; their corpses were counted by men stationed at the harbours, ferries and city gates to keep a check on the number of casualties, as the dead were carried out of the city. There were probably about three-quarters of a million people living within the city walls when the plague struck in May; if you add the number of people living in the suburbs, the total probably came to something like a million in all, and by the end of the summer 300,000 had died. At first, families and friends buried their own dead, but as the hurricane of death carried all before it, corpses were left lying in the streets where they dropped. How many lay rotting and forgotten in the warren of small, crowded houses lining the rat-infested back streets of the city no one will ever know; even in the homes of the rich bodies lay and stank for weeks, for the servants of such households were either dead themselves or too frightened to touch those who had died. Eventually, they were removed by sanitary squads organised by an imperial private secretary named Theodore, who was ordered by Justinian to tackle the urgent but repulsive task of cleaning up the city. Huge pits were dug at Sykae, and the bodies of the dead were taken there by boat across the Golden Horn to be laid in rows and trampled down tightly; but the burial parties could not keep up with the avalanche of corpses, and in desperation they mounted the walls of the suburb, tore off the roofs of the towers which stood at intervals along their length, and filled them with the dead. Not surprisingly, according to Procopius, 'an evil stench pervaded the city and distressed the inhabitants still more, especially when the wind blew fresh from that quarter'. But the need to get rid of the dead was so great that no one could afford to complain about a mere stink; even the Blues and the Greens agreed to forget their rivalry for the duration of the crisis and to work together until there were no more corpses to be buried.

By the time that the plague was taking its heaviest toll, everyone in Constantinople had given up all hope of surviving; despair had settled upon the city like the shadow of a monstrous cloud blotting out the sun, and it seemed as if nothing could depress them further; but the final blow was still to fall upon them. Justinian contracted the disease. He was not particularly popular; many people remembered with great bitterness the way in which the Nika revolt had been brutally suppressed; and his unceasing demands for more and more money, with which to pay for his wars, made many others hate him. But even those who disliked him intensely did not doubt for a moment that he was the vicegerent of Christ on earth, appointed by God and sustained by God to be the defender of all Christian people against the powers of evil in this world, whether those powers took the form of pagan countries like Persia, heretics, earthquakes, or epidemics. And if he, of all people, could be struck down by the plague, what possible hope could there be for anyone else? God had not only deserted his people, but the storm of death in which they found themselves was a manifest proof that he was desperately angry with them too. No one could fight against the wrath of God; Justinian's illness was the last and heaviest blow of all.

It also gave rise to some grave and immediate political problems. All court functions had ceased for many weeks, and with Justinian seriously ill, the central government of the Empire must have ground to a halt too, if Theodora had not taken over his duties in addition to her own; the conduct of the wars now fell into her hands, and the generals in Italy as well as those in Syria, where the Persians had recently invaded the Empire, had to take orders from her instead of from the stricken Emperor. Not all of them were very happy to do so, but their unhappiness about this sudden shift of power in Constantinople was nothing to their unhappiness about another and much more serious consequence of Justinian's illness;

for while he lay between life and death, everyone was acutely and uncomfortably aware that, if he should die, his successor had not been named, and there would be an ugly and dangerous crisis at the heart of the Empire while it was trying to fight two wars, one in the West and the other in the East, and finding itself badly over-extended in the process.

Justinian and Theodora had no children. The Emperor's closest blood relation was his cousin Germanus, and many people would have been delighted if he had been chosen to be their next Emperor; he was a brave and distinguished soldier, he had married into an enormously rich and noble family, and he was popular. But Theodora hated him; for years she had done everything in her power to keep him well away from the centre of affairs. Her own favourite candidate for the succession was one of Justinian's nephews, Justin by name, who had married her own niece, Sophia, Comito's daughter; but though no doubt she had tried to persuade Justinian to name his nephew as his successor, he had not done so. So one of the first things she did, when her husband fell ill, was to call a secret meeting of some of her most trusted ministers in order to discuss the succession in the event of his death, and to lay her plans accordingly.

She was not the only person to see the necessity of being prepared for the worst, and Belisarius, who had been hastily recalled from Italy and sent east when the Persians had attacked Syria, also called a conference of his senior generals to discuss the same eventuality. He was not normally a politically minded man, but he must have known very well that, as the senior and also by far the most popular general in the Byzantine army, he would inevitably be involved if Justinian were to die, and a crisis over his successor was to arise in the capital. Just what he and his generals decided is not known, but Theodora was secretly informed by one of her spies that they had agreed not to recognise any successor appointed in Constantinople without their prior knowledge and agreement. It is quite possible that they did indeed come to such an agreement, for they must have known that the choice of an Emperor against the wishes of the army would lead at best to violence and at worst to civil war; to decide therefore that they must have a say in arranging the succession was to be no more than realistic. But when Theodora heard of their action, it seems that all her old fears that Belisarius might one day become a successful candidate for Justinian's throne were aroused;

she may even have suspected that he was hatching an immediate plot to overthrow Justinian while he was too ill to defend himself. At any rate, she reacted with violence, summoning Belisarius and his second-in-command, a man named Buzes, to Constantinople and imprisoning Buzes on the spot, while Belisarius was dismissed from all his posts in disgrace. He was not restored to favour for two years.

Justinian did not die. He was one of the lucky ones, and after a long period of uncertainty and great anxiety he began to show signs of recovery, until eventually the fever left him. Theodora however remained in sole charge of the government for some months after it became plain that he was not going to die, for he took a long time to regain his former strength, and during his convalescence he was advised by his physicians to do as little work as possible. It was not an easy time for her, for so many people had died throughout the Empire that the problems of government were enormous. The entire population of some small towns and villages had been wiped out; in many cases they fell into ruins, and were never occupied again, while the tilled land around them was left untended, and eventually reverted to its natural state. Even in those places where enough people had survived for the community to recover over the years, it was a slow and painful process. While the disease had been active, it had filled the churches to bursting point, for during the months of the plague everyone had shared such an agony of fear that the most notorious of evil livers had fallen on their knees beside those who were more regular worshippers, and it had been difficult to distinguish the one from the other; but Procopius made a note of the fact that the reprobates who survived soon went back to their godless ways once the tide of death had receded. The army had been drastically reduced in strength, both by death and by panic desertion by men who had hoped to save themselves by flight into the country away from the worst centres of infection. The Empire, however, had been saved from serious attack by its traditional enemies, because the disease was a defence in itself: no one in their senses would ever have dreamed of sending an invading army deep into a plague-ridden country, and as it happened Persia had been busy trying to cope with as devasting an epidemic as that which had swept through Byzantine society. Meanwhile, the economy of the country, already badly over-taxed by Justinian's military adventures, had been reduced almost to the point of beggary by the cessation of all work while the epidemic had lasted and by the drastic reduction in the number of workers brought about by death. It took years for the Empire to recover and to return to anything like its former economic strength. When at last the disease started to lose its force, and people began to dare to hope once again, they were numb with shock. It was only gradually, timidly, and with incredulity that the Byzantines gathered together the broken threads of their lives and went back to their daily pursuits as best they could.

X

After a month or two, Justinian had recovered sufficiently to take up the reins of government again, and Theodora was able to go back to her own affairs. She was forty-three in the year of the great epidemic, and we know what she and some of the other principal actors in the drama of her life looked like at this time, for it was during the years which immediately followed the plague that the mosaics in the apse of the Church of San Vitale in Ravenna were made. If, once, there were other portraits of them, as there must have been, they have not survived; thousands of works of art were destroyed during the eighth century when iconoclasm was the official policy of the Emperors and all pictorial images were condemned as idols, and more were done away with by the Turks, but at least we have these superb works at Ravenna. Justinian is depicted with a small group of courtiers and guards, standing between a man in the white and purple robe of a Patrician, who may have been Belisarius, and archbishop Maximian, with an unknown man just behind the Emperor and the archbishop. Facing them on the opposite wall stands Theodora with, on her left, the figure of a lady who has often been identified with Antonina, while to her left again there is a younger girl, who may have been Belisarius' and Antonina's daughter Joanina. In order to enhance the majesty of the Empress, the artist has made Theodora taller than her companions, whereas in reality she was diminutive, but otherwise the portraits give the impression of being realistic and faithful likenesses. Theodora is represented as no longer young; her face is thinner than it was when she was a girl, a fine, delicate oval in which her dark eyes look enormous and rather sad. The whole effect is so life-like in its fragility and air of physical delicacy that it has sometimes been suggested that perhaps the disease which was eventually to kill her may have been already at work in her. For the fact was that, as life slowly returned to normal, and the Byzantine world began to pick up the threads of its previous existence once again, Theodora, although she certainly could not have known it, had only five more years to live. Time was running out for her.

For Justinian, picking up the threads meant returning once more to his great military adventure in the West, while for Theodora it meant resuming her struggle to make Pope Vigilius keep his unfulfilled promises to her on behalf of the Monophysites, and of course it also meant returning once more to the private life which she was accustomed to lead in the comfort and silken privacy of the *gynaeceum* amongst her women and her friends, including people like the deposed Patriarch Anthimus, of whose hidden existence still no one knew anything at all; it meant returning to her conversations with Antonina and those with the eunuch Narses, when he was not in Italy at the war; returning to her endless baths in the morning, her fastidious daily toilet, and her prayers; to her dinner parties with red wine from Cyprus and white from the volcanic island of Thera; to her expeditions to the sulphur springs in Bithynia and her summer visits to the Palace at Hieron, where Justinian usually joined her for a short holiday in early autumn; to her solemn processions through the streets of Constantinople to church to attend the holy liturgy or to thank God at Candlemas, which the Emperor had recently decreed should be observed annually as a feast of thanksgiving for deliverance from the plague; to her social duties as Empress, presiding at receptions for Sheikhs from Arabia, ambassadors from Persia, Gothic Princesses from the West, or parties of noble but uncouth barbarians from the steppes of what is now southern Russia, or taking her rightful place at some other ceremony of the Byzantine court, which was nothing if it was not rich in ceremonies; and lastly, it meant returning to her married life with Justinian.

Of that life nothing is known except that they were devoted to each other and consulted each other in everything; the inner citadel of their privacy was, and remains, inviolate. If they wrote letters to each other, they have not survived; they kept no diaries; no one was allowed to share or penetrate the intimacy of their domestic life together; when they shut themselves away from the world, the court, and the cloud of eunuchs and ladies-in-waiting, chamberlains and Patricians, chaplains and servants which normally surrounded them, to be alone together somewhere in the heart of the Imperial Palace, no one followed. Presumably, they spent much of their time as other couples do, talking about their friends or their enemies, or merely sitting together doing very little, saying nothing, and relaxing; they could not have spent their whole time discussing official business, politics, or religion. Yet during the years immediately after the disastrous visitation of the plague they must also have spent much time talking about these last two all-engrossing subjects, for the war was going extremely badly in Italy, and inevitably this had its effect on Justinian's religious policy. With his armies being pushed back almost to the point from which they had set out seven years earlier and Rome in danger of falling into the hands of the Goths once again, more than ever he needed to be careful not to offend the staunchly Catholic West by making the smallest gesture of reconciliation to the predominantly Monophysite East. So once again Theodora had to cultivate the virtue of patience, while Vigilius made no move to keep his promises to her. Yet Justinian was in a dilemma, for Jacob Baradaeus was having such an unprecedented success in reviving the deeply harassed Monophysite Christians throughout the East that no one could deny that the persecution, which had been expected to reduce them to an insignificant and negligible little sect or even to wipe them out altogether, had failed in its object, and if the eastern provinces were not to be finally and completely antagonised, some sort of gesture of reconciliation would have to be made towards them by the Emperor sooner or later. It was not a new dilemma; it was the old, old problem which had faced Emperor after Emperor of how to hold together in one undivided church the two great groups of which it was composed: groups of people who seemed to be of such radically different religious temperaments that they were incapable of agreeing with each other.

As time passed, however, Justinian found what he believed might turn out to be a solution to the problem, and since Theodora saw in his scheme a means by which she might at last bring Pope Vigilius to heel, she encouraged him to put the idea to the test. It had been suggested to him by one of his favourite theologians, a certain Theodore Askidas, who was archbishop of Caesarea in Cappadocia, an ambitious man with a talent for political intrigue. In essence the scheme which he put to Justinian was extremely simple, though in detail it turned out to be almost unbelievably tortuous and complicated even by the standards of Byzantine ecclesiastical controversy; but no one could have known in advance that it would do so, and it appealed to the Emperor partly at least because he was beginning to pride himself more and more at this time upon his ability as a theologian. Essentially, the idea put to him by Theodore Askidas was the simple one of trying to unite the Orthodox party and the Monophysites by providing them with a common enemy; it had proved impossible to unite them in love, but perhaps a shared hatred might do what nobler motives had signally failed to accomplish.

The dispute between them was over the two natures in the single person of Christ, the Monophysites appearing to believe in his divine nature only, while denying the reality of his human nature, and the Orthodox party affirming his dual nature; but in the previous century there had been a number of Christians, followers of a monk named Nestorius who had been the Patriarch of Constantinople for a time, and who had held yet another view of Christ's nature, which was anathema to Orthodox and Monophysite alike. He had believed that Christ had had two natures, one human and one divine, but he had also believed that in some way or another two persons had been combined in Christ too, and that the Virgin Mary had been mother of the human Jesus only and not of the divine Christ. As a result he had taught his followers not to refer to her as the Theotokos or Mother of God; she was no such thing; she was the mother of the man Jesus alone. Justinian hoped that if he could encourage both the Monophysites and the members of the Orthodox party to come together in a common condemnation of the Nestorians, perhaps their own differences might begin to disappear. In fact, there were very few Nestorians, if any, practising their particular brand of Christian faith within the boundaries of the Empire, though they were common enough in Persia and further east, and this was awkward; plainly, it would be useless to excommunicate the Nestorians of Persia, India, and Turkestan for, being outside Justinian's imperial jurisdiction, they would be unmoved by his anathemas or those of the Patriarch of Constantinople. But this was not an insuperable obstacle, and after much thought Justinian issued an edict condemning certain of the works of three long-dead theologians, who had been sympathetic to Nestorius in their day; their names were Theodore of Mopsuestia, whose person was also condemned along with his works,

Theodoret of Cyrrhus, and Ibas of Edessa. All three had lived in the first quarter of the fifth century, but apparently it did not occur to Justinian to think this persecution of their dust either unseemly or slightly absurd, though most people today would apply both adjectives to his action.

At first, it seemed as if the Emperor's plan might succeed. The Edict of the Three Chapters, as his condemnation came to be called, was greeted by most leaders of the Monophysite party with guarded approval, if not with much enthusiasm, and few of them refused to subscribe to it. The leaders of the Orthodox party in the eastern half of the Empire, led by the Patriarch Menas, did the same, though some of them had to be persuaded against their initial judgement to agree, and they did so reluctantly and only after a good deal of pressure had been put upon them. But in the western Empire the reaction was different. For one thing, no one was interested in the Nestorians, for they had not existed in any numbers in that part of the world for years; this did not matter very much, even though it meant that Justinian's edict failed to capture their enthusiasm, but what mattered very much indeed was that many leading Catholics were of the opinion that the terms of the edict itself were of doubtful orthodoxy, if indeed they were not downright heretical. The papal legate in Constantinople reacted to the Three Chapters with such righteous and assured indignation that, without even waiting for instructions from Rome, he excommunicated the Patriarch Menas for having signed the offending document. Plainly, Justinian's attempt to reconcile the Orthodox party in the West to their Monophysite brothers in the East had got off to a bad start. Unless he could persuade the Pope to disown his own legate and reverse the excommunication of Menas, the confusion in ecclesiastical affairs would have been made permanently more confounded by his ill-fated venture into the world of theological controversy, and the state of war in Italy made it impossible for him to bring much pressure on Vigilius for the time being.

For the better part of two years throughout 544 and 545 Justinian did nothing, in the hope that at least things would not get worse if he left everyone alone for a time; he was careful not to bring any pressure on Vigilius or to try to make the staunchly Catholic clergy of Italy change their minds about the Three Chapters. But in the autumn of 545 events there forced his hand. The Goths had turned the tables so completely on the imperial troops that most of the ground, which Belisarius had orginally conquered, had now fallen back into their hands, and Rome was once more in danger of a siege. If the city were to fall into enemy hands once again, the last thing the government in Constantinople wanted to see was Pope Vigilius fall with it; as a prisoner he would be an invaluable hostage and bargaining counter to the Gothic king. So Justinian sent a detachment of the Imperial Guard to Rome with express orders to bring him out of the city before it was too late. The sequel was dramatic. On 22 November, Vigilius was in the Church of Saint Cecilia in Trastevere for the celebration of the anniverary of its dedication; the place was packed with people when suddenly, in the middle of the ceremony, a body of soldiers burst in. The officer in command marched up to the Pope, and presented him with an imperial mandate ordering him to leave at once for Constantinople. Although the order was served with the greatest politeness, it was plain that Vigilius had no option but to obey, for in effect he was under arrest, and if he had resisted, he would probably have been removed by force. But, in fact, the Pope gave no sign of even wishing to resist; instead, he obeyed at once, not even waiting until the end of the service but leaving immediately. Not unnaturally, his sudden departure took the congregation completely by surprise, and most of the worshippers in the church followed in order to see what would happen next, accompanying him and the soldiers as they led their illustrious captive down to the banks of the Tiber, where there was a ship waiting for him. Before going aboard, he turned and gave the people his blessing, which they received devoutly enough; but once he was on board and the ship was under way, they seemed to realise that the Pope was abandoning them to the tender mercies of the Goths, and their mood changed. Shaking their fists, they pelted the ship with stones, shouting angrily at Vigilius, 'Famine and death go with you!'

It has sometimes been suggested that the Pope was kidnapped at Theodora's instigation, and she has been blamed for perpetrating yet another outrage upon one of her enemies; but the sequel makes this highly unlikely, for he was not carried in chains to Constantinople, there to face an implacable and vengeful Empress. On the contrary, he was taken by sea to Sicily, where he was allowed to live in peace on one of his own family estates, where he was treated with punctilious respect. If he had been dragged from Rome forcibly and against his will by Theodora's agents, she would hardly have prescribed such luxurious treatment for him. The truth seems to be that he was removed from Rome by Justinian because of the possibility of his capture by the Goths. It has also been suggested that, far from being reluctant to leave the city, he was only too pleased to do so, as long as his departure could be made to look like an abduction, so that the people of Rome could not reproach him for deserting them of his own free will in their time of greatest need; so the dramatic scene in Saint Cecilia's was carefully stage-managed to save his face and to give him an unimpeachable excuse for leaving his flock just in time to save himself. It is not a very kind suggestion, and it may not be true; but such behaviour would not have been out of character.

For ten months Vigilius held court in Sicily, welcoming many leading churchmen to his home, and discussing Justinian's Three Chapters with them. They were unanimously against the Emperor's edict, and as the Pope, pliant as ever to the wind of prevailing opinion, bent ever farther over in their direction, some of the Catholic clergy of Italy decided to urge him to take decisive action. The archbishop of Milan, who had been living in Constantinople since the massacre of the people of his city and its virtual destruction, made a special journey to visit Vigilius in Sicily, where he told him that he had broken off relations with the Patriarch Menas over the Three Chapters, and urged him to do the same. Encouraged by the massive support of the western clergy, Vigilius eventually decided to go to Constantinople in person to urge Justinian to revoke his edict, and in the autumn of 546 he set sail for Patras in southern Greece in company with the archbishop of Milan. He travelled slowly and in as great a comfort as he could manage, as was fitting both to his dignity and to his temperament, and when he reached Thessalonica, he decided to have a short rest from the exertions of his journey. While he refreshed himself, he wrote a letter to Menas explaining his opinion of the Three Chapters, and threatening to break off communion with him if he continued to support the edict. Eventually, when he was ready, he set out again, arriving in the capital on 25 January 547, to be greeted by the Emperor with exaggerated respect, and to be lodged in the Palace of Placidia, the residence of the papal nuncios. Menas, on the other hand, was less respectful; for since his original hesitation about Justinian's Three Chapters, he had become an ardent supporter of the edict, and he told the Pope flatly that he had no intention whatsoever of changing his mind. Egged on by the archbishop of Milan, Vigilius excommunicated him.

This was too much for Theodora. She summoned the Pope to her presence, and remonstrated with him. No one knows exactly what passed between them, but from that moment both she and Justinian maintained a relentless pressure upon him to change his mind, and being the man he was, he vacillated. It would be easy to feel sorry for him as he found himself torn between the approval of his own western clergy and the approval of the Emperor, if it was not so difficult to forgive him for dragging the honour of the greatest see in Christendom in the dust by his grovelling indecision and self-seeking; for it was not long before, once again, he was bending in the direction of the prevailing wind. He read extracts from the works of Theodore of Mopsuestia, which were translated for his benefit by some of the Greek clergy, and as the pressure upon him from the Imperial Palace became more and more uncomfortable, he began to come to the convenient conclusion that he had been wrong after all to withhold his agreement to their condemnation; plainly, they were extremely dangerous. To save his face, he still refused to sign Justinian's edict on the grounds that the Emperor as such had no right to dogmatise on matters of faith; but he promised Justinian and Theodora that he would publish an independent judgement in which he would pronounce in the same sense as the edict. Theodora, however, who was taking no chances, insisted that he should put his promise in writing, which he did. So it came about that, on the eve of Easter, 548, when he could put off the evil moment of decision no longer, he issued an official Judgment—a *Iudicatum*—addressed to Menas condemning the works of Theodore of Mopsuestia, but doing so in terms which he hoped would disarm the Catholic clergy of the West with whom, until recently, he had been hotly supporting precisely the contrary view. Menas was delighted to have won the Pope round to his own point of view; the Monophysites were pleased, though they were wise enough not to allow Vigilius' *volte face* to raise their hopes too high; and Theodora after years of frustration could at last congratulate herself that he had been forced to keep at least one of the many promises which he had made to her over the years.

The conclusion of the shabby saga of Vigilius' irresolution and recurrent changes of direction lies outside the scope of this story, for Theodora was not destined to see the subsequent humiliation inflicted on him, when the outraged clergy of the West forced him to withdraw his *Iudicatum* in yet another total change of mind. By the spring of 548 she was a very sick woman. She must have been aware for some time that she was ill, though for how long she had known, there is no way of telling; nor is it known whether she told Justinian or not. It would have been in character if she had acted a part for as long as possible in order to save distressing him, for she was a woman of great courage; on the other hand, in the normal course of events she shared everything with her husband, and so she may have shared this with him too. In any case, she could hardly have hidden it from him to the bitter end, and by the time of her small triumph over Vigilius at Easter, the end was desperately near. A few weeks later, on 28 June, Theodora died of cancer.

The news sent a shock-wave all over the Byzantine world. To the Monophysites, her death was a catastrophe; she had not succeeded in doing all that she wanted to do for them, but she had done an enormous amount to better their lot, and her loyalty and affection had not been in doubt for a moment. They would never again have such a protectress. But to her many enemies, the news of her death was a cause for great rejoicing. John of Cappadocia reappeared in Constantinople full of hope that he would once again become Justinian's favourite now that his arch-enemy was out of the way; Artabanes threw the wife who had been forced on him by Theodora out of the house, and joined a conspiracy against the bereaved Emperor; Germanus took courage again, and began to hope that perhaps he might succeed his cousin on the throne after all, now that the implacable Empress was no longer there to block his way; and the Orthodox party heard the news with grim satisfaction, offering prayers of heartfelt thanksgiving for her death as a deliverance from an evil more subtle but hardly less destructive than the great plague. She was barely cold before Orthodox churchmen were urging the Emperor to take more drastic measures to suppress the Monophysites; those who still remained as virtual prisoners and refugees in the Palace of Hormisdas should be evicted now that there was no one to protect them, and the Imperial Palace should be cleansed of their contaminating presence; the other deposed leaders of the heretics, for whom Theodora had found places of refuge, should be hunted down and forced to renounce their errors; meanwhile the eastern provinces should be purged of the foul corruption and sin of heresy by main force, until the enemies of

Christ were no more. There had been too many half-measures in the past; now was the time for ruthless extirpation.

But all these busy little enemies of the dead woman counted without Justinian's deep and lasting love of Theodora and without his lifelong habit of following her advice in all things whenever he could do so; for the better part of thirty years he had adored her, consulted her, and respected her, and he had no intention of throwing her policies on to the scrap-heap just because she had died. On the contrary, as one contemporary said at the time, he 'was determined to remain faithful in all things to the will of his wife, even though she was dead'. So John of Cappadocia, though he returned to the capital full of hope, was never reinstated in the Emperor's good books; Belisarius, despite all the honours showered on him and despite his lifetime of service, was still regarded with slight suspicion; Narses was still treated as a trusted favourite; and even Antonina, who had always been Theodora's *protégée* rather than Justinian's, was accorded a special place in his affections in memory of his wife. It is true that the fortunes of Germanus and his family seemed to be radically changed by the death of the Empress, for they were welcomed once again to court with every sign of warmth; but in fact the change in Justinian's attitude to his cousin did not affect the fundamental issue of the succession, and it was still to his nephew Justin, who had married Theodora's niece Sophia, Comito's daughter, that he turned when he came to consider the problem of who was to follow him on the throne. Meanwhile, the depth of his love and respect for Theodora was even more clearly shown in the way in which, after her death, he made her religious policy his own. Far from feeling free at last wholeheartedly to back the Orthodox party now that she was no longer at his elbow to plead for her friends, to the horror of their opponents he made many Monophysites his friends and counsellors. When the old Patriarch Anthimus was discovered after his years of hiding in the *gynaeceum*, Justinian greeted him warmly and with open respect, treating the old man as an honoured guest and begging him to stay in the Imperial Palace. A little later, he went even further, inviting Peter of Apamea and Theodosius, the deposed Patriarch of Alexandria, to come to Constantinople from their places of exile to try with him to find some way of bringing peace to the church once again. Until the day he died, he never gave up the struggle to win the battles, which Theodora had fought so

174

hard all her life, for religious unity between the warring factions in the church.

But on the day that she died, all this was in the future, and although Justinian must have been aware for some time that she was very seriously ill indeed, when she actually died he was prostrated by grief. He was sixty-five at the time of her death, and he never got over it; for the rest of his life he mourned her loss as irreparable; both in conversation and in official documents he loved to refer to her as the 'most glorious wife whom God had given him . . . his sweetest delight . . . the excellent, beautiful, and wise sovereign' who, after being his beloved consort in this life, was now praying for him in the next.

He could not hide the depth of his sorrow, as she lay in the Triclinium of the Nineteen Couches; dressed in purple and with the diadem of an Empress of the Romans on her head, she looked younger and a little paler than usual, as if she was sleeping on the great golden catafalque which had been placed in the centre of the hall to receive her body. Surrounded by a small forest of candles on golden stands and enveloped in clouds of incense, Theodora held silent court, as the Byzantine world came to pay its respects to her for the last time. In endless procession both her friends and her enemies filed past her body with impassive faces, masking sorrow and relief alike and giving nothing away. The Orthodox Patriarch Menas was there, accompanied by a dark retinue of bishops and bearded priests from the Church of the Holy Wisdom, which she and Justinian had caused to be built after the Nika revolt, and where she had so often worshipped. Pope Vigilius with his nuncio, his legate, and a thicket of bishops and monks walked slowly by with due solemnity. Members of the Senate came in their robes of office; Patricians, Prefects, magistrates, and government officials shuffled silently past the bier; the armed forces were well represented, though Belisarius was in Italy again, where the war had taken a turn for the better as soon as he had arrived. Then came the women: the long train of ladies-in-waiting, some of whom were in tears; wives of Consuls and Quaestors and Excubitors; women of all ranks, whom she had helped in various ways, and for whose rights she had fought; and a host of her own personal maids and servants; all came to bow their heads once more to the daughter of Acacius the bear-keeper, as the candlelight flickered and moved on her marble face and danced like little points of fire in the jewels in her crown.

Last of all came members of the family and Justinian himself with tears running uncontrollably down his cheeks, carrying a parting present for the wife whom he had adored; it was a set of jewels of great magnificence for her to wear in the tomb. Blinded by tears, the old Emperor placed it gently around her neck with hands which trembled; then taking her in his arms for the last time, he said goodbye to her. It was too much; he had to be assisted away from the bier by one of his aides, and for a time he could do nothing but stand and sob bitterly.

When he had sufficiently recovered, Justinian gave a sign to the bearers, and the master of ceremonies stepped forward. In a loud voice he cried three times, 'Go forth, O Empress! The King of kings and Lord of lords calleth thee.' Taking up the bier, the bearers moved slowly down the length of the great hall, and as Theodora passed out into the Palace grounds, the great procession of mourners re-formed behind her. Outside the Chalkê in the great square, the citizens of Constantinople had waited all night, and as the head of the procession came in sight, they fell silent. It seemed as if all of them were there, so dense were the crowds in the Augusteum and along the route of the funeral procession. The streets were lined with people; others hung out of the windows of the houses or stood motionless on the roofs, dark against the sky, as the *cortège* passed slowly and with sombre magnificence down the Mesê, through the Forum of Constantine and that of Theodosius to the Church of the Holy Apostles. Parties of priests and deacons preceded and followed the bier carrying candles and chanting penitential psalms; women mourners, their hair dishevelled, wept, piercing the morning from time to time with the thin, high-pitched, wailing cries of their ritual grief; the Blues and the Greens called out their ceremonial farewells in formal chorus, as they had welcomed her in similar formal unison in the Hippodrome on the day of her coronation; and at the head of them all a company of heralds with silver bugles gave notice of the coming of the Empress on her last journey to church through the streets of the capital of the Roman world.

In the Church of the Holy Apostles, which was not yet quite complete, a crowned and vested phalanx of bishops supported by a larger number of priests and deacons and sub-deacons sang the office of the dead. The light of hundreds of candles was reflected from the golden tesserae of the new and sumptuous mosaics on the walls and in the domes of the roof, and once again clouds of incense rose in the dark air like the prayers of the faithful rising to God for the soul of Theodora, as the great ones of Byzantium crowded in. Slowly the ceremony drew towards its end, and the diadem was removed from her brow to make way for a small band of purple silk. The master of ceremonies stepped forward for the last time, and cried again in a voice as loud as the voice of doom itself, 'Enter into thy rest, O Empress! The King of kings and Lord of lords calleth thee.' Her small body was lifted from the bier and lowered gently into a huge porphyry sarcophagus of verd-antique from Hierapolis, which she herself had caused to be made, and for a brief moment or two there was complete silence in the church, while the enormous lid was lowered gently and carefully into place, suspended on ropes and eased into position by well-oiled pulleys. Then and only then did Justinian, crushed and still in tears, go home to his empty Palace, and the Byzantines returned to their houses.

XI

ΘΕ
ΟΔΩ
ΡΑ History has not been kind to Theodora. Enough has already been said of the obsessional hatred she inspired in Procopius, who made no secret of the fact that he detested her, to make it unnecessary to discuss his attitude towards her again at length. His picture of her is so lurid that it is incredible; no one could ever have been quite as uniformly nasty as he makes her out to have been. More dangerous than Procopius, horrified churchmen, looking back down the long vistas of time from the vantage point of the assured triumph of Catholic Orthodoxy over all heretical rivals, have never found it easy to forgive her for the support she gave to the Monophysites or, more understandably, for her treatment of the unfortunate Pope Silverius. Generation after generation of righteously indignant and mercilessly uncharitable ecclesiastics have vied with each other in covering her memory with abuse; she was 'a second Eve in love with the serpent . . . a new Delilah . . . another Herodias thirsty for the blood of the saints . . . in league with the Devil and longing to destroy everything which had been won at so great a cost by the blood of the martyrs and confessors.' The propaganda machines of Fascist or Communist countries could not have done better, and Theodora's reputation has duly suffered down the ages. Lastly, the popular picture of her has been further distorted in recent times by salacious novelists, who have made the most of Procopius' account of her sexual adventures as a young girl to set her at the heart of their semi-pornographic works of fiction.

This persistent misrepresentation has been so unfair that it is tempting to swing to the other extreme in order to redress the balance and to present her as innocent of all the charges brought against her by a libellous posterity; but this would be to misrepresent her yet again. The truth is that she was a highly complex character capable of inspiring intense devotion and bitter hatred, and if on the whole her virtues outweighed her vices, she had her share of both. She was loyal, intelligent, brave, and genuinely devoted to two great causes: justice for members of her own sex and justice for Christians of the Monophysite party; for these she was prepared to go to almost any length and to fight with almost no holds barred. Indeed, the ruthlessness of which she was so often accused in her lifetime by her enemies, even if perhaps they exaggerated it, was both a by-product of her dedication to the things in which she believed as well as being almost certainly her greatest fault.

Her treatment of Pope Silverius was something which her apologists should neither forget nor lightly forgive, for it was indeed ruthless and wholly unjust. If it had been an isolated instance of ruthlessness on her part in a moment of frustration when things seemed to be going against her, it might more easily be excused, but it was no such thing. Although it was in all probability the most cold blooded and oppressive deed of her life, and although she may not have intended the old man to die, it would be idle to deny that there was an unscrupulous streak in her nature, which made her a dangerous enemy and one who was feared by many people. Like others before and since her day, as long as she was convinced that her ends were good, Theodora was not over-particular about the means she adopted to further them; justice for the persecuted Christians of Syria and Egypt, in her view, was well worth a deposed Pope.

Yet, having said all that, there are also other things to say, and the first of them is that, if she was ruthless from time to time, she was not unique in this respect; she lived in a ruthless age, and her Orthodox opponents were guilty of deeds at least as bloody as hers and often much bloodier. Even if she was privy to the death of Pope Silverius, and it is by no means sure that he was murdered, none of her other victims seem to have paid the supreme penalty. She threw some into dungeons; she banished others into exile; she had recalcitrant husbands whipped occasionally and possibly unjustly, but they all survived; and the stories of her thirst for blood were put about by her enemies, and are no more than stories. John the Cappadocian lived; Photius survived in her dungeons until released from them; and Artabanes nursed his revenge until after she herself was dead. Moreover, it would have been surprising if someone brought up in the harsh world of the Hippodrome, where the survival of the fittest was a fact of life, had treated her adversaries with less political realism and more generosity than Theodora's enemies received at her hands. Meanwhile, her Orthodox opponents regularly persecuted their rivals; they hounded them out of their sees, their monasteries, and their cures; they denied them the comforts of their religion; they rejected them as enemies of Christ, and even killed them without any apparent compunction. If it is impossible to excuse Theodora for what she did to Silverius, who was plainly a good man, it is at least as difficult to excuse her enemies for what they did to some of the Monophysites, many of whom were also good men.

But, of course, it can be argued that, although some of them may have been good men individually, their cause, to which Theodora was so devoted, was wholly wrong. The justice of competing causes, even in one's own day, is always difficult to determine, and it becomes almost impossible when it is a matter of causes which have long since ceased to divide the world because one of them, having triumphed over all others, has become universally accepted.

For fourteen hundred years since Theodora's death, the Monophysite Christians of her day have been at best discredited as mistaken and at worst reviled as heretics, while their history has been written exclusively by their victorious opponents; as a result their case has gone largely by default. But curiously enough in retrospect their worst crime seems to have been that they were too like their enemies, for both sides valued subscription to a set of theological propositions as the over-riding Christian virtue; doctrinal agreement, which often boiled down to the mutual acceptance of a verbal formula, was more important to Orthodox and Monophysite alike than love, justice, mercy, or peace, and failure to agree on a form of words was treated by both sides as a legitimate reason for hatred, hostility, and physical violence. This whole procedure was justified as the pursuit of pure truth, and so in a way it was; for the manner in which the arguments about Christ's nature were eventually resolved was bound to determine what Christians would believe about their own nature and value, since Christ was, in their view, the clue to their own true humanity. It would therefore be both naïve and mistaken to dismiss the furious theological disputes of the day as irrelevant and unnecessary; yet they are wide open to the criticism that they were ferociously propositional, and indeed this is what vitiated them. But although Theodora was fully engaged in the disputes of her day, she really does seem to have been much less wedded to that particular side of them than most of her contemporaries. Perhaps it was because she was a woman, and on the whole propositionalism is a masculine disease; but it is also certain that her early experience in Alexandria of the kindness of such men as the Patriarch Timothy and his exiled colleague, Severus of Antioch, had shown her the absurdity of judging such men to be sub-Christian because their theological opinions deviated from the strait and narrow Orthodox party line, and she seems genuinely to have fought for their recognition because she had met something very like the love of God and the courtesy of Christ in and through them at her moment of greatest need. It would be too strong to say that she was one of the first ecumenists in the modern sense of that word, trying to find a common denominator of Christian love and cooperation in those who found it impossible to reach intellectual agreement in all things without compromising their own integrity of mind, but she was certainly more ecumenically minded than most of her contemporaries, and infinitely more so than the bigots and the fanatics on both sides.

Meanwhile, there is no doubt that she was endowed with a remarkable insight into the political realities of her time, which gave her a firmer grasp of the real problems facing the Byzantine world than most other people including Justinian. Even those historians who have greatly disliked her have not been able to deny that she had the vision of a statesman; while her husband dreamed dreams of restoring the glory of ancient Rome in the West regardless of the cost of such an enterprise in lives and money, Theodora saw that it was in the eastern provinces that the future of the Byzantine Empire would eventually be decided. When Justinian died, although his armies had by that time reconquered Italy and much more in the West, the Empire was so badly over-stretched that his hard-won conquests were very soon lost again; yet part of the price he had had to pay for these ephemeral triumphs had been the bitter and permanent antagonism aroused by his ecclesiastical policy towards the Monophysite Christians of the East in Syria and Egypt. The consequence was that, a hundred years later, when the Arab world embraced the new faith of Islam with open arms, both those provinces were only too eager and happy to secede from the

Empire. The Muslims were more tolerant in religious matters than the inexorable Byzantine government and the fanatical and bigoted Orthodox churchmen had ever been, and the provinces which had been persecuted by successive Emperors in the name of Orthodox uniformity willingly succumbed one after another to the armies of the Prophet, greeting them more as liberators than as conquerors. Thereafter the Monophysites of Syria, Palestine, and Egypt regarded their Muslim rulers more as protectors from the Orthodox Christians of the Empire than as oppressors; the last thing they wanted was ever again to come under Byzantine rule; as loyal Christian minorities in Islamic countries they had more religious freedom than they had ever had in Byzantine days.

The ifs and ans of history are dangerous things to play with, but it is impossible not to wonder what would have happened if Theodora had had her way. Probably the mantle of the persecutors would have fallen on to the shoulders of the Monophysite party once it had gained power, and the tables would have simply been turned on the Orthodox churchmen without altering the basic situation in which fellow Christians fought each other over the manner in which to split doctrinal hairs. But it is at least possible that the Monophysites might have proved less ferocious to their opponents than the Orthodox heresy hunters had shown themselves to be, and indeed continued to be. Meanwhile, it is not only possible but even probable that the eastern provinces would never have been lost to the Empire, and if that had been the case, the history of Christendom in particular and the world in general would have been very different. It is even possible that the Arab world, which was deeply influenced both by Judaism and by Monophysite Christianity before the rise of Muhammad, might not have embraced the faith of Islam with such single-minded devotion, if Orthodox Christians had not been so obdurate and unloving. Admittedly, this is speculation, but the conjecture that the Christian church, which has reviled Theodora for centuries, might not have suffered such a crushing defeat by Islam in the seventh century, if she had had her way in ecclesiastical politics, is a beguiling one.

Meanwhile it is no speculation to say that she was a very remarkable woman. Few other people have ever been plunged by the whim of improbable circumstance into a life of such extraordinary contrasts as those which she experienced, and few other people can have had the grace, the competence, and the astonishing adaptability which she brought to the task. History has gloated over her sins; it has conveniently ignored, forgotten, or denied her many qualities of courage, constancy, faithfulness to those whom she loved, and dogged fidelity to the causes which she believed to be right. But perhaps her greatest gift was a genius for being able to see the wood, however many and alluring were the trees of which it was composed. It is a rare gift at all times, but in Byzantine days it was even rarer than usual; for the Byzantines, almost to a man, were devoted to an intellectual and analytical approach to life, which made them brilliant theorists, but which did not always help them to see the true nature of the problems they were examining, whether those problems happened to be political or theological in their nature.

Justinian had the mind of a great academic; indeed, it was this which enabled him to undertake his great work of codifying Roman law and bring it to such a triumphant conclusion; but his dream of restoring the Roman Empire to its former glory was so much more the dream of a scholarly historian than that of a practical politician that it was destined to have only the most ephemeral results. The theologians of Byzantine days had academic minds too; they loved nothing better than to analyse, argue, and define the nature of God, of Christ, and of the church, while apparently completely losing sight of the reality of Christian love and truth, and splitting the church wide open in the process; and the average Byzantine citizen followed admiringly in their leaders' propositional footsteps.

Theodora, on the other hand, with her unerring realism saw almost as if by instinct to the heart both of people and of problems without first having to analyse them intellectually. She had at least as brilliant a mind as that of Justinian or indeed as that of any other man of her time, but, perhaps because she was a woman, she also had what many of them lacked, an unfailing ability to see the real crux of any matter without getting bogged down in endless discussions and fruitless arguments about things incidental to it. Whether she was born a realist, or whether she learned to be a realist in the hard school of the Hippodrome, it is impossible to say; but combined with her courage, her intelligence, her ability to inspire great devotion in friends and followers, and her strength of character, it was probably her realism above all which helped her to survive that savage childhood, and which brought her through the notorious and corrupting years of her adolescence and early maturity relatively unscathed to become an Empress of great distinction and remarkable stature.

It used to be fashionable to pour scorn upon the Byzantines; Gibbon, their greatest English historian, said that their history was 'a tedious and uniform tale of weakness and misery'. It is only recently that many people have come to realise that that judgement was a travesty of the truth. On the contrary, Byzantine civilisation was one of the great civilisations of the world, and no one would now deny that in its thousand years and more of existence it produced some great men and women. By any standard, Theodora, the bear-keeper's daughter, was one of them.

BIBLIOGRAPHY

ORIGINAL SOURCES

The events of Theodora's lifetime were described by a number of contemporary historians, though not all their works have survived. Only the most important will be mentioned here, and then only when they are available in English translations. Potential scholars will have no difficulty in finding lists of works in Greek, Latin, and Syriac dealing with this particular period at the back of more learned works than this.

PROCOPIUS Procopius is far the most important of the contemporary historians. He wrote a number of books describing Justinian's reign, some official and one very unofficial indeed. His official *History of the Wars* in eight volumes is easily available in an English translation published in the Loeb Classical Library, and so is his scurrilous and highly unofficial *Secret History*. A more modern translation of the *Secret History* was also published by Penguin Books in 1966, but is now out of print.

EVAGRIUS Evagrius was a Syrian lawyer, who wrote a six-volume ecclesiastical history of the period, which also mentions a number of secular subjects. It was translated into English in the mid-19th century, and those with access to a good library may be lucky enough to find it there. It was published in Bohn's Ecclesiastical Library in 1851, and is entitled *Evagrius, a History of the Church from* A.D. *431 to* A.D. *594.*

JOHN OF EPHESUS John of Ephesus was a Monophysite, and his history of the Church was written from a Monophysite point of view. It was written in Syriac, but it is available in a 19th century English translation. It was published in Oxford in *1861*, and is entitled *The Third Part of the Ecclesiastical History of John, Bishop of Ephesus.*

JOHN MALALAS Another Syrian lawyer, Malalas wrote a history of the world up to and including Justinian's reign. It was translated into English and published in Chicago in 1940, entitled *The Chronicle of John Malalas.*

Together with these and many other works, Justinian's legal publications, including the *Digest,* the *Code,* and the various *Novellae,* contain much valuable information, but only some of them are available in English.

GENERAL WORKS

N. BAYNES & H. ST. L. B. MOSS. *Byzantium: Collected Essays.* Oxford, 1948.

C. DAWSON. *The Making of Europe.* London, 1939.

C. DIEHL. *Byzantium: Greatness and Decline.* Trans. into English by Naomi Walford. U.S.A., 1957.

H. DINER. *Emperors, Angels and Eunuchs: 1000 years of Byzantine history.* Trans. into English by E. & C. Paul. London, 1938.

H. W. HAUSSIG. *Byzantine Civilisation.* Trans. by J. M. Hussey, London, 1971.

H. ST. L. B. MOSS. *The Birth of the Middle Ages.* Oxford, 1935.

D. OBOLENSKY. *The Byzantine Commonwealth.* London, 1971.

G. OSTROGORSKY. *History of the Byzantine State.* Trans. by Joan Hussey. Oxford, 1968.

S. RUNCIMAN. *Byzantine Civilisation.* London, 1933.

S. RUNCIMAN. *Byzantine Style and Civilisation.* London, 1975.

A. VASILIEV. *History of the Byzantine Empire.* 2 vols. Wisconsin, 1958.

THEODORA AND HER TIMES

R. BROWNING. *Justinian and Theodora.* London, 1971.

J. B. BURY. *History of the Later Roman Empire from the death of Theodosius to the death of Justinian.* 2 vols. London, 1923.

C. DIEHL. *Théodora, Impératrice de Byzance.* Paris, 1904.

C. DIEHL. *Justinien et la civilisation byzantine au VIe siècle.* Paris, 1901.

W. G. HOLMES. *The Age of Justinian and Theodora.* 2 vols. London, 1912.

P. N. URE. *Justinian and His Age.* London, 1951.

P. CHARANIS. *Some Aspects of Daily Life in Byzantium.* The Greek Orthodox Theological Review. U.S.A., 1962-63. Reprinted in *Social, Economic and Political Life in the Byzantine Empire.* Variorum Reprints. London, 1973.

D. J. CONSTANTELOS. *Byzantine Philanthropy and Social Welfare.* U.S.A., 1968.

O. DEMUS. *Byzantine Mosaic Decoration.* London, 1948.

M. MACLAGAN. *The City of Constantinople.* London, 1968.

G. MATHEW. *Byzantine Aesthetics.* London, 1963.

D. TALBOT RICE. *Byzantine Art.* Oxford, 1935.

D. TALBOT RICE. *The Beginnings of Christian Art.* London, 1937.

A.D.

258-263 The first really serious barbarian invasions of the Roman Empire take place.

330 Constantine founds the city of Constantinople as capital of the Roman world on the site of the old Greek city of Byzantium.

364 The Empire is divided for administrative purposes into two parts with a Western Emperor in Rome and an Eastern Emperor in Constantinople.

378 Gothic invasion of the Balkans and defeat of the Roman army at Adrianople, but Constantinople holds out.

401-403 Invasion of Italy by the Visigoths under Alaric.

406 The whole of France and Spain overrun by German barbarians: Vandals, Suevi, Alans, and Burgundians.

407 Abandonment of Britain by the Roman army.

410 Capture and sack of Rome by Alaric.

413 Theodosius II enlarges the city of Constantinople by building a great wall from the Golden Horn to the Sea of Marmara three-quarters of a mile further west than the wall of Constantine.

429-435 The Vandals invade North Africa.

434-453 Attila and the Huns invade the Empire.

476 The last of the Roman Emperors in the West is deposed, and Italy is ruled thereafter by German barbarians.

482 The birth of Justinian.

493 Theoderic the Great, an Ostrogoth, becomes King of Italy.

500 (or thereabouts) The birth of Theodora.

518 Justin I made Emperor by the army in Constantinople.

524 The marriage of Justinian and Theodora.

527 The death of Justin; Justinian and Theodora crowned as Emperor and Empress.

532 The Nika Revolt.

533 Belisarius invades and reconquers the Vandal kingdom of North Africa.

535 Belisarius reconquers Sicily from the Goths. The same year, Agapetus is made Pope.

536 Belisarius invades Italy, and lays siege to Naples. Agapetus dies, and Silverius is made Pope.

537 Vigilius is made Pope.

539 The massacre of Milan.

540 Ravenna surrenders to Belisarius.

543 Plague in Constantinople.

548 The death of Theodora.

565 The death of Justinian.

INDEX

Monastery of St Conon, 65
St Sampson, 136
Monophysites, 29-33, 39, 88-90,
122-31 *passim*, 134-43, 167, 173,
174, 179-82
Monophysitism, 29-31, 168
Moors, 99
Mundus, general of Justinian, 71,
73, 75-80 *passim*, 84
Mysia, 118

Naples, 146, 149, 186
Narses, 48 ff., 53, 73, 76, 78, 84,
111, 116 ff., 128 ff., 166, 174
Nestorianism, 168
Nestorius, Patriarch of Constan-
tinople, 168
Nicaea, Council of, 133
Nika Revolt, 68-81, 101, 108, 109,
123, 161, 175, 186
Nisibis, 140
Numidia, 99

Palace Guards, 34, 36, 45, 47, 52
ff., 68, 71, 73, 75, 78, 79
Palestine, 28-31, 182
Pamphylia, 50
Paphlagonia, 33, 157
Patara, Bishop of, 149
Patras, 171
Paulinus, 131
Pelusium, 155, 156, 157
Pentapolis, the, 20
Persia, 45, 55, 60, 84, 106, 140,
157, 161, 163, 166, 168
Peter, Bishop of Apamea, 123,
130, 137, 138, 142, 174
Peter Barsymes, 118
Peter, general of Justinian, 120,
121
Peter, Patriarch of Jerusalem, 125
Phantasiasts, 127-9
Philadelphia, 63
Photius, Antonina's son, 102,
106-8, 179
Phrygia, 157

Placidia, Palace of, 171
Pompeius, nephew of Anastasius,
70, 73, 80, 81
Pontia, Island of, 149
Praejecta, Justinian's niece, 100,
101
Praetorium, 64, 68
Probus, nephew of Anastasius, 70
Procopius, 12, 16, 17-21, 36, 38,
49, 82, 108, 118-21, 150, 158 ff.,
161, 177, 187
Prostitution, 95-7
Pythia, hot springs, 86

Ravenna, 83, 108, 165, 186
Church of San Vitale, 83, 165
Relics, 72, 93, 94
Reparatus, Prefect of Italy, 152
Rimini, 153
Rome, 143-9, 166, 169-71
Asinarian Gate, 147 ff.
Avantine Hill, 148
Church of St Cecilia in
Trastevere, 170
Circus Maximus, 10
Lateran Palace, 147 ff.
Pincian Palace, 148
Siege of, 147
Rufinianae, 116
Russia, 1, 27, 166

Senate, 36, 52
Senate House, 13, 68
Senators, 36, 52, 59, 70, 73, 74,
118, 175
Severus, Patriarch of Antioch, 32,
89, 90, 123-5, 129, 137, 138,
142, 181
Sicily, 84, 103, 108, 115, 157,
170, 186
Side, 50
Silverius, Pope, 146-50, 177, 178,
186
Sittas, general of Justinian, 47
Slavs, 45, 55
Sophia, Empress, Comito's
daughter, 162, 174